The Therapeutic Purposes
of Reminiscence

WITHDRAWN

The Therapeutic Purposes of Reminiscence

MIKE BENDER
PAULETTE BAUCKHAM
AND
ANDREW NORRIS

SAGE Publications
London • Thousand Oaks • New Delhi

SAGE Publications Ltd
6 Bonhill Street
London EC2A 4PU

SAGE Publications Inc.
2455 Teller Road
Thousand Oaks, California 91320

SAGE Publications India Pvt Ltd
32, M-Block Market
Greater Kailash – I
New Delhi 110 048

British Library Cataloguing in Publication data

A catalogue record for this book is available from the British Library

ISBN 0 8039 7641 0
ISBN 0 8039 7642 9 (pbk)

Library of Congress catalog record available

Typeset by Mayhew Typesetting, Rhayader, Powys
Printed and bound in Great Britain by Athenaeum Press, Gateshead

The first thing I remember I was lying in my bed.
I couldn't have been no more than one or two.
I remember there's a radio comin' from the next door.
And my mother laughed
The way some ladies do.

For our children

CONTENTS

LIST OF FIGURES

LIST OF TABLES

PREFACE

Some time ago – it seems a very long time ago – we collaborated in writing a book called *Groupwork with the Elderly*, which was published by Winslow Press in 1987. While the book aimed to cover all types of groupwork, we used as a working assumption that the group the reader had in mind was a reminiscence group, so there is a lot about reminiscence groupwork in that book. We went our separate ways, each continuing to work with reminiscence. In the time since, books and articles on reminiscence have been produced at an ever-accelerating rate. Another feature has been the increase in commercially produced memorabilia for use in hospitals, day centres and other such units.

So there is undoubtedly tremendous interest in reminiscence work; but there are also worries and concerns. Is reminiscence work becoming routinized (will it be bingo or reminiscence today)? The term 'reminiscence therapy' is used a lot, but in most units untrained staff do reminiscence work, so what does the 'therapy' bit actually mean? If they are doing therapy, then why haven't they had a subsantial period of training and supervision?

Another concern is that we have here a very popular technique, but there is little hard research evidence to testify that it does any good.

And to add one final bit to the puzzle: how many reminiscence activities are there? Is there one basic model, with small variations, or are there actually a number of quite different ideas being lumped together?

Discussing these features of the contemporary reminiscence scene, we decided we wanted to write a book that tried at least to clarify, even if it could not answer, these questions. We hope you will find our efforts useful in your work.

We should like to thank Alison Bender for her unfailing support, Anthea Sperlinger for her comments on her reminiscence work, and Kay Harding for producing and re-typing innumerable drafts of this manuscript.

We must also pay tribute to the memory of Charles Goodson; and to Faith Gibson, who for so many years, has taught so many people how reminiscence work can improve the human condition.

INTRODUCTION: THE MAIN UNDERLYING THEMES OF THIS BOOK

It will be useful for the reader to know our basic assumptions about reminiscence. They can be summarized as follows:

1 Reminiscence work can be useful and beneficial to everyone, that is to *all* client groups, *not* just the elderly.
2 Reminiscence work is age-independent. It can be used as soon as human beings have memories. Certainly, it has been used with young children in care.
3 For reminiscence work to be effective, each piece of group or individual work has to have a clearly specified and understood purpose.
4 This purpose must relate to the needs of the people being considered for that group or individual work.
5 It must also consider the needs of the workers – our needs.

This approach contrasts with the usual attitude of grouping a large number of activities with different purposes and calling them by the same term – reminiscence. The act of cataloguing and describing these different aspects should help clarify our understanding. Once we have understood the various and separate purposes that reminiscence work can be put to, we can start to resolve the paradox regarding training: reminiscence work is done mainly by untrained staff; and yet psychologists and others claim it as a therapy. If it is a therapy, should it not be done only by trained therapists?

This paradox can be resolved if we stop seeing reminiscence as a single activity. Rather, it can be used for many different purposes. Each purpose requires a different mix of experience, personality and training to be most useful. In this book, we will indicate for each purpose, the training required.

Throughout this book, we urge that the worker gains regular supervision. Since you cannot predict how reminiscing will affect people or what memories it will stir up, workers need to have help available to discuss how to handle the unpredictable. Thus all group leaders – whatever the purpose of the particular group – should have regular supervision. Additionally, supervision helps group leaders look at their work more reflectively and therefore more objectively.

We will elaborate further on these ideas.

Reminiscence for all

The first point we want to make is simple. Reminiscence work has been tied to working with the elderly. There may be theoretical reasons for this. For example, the psychotherapist Robert Butler suggests that the older person undertakes what he termed a 'life review' towards the end of their life. But these reasons for offering reminiscence work to older adults are *not good reasons for not extending such work to other clients*, or indeed, *to most people*. The literature search for this book revealed an article recounting studies of the reminiscences of 2-year-olds! (For the sceptical, we give the reference at the end of this chapter.)

If we limit reminiscence work only to older people, it gets the tag of merely being used to pass the time, because what can you usefully do with or for the old? Of course, in fact, our own work and experience, and that of countless other professionals, has shown us that this is a quite unnecessarily pessimistic and nihilistic stance. Indeed, Robert Butler argues that the older person is more hungry for change as they know they have not got time to spare.

However erroneous this common stereotyping of the elderly, it can limit creativity about reminiscence. Equally important, this stereotype also limits the range of utility of reminiscence. Again, our experience, in common with that of many other workers, has taught us that many other types of clients – people with a learning difficulty, people who have been in the psychiatric system for a long time, schoolchildren listening to their elders, can all enjoy and benefit from reminiscence work. We suggest that anyone who has some speech and long-term memory capability can reminisce, and we hope that the examples of work by ourselves and others that we describe in this book will prove this to be the case. So, our first goal in this book is simply to advocate **Reminiscence for all, from 5 to 95**. Restricting its use to the elderly limits vision and opportunity quite unnecessarily and stops the flow of ideas and methods that are useful across client groups. Because, for all three authors, our experience has mainly been with older adults, especially over the past few years, our fieldwork examples will be mainly drawn from this area. But this limitation in our experience does not decrease the validity of the point that reminiscence is useful across the age range.

Clarifying the various different approaches

We need to clarify the various approaches to reminiscence. We are clear that different authors have different activities in mind when they use the term 'reminiscence'. Such uses include therapy, life review, stimulation, oral history etc. These different approaches come from quite different philosophical backgrounds and aim to achieve quite different ends. We outline a score of different purposes in the following chapters. Our hope is that by doing this, we will increase the theoretical and practical utility of the term 'reminiscence'. If we are successful, the reader will be able to see more clearly where within the family of reminiscence methods, the type of reminiscence work they would like to do is coming from – its historical roots and underlying values, and its goals.

Relating our work to client need

We are concerned that reminiscence work has often been seen as an end in itself. A unit may set up a reminiscence group with little idea of why except that reminiscence work is always a good thing, isn't it? It may or may not be a good thing. That depends on the purpose of the group. It probably is not a good thing if it is being undertaken without a clear purpose. Without a clear purpose, it becomes impossible to select appropriately; it is impossible to accurately pitch the level and content of the group because people with quite differing needs and abilities will have been selected to join; and it is most certainly impossible to evaluate, because the goals or aims are undefined.

Perhaps even more importantly, a lack of clarity greatly increases the chances of clients getting damaged or feeling used. They are asked to self-disclose, and then, because the worker, literally, does not know what they are doing, that self-disclosure 'goes nowhere' and the client is puzzled and hurt, even though the group leader may be ignorant of their feelings.

We therefore suggest that you need to work out what the unmet needs of the unit's clients are, and then design the most appropriate activities or treatments. *The process must be needs-led.*

We shall outline 20 different purposes for reminiscence, each requiring somewhat different procedures to achieve success. We will describe these procedures, drawing on our work and that of other workers in the field. We hope that this will enable you, having established the unmet needs of your clients, to match your reminiscence work more accurately with their needs.

The client, the carer, the context

There is another sense of purpose that we wish to develop in this book. We said earlier that reminiscence work has on occasion be seen as an end in itself, without asking 'Why?' for the clients; but it is also very important to ask 'Why?' in the context of the unit in which that work is being delivered. Sometimes the group is actually for the *staff* – for example to help them develop groupwork or evaluation skills. If that is the case, what does a good group to help staff learn look like? And finally, sometimes a group's purpose is to make *the unit* a better place, to help staff and clients get to know each other; to help staff individualize each client. It is a well-repeated finding that groupwork helps staff become more positive towards their clients, as they get to know them so much better, and that is a very worthwhile goal. Again, how do we target that achievement? So, we have both a vertical and a horizontal axis of two interwoven strands: one is the purposes of the group, while the other is the target population – the clients, the carers, be they professional or personal, and the context (the place in which the work takes place and its culture).

The needs of the group leaders

Quite often, staff wish to run a reminiscence group to improve their groupwork skills. We would like to highlight this purpose. Once we recognize the validity of this need, we can plan that the experience is as useful as possible. Of course, we need to make sure the clients know what is going on, give their consent and enjoy the group, and we will have to ensure that these things happen; but what we should not do is to apologize for trying to meet *staff* needs. Within the assumption of several different types of reminiscence work, there will need to be a core training to make the staff member a competent group leader – competent to run most types of group. But staff will also need to understand the various types of reminiscence work, and receive training in the ideas and aims of the various purposes to which reminiscence can be put, with their different emphases.

   This will be a strong theme in this book – the need for good training and continuous, high quality, independent supervision. As long as reminiscence work was and is being written about as one homogenous pudding, it was very difficult to specify the training and supervision needs. Once we can tease out the various, and often quite different and disparate purposes to which reminiscence can be put, so the training required becomes much more sharply in focus for each type of purpose. The same is true for supervision.

The need for supervision

Another theme we want to highlight in this book is the need for supervision for any group and certainly for reminiscence groupwork. The necessity of supervision has often been ignored or understated because of two British hang-ups: the first is professional defensiveness – I'm professionally trained, how dare you suggest I don't know what I'm doing.' This claim to perfection is of course a ridiculous pose at any time, but completely misunderstands what supervision is about, which is to make your groupwork better and more effective. The second hang-up is the British 'stiff upper lip', the idea that looking after your mental health and keeping your communication and listening antennae sharp by receiving supervision is somehow wimpish, a soft luxury. Again, it is a pathologically defensive reaction, albeit a very common one.

Seeing reminiscence work in the context of positive mental health

Another major theme is the need to look at the needs of our clients and of ourselves in a positive light, if we are to make sense of what reminiscence can achieve. There are two philosophies we need to move away from.

The model of therapy

The first model we need to challenge is that the only real treatment is an assess–treat–cure model. This of course apes the model of medical treatment. Diagnose tonsillitis, treat it and close the case when the person gets better. This model does not make much sense when we consider emotional problems or difficulties which rarely come in such neat packages. It devalues attempts to look at people in a more holistic manner that takes account of their subjective experience. It is near useless when dealing with people with long-term problems, or with real problems that won't go away, like a bereavement or an amputation. An unfortunate implication of this model is that it emphasizes helping people who are likely to show improvement, so resources go towards people with acute, short-term difficulties, not long-term conditions, like being old.

Secondly, the model has another nasty insinuation. The outpatient mental health model, which most closely apes the medical assess–treat–cure, is invariably individually based. The therapist sees the patient alone for an hour. This prestige model of *individual* therapy undermines *groupwork*, which in fact can do many things that individual work cannot do. For example, if you want people to feel they can act together to change their lives for the better, groupwork is a far more effective medium. If you want people to feel their lives were valuable, again groupwork would be the method of choice. We need to see groupwork not as competing with individual work, but as different, aiming to achieve different ends, and certainly not as inferior. (Irving Yalom (1995) is particularly clear on this point.)

A different model of human needs

The argument about therapy is in no way academic. It is vitally important in deciding who gets help. In a similar way, it is important that we
use a more positive model of what people need. And this comes up
against a second philosophy that gets in the way – the concept of need
as only relating to deprivation. By this we mean that it is often argued
that the only needs we need to intervene in are those that relate to a
deprivation state, such as hunger, thirst, cold and shelter (although we
in Britain don't even seem to be providing for the last need properly,
judging by the number of homeless).

These are definitely real needs but, as Abraham Maslow pointed out
as long ago as 1954 in his book *Motivation and Personality*, this is *not* the
complete picture of a human being's needs. People also need to feel safe,
to feel they belong, to feel loved, to feel they are achieving something
with their lives. If we use a deprivation model, then reminiscence work
won't be seen as relevant. If we look at a positive model of needs, then it
can be very relevant indeed. The two traditional concepts of treatment
and of need hinder us in developing reminiscence work because they
marginalize groupwork aimed at helping the human condition and
working with positive needs.

As Faith Gibson wrote in *Reminiscence Reviewed*, 'therapy implies that
a person is a patient with a problem'. And when we try to make reminiscence 'respectable' by calling it a therapy, we make it unnecessarily
pathological, and more treatment-oriented than it can really stand; we
load it with expectations that it will never fulfil. Also, it restricts what
reminiscence can do, and do well – that it can also be fun and stimulating and have no thought about 'making you better'. So, we are not in
the business of making reminiscence a new therapy and calling all
reminiscence workers therapists. Rather, we would suggest other meanings for the term 'therapy' so that we can break through the Gordian
knot of 'if it's therapy, then where are your qualifications as a psychotherapist?' We hope that by the end of this book you will agree that
there are many therapeutic uses to which reminiscence can be put, and
that these different uses require differing skills from the practitioners.
There are many ways of being therapeutic, of helping people to feel
good about themselves, and to feel valued. Once they get to that stage,
that level of self-esteem, they may well be able to change their lives for
the better.

A way of improving research in the field

One of the striking features of the current state of reminiscence work is a
great deal of interest among therapists and workers in units for older
people; but little research has been done, and what research there is does

not provide very strong evidence for the effects of reminiscence. We believe that one of the reasons for this is that both the purpose and the process of a given intervention are often poorly defined. There seems to be an assumption that reminiscence in any shape or form is a good thing; and that everyone knows, more or less, what happens in a reminiscence group. We believe that both these assumptions are incorrect. In this book we try to focus on a number of different purposes which have different goals; and we try to spell out how these goals might be achieved. It should then be possible to conduct better-focused research, with (one hopes) positive results.

About the book itself

In this book we hope to hand on what we have learned from running, supervising and teaching about reminiscence groups. Two things this book is not. It is not a guide to the literature. We will give relevant readings at the end of each chapter, but the literature is now vast and to try to be exhaustive, besides dating very quickly, would have drowned the purpose of the book. What we will do is give you enough references to get you into the literature. Nor is this book a manual on how to run groups. We have, however, provided sufficient suggestions for resources and further reading to allow the reader to develop their own ideas further.

Two final points. While each purpose we describe has a separate identity and use, there is often overlap in the means of reaching the desired ends. This creates a small amount of overlap or repetition in the book. Also, we expect that readers will be more interested in some purposes than in others. To this end, we have tried to make each purpose stand alone, so that the relevant chapter can be read without having to cross-refer. We hope the inevitable amount of overlap is insufficient to cause tedium and irritation.

We would hope, however, that the reader will read Parts One and Four in order to understand our conceptual framework and its implications for units such as the one they work in.

Finally, when we give examples of the purposes in action, the author whose experience it was writes about it in the first person but without being identified. This is because we don't like nit-picking sharing of the spoils ('Harry wrote Chapter One, except for the second paragraph on page 6, which was Fred's idea') and yet wanted to convey a personal sense of what it felt like undertaking the work. We hope this will make for more lively reading, and also, by giving a more warts-and-all view, show that we didn't have any magical skills; it was often hard graft for us, and we made our share of mistakes.

We do hope you enjoy this book and, when you've finished reading it, you feel stimulated, and try out some of these ideas. We hope that this

book is a journey, where you travel with us for a while and then stride
out on your own.

Relevant reading

If you want to check out that 2-year-olds can reminisce, see Robyn
Fivush, Jacquelyn Gray and Fayne Fromhoff's article 'Two-year-olds
talk about the past' in *Cognitive Development*, 1987, 2, pp. 393–409.

A very useful collection in which most of the leading British reminis-
cence workers have contributed a chapter on their work and ideas is
Reminiscence Reviewed: Perspectives, Evaluations, Achievements, edited by
Joanna Bornat (Open University Press, 1994)

The best introduction to therapeutic groupwork is Irving Yalom's *The
Theory and Practice of Group Psychotherapy*, 4th edition (Basic Books, 1995).
Its focus obviously is on psychotherapy and it is long – 600 pages; but it
is strong on what can make groups beneficial to their members.

A review of research into reminiscence work is provided by S.
Thornton and J. Brotchie in their article 'Reminiscence: a critical review
of the empirical literature', *British Journal of Clinical Psychology* 1987, 26,
pp. 93–111.

PART ONE

SETTING THE SCENE

Chapter 1

AN INTRODUCTION TO THE PURPOSES

We believe it is very important to embed reminiscence work into the context of actual needs – the needs of the client, of the carer/staff or of the unit itself. We call this the 3C approach (client/carer/culture) and we discuss it at much greater length in Chapter 2. We want to get across that the assessment of needs always has to come first, because it is only after you have assessed need that you can know whether reminiscence work would be useful in meeting those needs; so we shall discuss these 'setting conditions' in detail.

Having considered what the client needs, we can examine, in the context of this book, what reminiscence might offer to help fulfil any or all of these needs. In this section we shall list and briefly overview the different purposes to which reminiscence work can be put. We shall make clear the needs that each purpose is relevant for.

That done, we shall look at which uses may be most appropriate for particular client groups. While, as we wrote earlier, we feel strongly that reminiscence work can be of benefit independent of age and within a very wide range of cognitive ability, most readers will only be working with one client group and may therefore want to know which purposes of reminiscence work would be most appropriate with their particular clients.

Before we start describing the various purposes, there is an important point to make. There are inevitably areas of overlap between the purposes, but we suggest that *one* purpose should be outstanding and be the clear and focused aim of the group leaders. Table 1 lists the 20 major

Table 1   *The major purposes of reminiscence*

Purpose One	Reminiscence to encourage spontaneous conversation between clients
Purpose Two	Reminiscence to encourage informal conversation between staff and clients
Purpose Three	Reminiscence as fun
Purpose Four	Reminiscence to promote emotional and social stimulation
Purpose Five	Reminiscence to promote emotional and social stimulation with people who are severely disorientated
Purpose Six	Individual reminiscence work
Purpose Seven	Reminiscence to create group cohesion
Purpose Eight	Reminiscence to teach people how to use groups effectively
Purpose Nine	Reminiscence to re-use old skills or learn new ones
Purpose Ten	Reminiscence as oral history to maintain or improve skills
Purpose Eleven	Reminiscence to aid intergenerational communication
Purpose Twelve	Reminiscence to achieve cultural legacy
Purpose Thirteen	Reminiscence and spirituality
Purpose Fourteen	Reminiscence in the assessment process
Purpose Fifteen	Reminiscence for life review
Purpose Sixteen	Reminiscence to aid the creation of a positive identity
Purpose Seventeen	Reminiscence to aid communication between a person with a disability and their family
Purpose Eighteen	Reminiscence to train staff in groupwork or to improve staff groupwork skills
Purpose Nineteen	Reminiscence to improve staff understanding of the individual
Purpose Twenty	Reminiscence work as the working philosophy of the unit

purposes of reminiscence, which are then each discussed in terms of the benefits offered within the 3Cs approach.

Client benefit uses

Purpose One: Reminiscence to encourage spontaneous conversation between clients

We may wish to encourage people to talk to each other informally – that is to say, not in groups and without staff present. They may find they enjoy the conversation; that they have experiences in common, which they enjoy sharing; that sharing can help them feel that their life *is* worth talking about; that it has had some purpose and sense; and that therefore their life, and therefore they themself, have value.

People can get out of the habit of talking to other people, because they have become psychologically or physically isolated. Talking to other people is a skill which needs to be practised and maintained.

Thinking of things to say to strangers or near strangers is not easy; and the more anxious people get about whether they will make a fool of themselves, the more difficult it becomes. Reminiscence material – photos on the wall, objects that are readily touchable – are easy points around which to start a conversation. Starting a conversation is probably much harder than continuing it, so if we can help people get started talking to each other, then it becomes much easier for them to keep talking; and to talk to the person again, at some later date.

Once people have started talking to each other, they will have some group feeling and then lots of other activities become possible. So, using reminiscence to start off the communication process can have surprisingly important long-term benefits.

Purpose Two: Reminiscence to encourage informal conversation between staff and clients

Just as we may have the goal of getting clients to talk informally to each other, so we may have the goal of getting clients to talk informally to staff – in the canteen/over coffee/on the bus. Again, there is the problem of starting the conversation – what to talk about? What happens if the person rejects your overture? And so on. These anxieties will be present for both staff and clients. It can also happen, in these days of rapid change, that both staff and clients start in a new unit at the same time, so everything is unfamiliar to them both. In such a situation it is helpful if there are pictures, music, objects etc. relevant to the clients' lives and experiences, which may be very useful as conversation starters. Such conversations have the added benefit of allowing the staff to get to know the clients better; to get a more rounded picture of them. And this increase in their knowledge is attained in an informal way, avoiding the anxiety that often comes with assessments. The same reminiscence stimuli can be used for conversations on a one-to-one basis or with a small number of clients. The key point is that the stimuli are being used to encourage *spontaneous* conversation in informal settings. With this purpose, they are *not* part of assessment or treatment.

Purpose Three: Reminiscence as fun

Being disabled or disadvantaged in Britain today is not much fun. It almost always means you are poor. It always means that you are in pain or discomfort of some sort. So, any activity that is effective in helping you forget your problems and pains for an hour or two will be very welcome; and you may even come out from the pleasurable experience able to cope or problem-solve a bit more effectively.

A well-run reminiscence group can be fun, if that is what the group leaders want to achieve, and they are competent. If the group leaders have done their homework – they know their clients' likes and dislikes, they know their life histories – then providing enjoyable memory prompts is not difficult. The clients' ages are quite unimportant: we all have a past and we all have life experiences. Films, records, tunes etc. – all can prompt reminiscences in any age group.

This purpose is all too often looked down upon – it is too low-level, it is not goal-planned or whatever. This puritanical attitude is actually punitive – should the disadvantaged be denied enjoyment in our units? People in full-time employment don't spend all their time working; we need relaxation to charge our batteries and then carry on. And when we're having fun, we may well find out that other people make us laugh, share our sense of humour, so we feel part of something and not so alone. How much more necessary is this for people with difficulties? So, a fun reminiscence group can easily be combined with a very active treatment programme.

Purposes Four, Five and Six: Reminiscence for emotional and social stimulation

Reminiscence for stimulation may sound very like reminiscence for fun but there is an important difference. Reminiscence as fun can be provided to anyone who's likely to enjoy it. Reminiscence as stimulation is more focused in its purpose of achieving mental stimulation and social interaction. There are two targets with rather different goals under the heading of 'stimulation'.

PURPOSE FOUR: TO PRODUCE EMOTIONAL AND SOCIAL STIMULATION   The first sub-type of reminiscence for the purpose of *social* stimulation is its use with people who do very little socializing during the rest of the week. This, of course, can be for a variety of reasons. The people they live with or near may not know how to talk to them, or what to talk to them about; they may be too busy, or think talking to them pointless. Alternatively, they may live by themselves and literally see no one to talk to, to pass the time of day with, from one visit to the unit to the next.

If a person doesn't talk to anybody, then the information they receive – from the television or the radio – is passive; it doesn't engage them in debate and dialogue. So, one aspect of reminiscence as stimulation is cognitive stimulation – stimulation of the brain. Another aspect of living alone is that people often shrink emotionally; they develop a set routine to see them through the day. They cut themselves off, and if they meet other people they only express minimal courtesies: 'How are you?' 'Fine.' When they come to a day unit, they almost need thawing out emotionally; reminiscence, by giving them a task and allowing them to share their lives, can thus provide both cognitive and emotional/social stimulation.

This is a major use of reminiscence and one clients often value very highly. They will humour the staff by going to treatment groups, to help the staff feel professional; but it is the spontaneous and group interactions that they look forward to and gain nourishment from.

PURPOSE FIVE: AS A MEANS OF ENGAGING COGNITIVELY DAMAGED PEOPLE
Secondly, we can use reminiscence material as a way of engaging people
who are very cognitively damaged, with whom most means of communication are closed or very difficult. Such reminiscence work will
be in small groups, with a high staff ratio. It will avoid the use of
reminiscence conversations as such long speech sequences will not be
possible for this target group. Rather, physical and non-verbal means
will be used. Physical objects, such as household objects, will be
available and music, whether played by the staff or records of familiar
songs, may elicit a positive response.

PURPOSE SIX: INDIVIDUAL REMINISCENCE WORK   People think of individual
work as being most relevant to people with severe dementia. This is
incorrect, as most can take part in groupwork. (Ways of encouraging
them to do so are discussed in Purpose Five.) Rather, individual work is
probably most relevant to the housebound and very physically frail.
There are people who are cognitively fine but physically very disabled.
Every attempt should be made to help them socialize with others. But
they may refuse to go out, or the cost of transporting them may be
considered prohibitive; we shall look later at bringing reminiscence into
the home.

With the very physically frail, it is likely that they will have difficulty
concentrating for any length of time. The reminiscence material should
be predominantly non-verbal and attention must be paid to the physical
comfort of the person. The use of individual work in palliative care is
discussed. In both settings, what is needed on the part of the worker
implementing this purpose is to understand reminiscence ideas and to
have the ability to modify the techniques to the individual situation.

Purpose Seven: Reminiscence to achieve group cohesion

Part of intimacy is shared experience. You are relaxed and don't feel
cramped with your old school friend, because you share such a long
history together. We can help people realize that they do have experiences in common by running a reminiscence group. These experiences
can either be historical – they went through a war together – or geographical – they come from the same part of the country, with its ways
and customs. Or they may share or have shared a common treatment or
regime – they spent many years in a particular hospital or they all went
to a special school. In fact, with a bit of homework it is usually quite
easy to find experiences common to potential group members. Of
course, they may not have the same emotions about those experiences –
some may have found them hateful, others OK, and a few very pleasant
– but this diversity will add a positive tension, a positive charge to the
conversations between members of the reminiscence group. So, when

we have many new people coming into a unit, one very useful way of getting them to feel that they belong is to start by asking them to join a reminiscence group.

Purpose Eight: Reminiscence to teach people how to use groups effectively

Groups are a strange environment in which to operate. Most 'natural' interactions take place in two, threes, sometimes fours. Seven to ten people is a large number of people to interact with. They might all turn on you and confirm your worst fears about yourself. What are the rules of this strange phenomenon; do you talk first or hold back? Do you laugh at every person's attempt at a joke? People wonder: Will my troubled and shaky identity be crushed? Will I have to pretend to be one of the boys or girls in order to survive? And what will that do to my feelings of uniqueness? The unstructured staff group, the away day, the brainstorm – these are all fairly recent organizational phenomena. It is unlikely that older people have taken part in them, and so they have little experience of *formal* small groups.

The learning of the rules of the game is particularly important for people with a learning difficulty. The idea that staff might want to create time and space to listen to them may well be a totally unique experience, and one which they need time to adjust to and learn the rules of. The reminiscence group can be a very useful forum for that achievement. Once they have learnt the rules of a group and how to use and enjoy them, they can then move towards more assertive forms of groups, ones in which they are expected to make decisions (see Purpose Sixteen: to achieve a positive identity).

Everyone, then, on entering a group is scared and insecure. For people with a shaky identity, such as psychiatric patients, this is double trouble as the insecurity of being in a group *and* having an insecure identity compound the problem. So one thing that reminiscence groupwork can do is provide a relatively nonthreatening forum in which, first, being in a group can be desensitized – people can go to sessions and find they come out alive! They may even get to enjoy them. Secondly, this positive experience can then be used either to 'gear up' a reminiscence group or as a preparation for a more traditional therapy group. When we say 'gear up' we mean that the areas the group can look at can be more or less innocuous or frightening. For example, if the group members enjoy a group on 'holidays I have had', we might move on to 'my family', which is likely to be a much more troublesome area. Obviously there must be no under-the-counter sliding from one theme to the next. Rather, the members will need to give their informed consent to joining this second group. In this way, always going at the members' pace, people with troubled lives may feel safe enough gradually to explore more potentially difficult areas.

Purpose Nine: Reminiscence to re-use old skills, or learn new ones

We can use reminiscence to get members to a point where they do something that we think would be useful and helpful to them. An example from Northern Ireland was a project run by Faith Gibson to help old people become computer-literate. If we encourage people to reminisce and we and they value those reminiscences, then it is helpful if they can get those reminiscences down in a more permanent form – which is where learning to use a word processor comes in. Or if we have people who were once keen gardeners but now feel 'they're past it', talking about what they grew – say a six-session reminiscence group based on the seasons of gardening – can end with a discussion of how we may have to adapt our ways a bit but certainly gardening is not beyond us. (What about taking responsibility for the centre's garden?) And so on. In these ways we are using reminiscence to point to and encourage people towards another activity that we think they will enjoy or benefit from but which they might not take up if it were suggested to them straight away.

Purpose Ten: Oral history as a beneficial technique to use cognitive skills

Oral history argues that history, as conventionally taught, is the recording of the deeds of the rich and the powerful, in written form. Since the poor are rarely powerful and, until recently at least, not great users of the written word, this led to a grave distortion of the ways events were recorded. While having considerable sympathy with this view, we are not proposing oral history as a purpose in its own right. We are not particularly interested, rightly or wrongly, in correcting history. What we are interested in, when considering oral history, is how it can be used for the benefit of our clients. Oral history demands factual accuracy. It wants to substitute or add facts and experiences recorded orally to facts written in dusty documents. It is *not* about substituting written records with unsubstantiated reminiscences. A round of group-cohesive, rose-coloured 'Good Old Days – poor but honest' reminiscence is *not* oral history.

The demand for accuracy can be a very useful tool. First, it avoids the inevitable hint of being patronizing that exists when a staff member listens to accounts, say, of the 1920s – why, in our society, would they be interested in listening if they weren't being paid? Secondly, the need for accuracy can help the older person re-frame their experiences because the facts may well be at odds with their coding of experiences. Thirdly, it can motivate them to seek out long-lost relatives and friends to gain their accounts. It can take them to the library and the museum, perhaps for the first time. And if the oral history is interesting, when recorded, they can have the satisfaction of seeing it perhaps in print in the local paper. We shall give a number of examples of such uses of oral history.

Purpose Eleven: Reminiscence to encourage intergenerational communication

We have observed, as indeed have many other workers, that the elderly have a strong wish or need to impart their legacy, especially to the young, to the children. It is as if their need to leave a legacy skips a generation (or two!). There are very real benefits to such communication. There is the mental stimulation of preparing the material – visiting the museum and the library, selecting slides etc.; stimulation due to the challenge of learning new communication techniques, such as using a slide projector or overhead projector; the development of new skills, such as lecturing or talking to children; the beneficial effects of trying to answer children's questions, and being valued by them for their experience. There are, in short, large numbers of important cognitive stimulation and social skills and social interaction benefits. We will describe a number of such projects.

Purpose Twelve: Reminiscence to achieve cultural legacy

Probably most elderly people in British society today feel that the young don't understand or value them (and the same probably goes for the young with regard to the old!); but whilst stereotypes can be written off as irrelevant and unimportant (which unfortunately they aren't), the fact remains that the older person has a wealth of experience and knowledge of past times that if it is not communicated to the younger members of their society will be lost forever. Society has changed rapidly in the past 70 years. When we ran reminiscence outings for people in residential homes in the East End of London, we would take them to their old home addresses to find that there was a tower block there instead of their two-up, two-down. This loss of continuity must be even sharper for ethnic elders, whose children have never seen Southern India or Jamaica. But not only may the elders be sad and unfulfilled if they cannot hand their legacy on, their children and their grandchildren will be impoverished if they cannot see the continuity of experience that links them with their grandparents, and the experiences and the decisions that link the two generations. In most cities there is more than one cultural or religious group and the act or fact of members of a given ethnic or religious group working together in reminiscence or oral history projects allows for the creation of or re-affirmation of a common history.

Purpose Thirteen: Reminiscence in the context of spirituality

Many of the values implicit in reminiscence work – respect, valuing, listening – clearly overlap with religious and spiritual practice. They also share a concern with the meaning of dying and the need to give life and living a meaning and shape. We will consider and explore this conjunction, looking at how a person's spiritual values can structure their lives and how the values and uses of reminiscence could benefit the work of the clergy.

Purpose Fourteen: Reminiscence in the assessment process

Assessment techniques, such as rating scales and questionnaires, leave a lot to be desired because they leave out so much of the person. Staff who take such techniques seriously will really hardly know their clients at all, and – if they are honest – will be continually surprised by how badly they understand them and how often they are caught out by behaviour they did not expect.

The reminiscence approach indicates the need to understand a person's present behaviours and beliefs in the context of their life. So, reminiscence can add depth to our understanding of a person and therefore can be a useful adjunct to more formal techniques, such as questionnaires. It has been used to help develop care plans and as a way of relating to clients.

Reminiscence as psychotherapy

Reminiscence has been used as a type of psychotherapy. We overview some of these uses and advise caution since such approaches seem to have a weak theoretical grounding.

PURPOSE FIFTEEN: AS LIFE REVIEW   This purpose dates from the writings of the psychotherapists Eric Erikson and Robert Butler, who suggested that the older person wants to undertake a review of their life; this undertaking may need professional help. Mental health professionals have worked out techniques to help the older person undertake their life review. Barbara Haight's procedures, which will be described, are perhaps the best known.

PURPOSE SIXTEEN: TO AID THE CREATION OF A POSITIVE IDENTITY   Perhaps the most obvious use of reminiscence in this context is the use of Life Books for children who have been adopted. Losing their 'natural' parents, they frequently feel discarded and rejected. If we can help them construct a history of their lives – however young they are (to repeat, reminiscence is age-free), then we may go a little way towards assuring them that their lives are of worth and will continue to be so. In a way, a person feels as worth-ful as they feel their life to have been. Increase the value they attach to their lived experience, and you increase the value they attach to their self, as long as they can extend this self-value into the present and future.

A common feature of almost all disadvantaged and disabled people is low self-esteem. In the case of people with a learning difficulty, it might be argued that they have very little concept of self-worth. They may feel

loved but they do not feel able to do anything independent with that
love – they cannot use it as a stepping-stone to generate activities which
would confirm their self-worth.

Reminiscence groupwork can help in various ways: it can decrease felt
isolation – they can discover that experiences that they feel ashamed of
or are puzzled by are common to other members of the group; the
interested listening by and respect from positive figures like staff
members (the group leaders) can light the spark of possible self re-
evaluation – 'if they think my life and my experiences are worth
listening to, maybe my life has some value'; they most certainly have
historical and geographical identities – they have to have because they
exist and existed in time and space, and these realities, these parts of
their identities, just as with any one else's identity, cannot be denied.
From this platform of self-worth, perhaps they can move on. We look at
groups aimed at helping people who have relocated from large mental
handicap hospitals, or who have very little information about their lives,
and use of Life Books with children in care.

We see the creation of positive identity as a very central use of
reminiscence and one with huge therapeutic potential.

Carer benefit uses

We now move on to the second C, the carers – be they relatives or
professional carers – and the purposes of reminiscence that can be
useful in terms of their needs.

*Purpose Seventeen: Reminiscence to improve communication between
disabled people and their families*

One obvious use of reminiscence is as a means of communication with
people who are suffering from dementia. This is because, in this condition, the short-term memory function is far more severely affected
than the long-term memory. This means that, while it is often quite
frustrating trying to discuss current affairs, very rewarding conversations can be had between dementia sufferers and their carers/relatives
about their past, during which, in fact, the carer may learn about facts
and events that they did not know. So, if we can make carers and
relatives skilled at eliciting reminiscing – for example, not pestering for
exact dates – they and the people they are caring for can find a whole
world of communication that they thought was forever lost to them.

More generally, one of the striking features of the usual pattern of
communication between a disadvantaged person, say someone in a
long-stay hospital, and their relatives is what is called 'the gift relationship' – namely that all the giving is one-way. The relatives give their

time by travelling and visiting; they may bring and give a gift; in the interaction, it is they who will make most of the conversation, desperately trying to find something cheerful to say. So, all the giving goes from relative to patient and very little the other way. Reminiscence work can go a small way to equalizing the gift relationship. Quite often, the person who is disadvantaged would be interested in getting their house of memories in order. The snaps are just in boxes, uncatalogued: they will never go back to the farm but would like to take some reminders of it when they move to their new accommodation; they would like the grandchildren to understand where the family came from etc.

All these projects can be very valuable ways for family groupings to communicate and participate, so that the gift relationship is reversed and a much greater degree of equality is achieved. Because there is a shared task, this can be used to make contact with relatives and friends who have not been spoken to for years. Re-establishing such contact without such a task would be very difficult and almost certainly not undertaken. Now, with the desire to get hold of old photos, or to see if they know where the people in the old school photograph are now, there is an opening, the opportunity for a re-start.

These uses of reminiscence are framed in terms of Maslow's Hierarchy of Needs and the importance of achieving satisfaction, creation and communication. The importance of stimulation, getting out and maintaining networks is also stressed.

Purpose Eighteen: Reminiscence to train staff in groupwork or to improve staff groupwork skills

It is a sad fact that the utility of groupwork is much under-appreciated, and as a result, there is a real dearth of training courses for staff in groupwork. This means that many staff who would like to run groups are put off by the lack of courses that could prepare them. Fortunately, whilst some theory is useful, the key ingredients of learning how to run groups are (1) running groups, preferably as varied as possible, and (2) being supervised when so doing. Reminiscence groupwork is a good place to start, as most of the time good preparation and a warm, respectful personality will carry the day; but occasionally, and sufficiently frequently to aid learning, the group leaders are faced with difficult situations, such as distress, arguments, wandering, aggression etc. So, if a unit wants its staff to start running groups and understanding what is involved, reminiscence groups provide good opportunities for learning.

Reminiscence as the philosophy of the unit

We turn to the needs embedded in the third C – the context or culture of the unit.

Purpose Nineteen: Reminiscence to improve staff understanding

The disabled – be that disability physical or intellectual – are kept away from the eyes of the working population. They lead separate lives. This means that new staff may have surprisingly little experience of working with disabled people. They may bring quite prejudiced attitudes with them – they may well be scared and a bit frightened in entering this strange world. So, we need to help them stop seeing the disabled as very different from themselves. In this, reminiscence work can provide a very useful listening and interacting platform.

This purpose is particularly apposite when either a new unit is opened and new clients are meeting new staff, or where there is a large influx of new clients into an existing unit, because, for example, another unit is closing. Here, a number of reminiscence groups pairing clients with their key workers may be extremely useful in increasing staff understanding and promoting the formation of positive staff–client relationships.

Purpose Twenty: Reminiscence as a working philosophy of the unit

We can use reminiscence to specify the philosophy that we wish our unit to work by, to live by. This is because reminiscence has as its core values:

- respecting the individual, and respecting the diversity of historical, cultural and geographical experiences that they embody;
- aiming to work with them within the framework of their experiences;
- encouraging them to value themselves and others.

The final chapter spells out these core values and then looks at how they can be implemented and maintained. A central theme is that, while the values are not negotiable, their successful implementation requires active staff and client participation and involvement.

Relating the purposes to your work

You are most probably reading this book because you want to use it in your work. Table 2 shows you quickly with which target group – clients/carers/the unit – a given purpose might be most useful. If you know your overall aim – to help clients, improve staff skills, or change the unit's culture and values – then Table 2 shows you the purposes of reminiscence that may be relevant to those aims. Because the needs and interests of relatives or other personal carers are often different from those of paid carers – staff – or even voluntary carers, we have separated the two within the table.

Table 2 *Particular benefits of the purposes of reminiscence*

Purpose		Likely benefit to:		
		Clients	Relatives	Staff	The unit
1	Encouraging spontaneous conversation between clients	Yes			Yes
2	Encouraging informal conversation between staff and clients	Yes		Yes	Yes
3	Fun	Yes	Yes		
4	Stimulation	Yes			
5	Group for severely disorientated	Yes	Yes		Yes
6	Individual work	Yes		Yes	Yes
7	Achieving group cohesion	Yes			Yes
8	Teaching people to use groups effectively	Yes			Yes
9	Re-using old skills, learning new ones	Yes			Yes
10	Oral history to maintain or improve skills	Yes	Yes		
11	Encouraging intergenerational communication	Yes	Yes		
12	Achieving cultural legacy	Yes			
13	Reminiscence and spirituality	Yes	Yes	Yes	Yes
14	Reminiscence in assessment	Yes		Yes	Yes
15	Life review	Yes			
16	Creating an identity and increasing self-esteem	Yes			Yes
17	Improving communication between clients and their families	Yes	Yes		
18	To train staff in groupwork skills	Yes		Yes	Yes
19	To improve staff understanding	Yes		Yes	Yes
20	To improve the culture of the unit	Yes			Yes

One may be a bit sceptical as to how different the various client groups actually are. For example, we have a strong suspicion that much of what we think of as useful for older people is also useful for people with learning difficulties, and it is sad that people have to be categorized in these artificial ways. However in the 'real world' most readers will be working only with one type of client and it may be useful to know which purposes we think of as particularly relevant to each client group. This is set out in Table 3.

Before you apply a particular purpose to a given client, it will help to have some understanding of the basic ideas of reminiscence and the context in which such ideas can be applied. This forms the subject of the next chapter.

Table 3 *Suggested purposes for use with various types of client group*

Purpose	Client group: Severe learning disability	Moderate learning disability	Chronic psychiatric condition ('rehab')	Physically infirm but cognitively intact (e.g. physical handicap, elderly)	Severe cognitive damage (e.g. dementia)	Moderate cognitive damage	Ethnic minority or those whose culture has changed greatly in their lifetime
1 Encouraging spontaneous conversation between clients		✓		✓		✓	✓
2 Encouraging informal conversation between staff and clients		✓	✓	✓		✓	✓
3 Fun	✓	✓	✓	✓	✓	✓	✓
4 Stimulation	✓	✓	✓	✓	✓	✓	✓
5 Group for severely disorientated	✓	✓	✓		✓		
6 Individual work	✓	✓	✓	✓			
7 Achieving group cohesion	✓	✓	✓	✓		✓	✓
8 Teaching people to use groups effectively	✓	✓	✓	✓		✓	✓
9 Re-using old skills, learning new ones		✓	✓	✓			✓
10 Oral history to maintain or improve skills				✓			✓
11 Encouraging intergenerational communication		✓		✓			✓
12 Achieving cultural legacy				✓			✓
13 Reminiscence and spirituality		✓	✓	✓	✓	✓	✓
14 Reminiscence in assessment		✓	✓	✓			✓
15 Life review	✓	✓		✓			✓
16 Creating an identity and increasing self-esteem							
17 Improving communication between clients and their families		✓	✓	✓	✓	✓	✓

Chapter 2

THE HISTORY AND DEVELOPMENT OF REMINISCENCE-BASED ACTIVITIES

It is some 40 years since reminiscence-based work was first recognized as having the potential to make a positive impact on the quality of life of individuals, particularly the elderly. Old age, up until the 1960s, was seen merely as a necessary, if unfortunate, consequence of extended life. In earlier pre-industrial societies the older person had the highly revered position of the person to whom people turned for advice and whose job it was to communicate the wisdom of one generation to the next. However, this became undermined with the advent of technology, the media and developments in other means of communication, and the place of the elder in society became increasingly undermined and undervalued. But it was at this time, in the late 1950s, that it was just beginning to be recognized that growth and development, in psychological terms, happen throughout life and are not confined just to childhood and adolescence. Up to that point, psychologists, who were concerned with how our abilities to think, learn and use language develop, and psychotherapists had channelled much of their energies into examining what happens to people *in their early years*. For instance, Jean Piaget, Professor of Psychology at the Universities of Geneva and Paris and famous for his detailed study of children's behaviour, produced experiments to show that between the ages of 4 and 7 children undergo a revolution in the way they think. Instead of dealing with things as they see them, an older child begins to construct a theory which tells him that the same object may appear in different forms, for example a ball of clay will be recognized as still being the same clay whatever shape it is moulded into. However, it is only when the child is even older that he will be able to talk about how this can be so. Similarly, Sigmund Freud, who founded psychoanalysis as a school of psychotherapy, was mainly concerned with how childhood influences affected the rest of a person's life. In writings like *The Interpretation of Dreams* (1900) and *The Psychopathology of Everyday Life* (1904) he outlined his ideas on how these influences would express themselves in a person's later years by means of the unconscious. Implied in all this work was that once an individual had reached maturity as a teenager, their pattern of life was fixed and set for the future with only minor refinements making any impact on individual lifestyle thereafter.

Although he himself worked primarily with adults, Eric Erikson was one of the first psychologists to acknowledge that the events which people face at particular points *throughout* their lives could be equally significant in determining how well they adapted to future life events and challenges. His theory of psychosocial development, outlined in *Childhood and Society* (1950), proposed a number of periods of psychosocial crisis or landmarks in each person's life. The way these stages were faced and dealt with would determine how well equipped the person would be to deal with the future. In particular, Erikson suggested that towards the end of their working life people would face a crisis regarding the meaning and value of what they had contributed to life. According to the person's unconscious assessment of themselves and how they had faced the challenges of what they had experienced in the past, this would lead to either a positive sense of 'generativity' (that they had made a worthwhile contribution to society), or 'stagnation', where the person was left wanting, feeling undervalued or with a sense of failure. Later still, as the person comes towards the end of their life, Erikson suggested that they seek to bring together all the strands of their life as a psychological preparation for death in order to face that death with a sense of a life completed. This he termed 'ego-integrity', as opposed to 'despair'.

The importance of Erikson's theory was that it suggested that growth and development occur throughout life and that to facilitate the optimum quality of life over the whole life span necessitates serious consideration of the influences upon a person throughout their years.

Erikson was followed in the early 1960s by Robert Butler, who focused on the behaviour of people at various stages in their life who were being confronted with the imminence of their own death. He observed that people nearing the end of their life seem to reminisce more frequently. This led him to put forward the suggestion that reminiscing over past life events might have a positive, adaptive significance at this stage of life. He suggested that what was occurring was a 'life review' process in which people engaged, psychologically speaking, in looking back over their life in order to address unresolved conflicts. This suggestion tied in quite neatly with Erikson's concept of 'ego-integrity' as the positive adaptive state reached when the loose ends of yesteryears had been tied up, so preparing the person for the process of letting go.

What was particularly significant about Butler's suggestion was that he threw a new, positive, light on the reminiscence process which, up until then, had almost been regarded as an unwanted, pathological side effect of the ageing process. As part of life review, Butler suggested that reminiscence was most particularly, but not exclusively, associated with the aged as a necessary, positive part of life span development. This led to a greater interest as to the role and function that reminiscence might have in the life of the individual, particularly in enhancing self-esteem and a sense of personal identity through a recounting of personal achievements and experiences unique to the individual.

As interest in reminiscence continued to grow, however, it became evident that not everyone reminisces in the same way. McMahon and Rhudick (1964/67) for instance, identified four different ways in which people reminisce:

1 The *storytellers*, who recounted their past exploits and experiences with great vigour and an obvious degree of pleasure.

2 Reminiscers who seemed to use the process *as a means of preserving their self-esteem* and *reinforcing a sense of identity*. Their reminiscences tended to be characterized by somewhat grandiose ideas and exaggerated achievements and conveyed an intention to impress the listener with past accomplishments in order to avoid having to face their current predicament.

3 Those whose reminiscences were characterized by themes of *guilt and unrealized goals*. In the light of Butler's ideas it was suggested that these people might be those who have yet to undergo life review successfully (if ever).

4 Those whose reminiscences were interrupted by *anxiety and concern* over physical health, failing memory, personal losses and a sense of inadequacy, together leaving an impression of hopelessness and lost self-esteem – Erikson's 'despair'.

Table 4   *Types of attitudes to reminiscence and related morale*

		Percentage of sample
Reminiscers		
Value memories of past	High morale	42
Troubled by memories of past	Low morale	16
Non-reminiscers		
See no point in reminiscing	High morale	30
Have to avoid because of contrast between past and present	Low morale	12

Source: Coleman, 1986, p. 37

The view that reminiscence has a differential function for different people was supported in a major longitudinal study conducted by Coleman (1974). He identified four groups of people who differed in their attitude and response to reminiscence. As Table 4 shows, these fell into two sub-groups – those who engaged in reminiscence and those who did not. Within each of the sub-groups there were those who found reminiscing as disturbing or something to be avoided. From his work,

Table 5   *Why did reminiscence become so influential?*

1   An ageing population
2   An increasing awareness of this change in demography
3   (a) The drabness of institutional life
    (b) Concern particularly about the quality of residential life for the elderly
4   The feeling that 'something had to be done' and some financial resources being made
    available
5   Increase in day care and day hospital places and the need for such units to fill the time
    available in ways that appeared therapeutic
6   Increased training opportunities for day care and residential staff working with low
    status groups, such as the elderly, the mentally ill and people with learning
    difficulties
7   (5) and (6) led to a receptivity and hunger for new assessment and treatment
    techniques that could be used by such staff and claimed as validly theirs (as opposed
    to being watered down versions of the methods of professions with longer training,
    such as psychotherapy and clinical psychology)
8   The development of the *Recall* tape–slide pack, which provided a method of eliciting
    reminiscences, fulfilled these criteria
9   The development of reality orientation led to an interest in other psychological
    techniques, such as reminiscence
10 There was a confusion of identity between work using the *Recall* pack and
    reminiscence, allowing *Recall* work to be linked to the desires and pretensions of staff
    to be providing therapeutic activities
11 Commercial interest in the spin-offs from recall/reminiscence meant further attention
    was drawn to reminiscence work
12 The increasing interest in oral history, while working with quite different populations
    and to quite different ends, increased the field of relevance of reminiscence and
    provided cross-fertilization of ideas between workers in clinical settings and those in
    community settings
13 A general social demoralization with the present state of government and the society
    it was creating increased interest in previous ways of thinking and behaving; the
    reminiscences of old people is one major technique for finding out about the ways of
    thinking and behaving of previous generations

Coleman also suggested that reminiscence may be a significant predictor of an older person's ability to cope with difficulties.

In spite of these threads of theoretical interest in reminiscence, it was not until a few years later that they were converted into practical results with the notion that reminiscence-based activities might have a positive part to play in enhancing the quality of life for people as they faced the possible impoverishment that older age can bring with it. In the intervening years – between the early 1960s and late 1970s – society was changing in ways that gave the needs of older adults a higher profile, and led to an increased valuation and appreciation of what they had been through, and their reminiscences. A number of such factors are listed in Table 5. So, in the late 1970s, recognizing the increasing isolation of elderly people in various institutions and, in particular, their isolation from younger members of the community, Mick Kemp, an architect, and a group of co-workers, from the DHSS in London, set about constructing a series of reminiscence aids to present to and stimulate older people and to act as a catalyst in mediating interaction in and with the elderly.

Their stated aims were to:

1 provide a framework for caring interaction between old people, care and nursing staff and others;
2 by evoking Reminiscence in the presence of an interested listener, to restore a sense of personal value to the old person;
3 enable old people to regain a fuller perspective of their own past lives and so relate themselves better to the present . . . (DHSS, 1979)

The efforts of the London group concentrated mainly on collecting a sufficient amount of information to produce a number of audio-visual sequences which would act as effective stimulants of reminiscences in mildly confused old people. This they achieved through various radio and newspaper campaigns which provoked a substantial correspondence from old people whose reminiscences formed the basis of the final audio-visual presentation. Their presentations were then used for a field testing study where they were shown to a selected group of old people whose responses were compared with those of a control group with whom the interviewer just chatted instead. Although the results showed no significant differences in increased wellbeing between the two groups, a number of interesting factors highlighting the nature and significance of reminiscences in the elderly emerged.

1 Old people enjoy reminiscing.
2 Reminiscing produces an increased spontaneity of conversation.
3 Reminiscence acts as a point of contact between the old person and others; and between the person and their environment.
4 Reminiscence produces an increase in the responsiveness of old people.
5 Reminiscing tends to be about the interface between an individual and various aspects of [their] world rather than about objective facts.
6 Reminiscing occurs along various dimensions of content, e.g. extending from intimate/personal life experiences outwards to more world-wide events.
7 Certain topics remained, even amongst the most confused, a focal point in reminiscence around which was often built a network of connected or related events.
8 Making use of multiple sensory channels produced better recall. (DHSS, 1979)

Reading these conclusions now, they may not seem very surprising but, at the time, given the low level of interest in older people, these findings were revolutionary. What they suggested was that reminiscence and the material it generates is not just a coincidental consequence of a progressive deterioration of short-term memory faculties but that it

constitutes a functional activity which is of meaning and significance to
the elderly person. The potential impact on these findings might have
been lost because DHSS funding for the project ran out. Fortunately,
however, the interest of Help the Aged, a charitable trust concerned
with promoting the welfare of the elderly, was aroused and in 1981
Recall, a series of 6 tape–slide packs covering a period from the beginning of the twentieth century to 1980, was published.

Recall was London-based and indeed focused on the culture of one
area of London, predominantly the East End. It was intended that it
should provide a model and encouragement for others to produce their
own sets of stimulation materials. Despite its geographical restrictive-
ness, *Recall* was a huge success and copies were bought all over the UK
by people who were anxious to open the gateway for interaction
between old people and those around them.

Interest in whether and how reminiscence-based activities could be
applied in clinical populations was also evident right from the early
stages after *Recall* became available. One of the present authors (A.N.)
had been involved with Kemp's team and helped in the development of
the tape–slide packs. He and a nursing colleague were among the first
workers to report their efforts in using reminiscence as a means of
making more meaningful contact with 'psychogeriatric' patients in a
hospital setting at Stone House, Dartford (Norris and Abu El Eileh,
1982). They got together groups of six patients with a wide range of
diagnoses (from senile dementia to chronic depression) who met for
ten half-hour sessions. A variety of means of stimulation were used,
including interview questions, audio and visual presentations based on
early versions of *Recall* and the use of personal mementos of the patients
themselves. They observed increased levels of interaction and spontaneity of patients within their groups which gave the first encouraging
signs that there were positive directions that could be followed in work
with what had otherwise become a rather neglected group. For the
ward staff too these reminiscence groups became an important
mediating influence in their relationships with the patients under
their care. Gradually the staff became more aware of their patients as
individuals, each with their own life history and as people who had
emotional as well as physical needs. Indeed, the reminiscence groups
had a profound effect on the morale and caring philosophy of the ward
as a whole.

During the mid-1980s, reports of a huge number of reminiscence-
based activities began to appear in all kinds of settings from community
groups to day centres to long-stay hospitals. The variety of activities
being generated was also mirrored by the enormous variety of different
people who began to show an interest in being involved in reminiscence
work. These included not only professional nursing and care staff,
psychologists and occupational therapists, but also voluntary workers,
carers, schoolchildren and so on. What also became evident was that the

declared purpose to which these activities were being put was incredibly diverse. Thus reminiscence was variously seen as being fun, therapeutic, educational, important for the recording of local history and so on.

The hope of the creators of the original *Recall* pack that many examples of locally produced material might evolve was rarely met in as complete and detailed a way as their own. (The Northern Ireland pack, created by a team around Faith Gibson, is an exception.) However, what *Recall* did give rise to was a mushrooming of a whole variety of commercially available reminiscence stimulation materials. These ranged from photographs, tapes, jig-saws, to games and memorabilia packs so that by the mid-1980s there was a plethora of reminiscence aids to chose from. This large amount of commercially available material and its promotion and advertising in turn stimulated yet others to engage in reminiscence work.

But this unrestrained escalation in reminiscence-based activities was not greeted with unreserved enthusiasm. In 1987, two psychologists, Sue Thornton and Janet Brotchie, decided to review the research evidence upon which reminiscence work was being conducted. They found a number of flaws in the ways in which the research had been conducted and the means by which the outcome had been assessed based on the reports of these activities in the research literature. Their conclusion was to advocate strong caution in viewing reminiscence as a panacea approach, applicable to everyone in every situation. (Coleman had of course already provided evidence showing that a sizeable number of older people did not think reminiscence of value to themselves, see Table 4.)

Nevertheless, interest in reminiscence-based activities has continued to grow and enthusiasm for them remains unabated. The latest major initiative in stimulus material came in 1990 with the version of *Recall* created in Northern Ireland by Faith Gibson. Currently, reminiscence work boasts both its own journal, entitled *Reminiscence*, and several theatre groups and organizations, including the Age-Exchange group based in Blackheath especially dedicated to the encouragement of reminiscence activities. Most recently, Joanna Bornat, who was involved in the later stages of the London *Recall* and who has been a real force in the oral history movement, has edited a book, *Reminiscence Reviewed* (1994), which provides a comprehensive review of the current state of developments within the field.

In summary, it can be seen that despite the paucity and quality of empirical research on the subject, reminiscence-based activities have had a considerable impact on the (re-)enhancement of the status of old people in society. Also these have provided an interactive framework within which old people and those from younger generations have been brought together.

It is outside the remit of this book to look at the research data, but one relevant point may be that 'reminiscence' of itself, cannot successfully be researched, as if all the various ways of undertaking it were the same, and used/activated by the same processes. Rather, each group needs to have its purposes spelt out. Once this is done, research can usefully be undertaken to investigate what is happening in each type of group and to see if these purposes were fulfilled.

Chapter 3

THE 3 Cs – CLIENT, CARER, CONTEXT

Since the time when reminiscence-based activities first began to have an impact, there have been many changes to the settings in which care takes place. These include changes of philosophy, pattern and provision of care, particularly within health and social services situations. The advent of community care, the care planning process and an emphasis on key workers and needs-based assessment has meant a radical change in ethos and approach as to how care services have been organized.

Those who currently work in the field would probably argue that provision for older adults is still the Cinderella amongst health and social services. But it has to be acknowledged that the needs of older people and ensuring that care of an acceptable standard is available to them, has had a much higher political and ethical profile than was the case a few years earlier. Devolution of residential care from local authority control to the private sector has been a mixed blessing. On the one hand, it has necessitated a closer monitoring of standards of care but, at the same time, this has tended to mean a concentration on physical and safety aspects of care rather than attention to the whole range of needs of the older adult. Provisions for programmes for activity and stimulation are, at best, sporadic while consideration of emotional and spiritual needs is as incidental as ever it used to be. Indeed, economic considerations often mean that attention to these areas is seen as a luxury if considered at all.

Overall, the way that services have evolved has meant that what currently exists is a diversity of provision which varies both in its quality and the degree to which it adequately addresses the full range of needs of the clients for whom it has been designed. The importance of a particular service should be assessed in terms of how well it meets client needs, rather than because it is seen as having an inherent value of itself. For instance, the changed emphasis towards community care is claimed to reflect the desire that older adults have to remain in their own homes for as long as possible. Certainly it challenges the long-established view that residential or nursing home care should be the automatic means of providing long-stay care for the frail and elderly. This is highly commendable providing that community care is *actually* what the individual older adult wants and needs. The danger is that community care becomes the new, substitute answer to everybody's problems and the needs of those who are highly dependent become lost.

There are, however, a number of factors which will determine the effectiveness and suitability of what services are provided. Devolution of services out of local authority control; the resultant increase in the variety of types of care available, plus a wider range of attitudes and philosophies on which the care is based, are just some of these. As well as considering the needs of the older person, nowadays, possibly more than ever, it is important to consider what needs and attitudes those who *provide* the care bring with them. In these times of rationalized resources, financial constraints and the emphasis on increased efficiency, it is important to determine precisely what are the resources available. But it is also vital to know the kind of environment and philosophy which will underpin that care. Experience, stress levels, training, supervision, commitment and motivation are just some of the things that will affect the caregivers and what they can provide.

The emotional, moral, cultural and spiritual values implicit in particular care philosophies will also have a profound effect on whether needs-appropriate care is given. For instance, the distinction between a nursing home and a residential care setting is well known. In the former, it is likely that the regime will be centred around providing good medical care and maintaining optimum levels of physical functioning. In contrast, residential care often starts from the basis of attempting to provide a homely setting in which older people can be cared for. Neither kind of establishment will necessarily neglect the type of provision offered by the other, but the starting point and priorities offered by each is likely to be different. More subtle permutations on this theme include whether old people are seen as primarily needing 'tender, loving, care' or to be 'kept comfortable' or to be 'helped to be as fully independent as possible'. However implicit or explicit these kinds of expressions of care philosophy might be, they will affect all aspects of what happens to a person under their influence and they need to be fully considered if we are to understand how effective and appropriate a given service provision is likely to be.

One of the particular contributions that reminiscence-based work has made to the increased quality of care for the individual is the way it has placed value on the whole person – particularly the emotional, psychological and spiritual dimensions which make up their lives. So, in the current climate, where there is a danger of de-individualization in the way that care is provided, reminiscence-based work has the potential for helping to reassert the importance of ensuring that services are planned on the basis of client need. However, it is very important to understand that reminiscence will only increase the perceived individuality of a client *if it is undertaken in a context which values individuality*.

Reminiscence work, as a block activity, 'to fill the Tuesday morning slot' or 'all our residents get reminiscence therapy' is hardly likely to achieve much in the way of establishing individual identities.

Summarizing this section: to understand reminiscence work, we must look beyond the immediate needs of the clients that we are trying to meet. One of the major purposes of this book then is to help us identify the many different factors which will influence the effectiveness of the reminiscence-based activities in which we might seek to engage.

To help us fully understand the range of factors determining the quality of reminiscence work, we have classified these factors under three headings – **client**, **carer** and **context** – in what we have called the '3Cs' approach.

Our brief overview of the history and development of reminiscence-based activities in Chapter 2 showed the substantial amount of interest which work in this area has created. This can only be for the good, since, in turn, it reflects an increase in interest in work with potentially disadvantaged and isolated groups, such as older people. The effect of heightened involvement in reminiscence-based activities can only mean that the interface between older people and those with whom they come into contact is enhanced.

However, it is important that the enthusiasm and energy which reminiscence work has generated for older people does not become misdirected. In particular, we must ensure that, in our desire to improve the quality of life for older people, that same enthusiasm doesn't blind us to the needs of the people we are seeking to provide for. The possibility of this happening arises because, as care-providers, we have needs, motives and desires of our own. That is not to say that these needs will be incompatible with those for whom we care. After all, every saint needs a cause! However, it is important to ensure that the needs of those who provide care and stimulation do not predominate over those for whom an activity is designed. This particularly applies in the case of reminiscence-based activities because, as we shall see, the basic principle of reminiscence is to create and sustain personal identity and self-esteem (see Purpose Sixteen). Any activity which is applied in blanket fashion without regard to the needs and preferences of the individuals concerned would undermine such a purpose.

Equally, it is important for any activity not to become an end in itself. As marvellous as we might think reminiscence to be, it is not the panacea for all people in all situations and, indeed, as has already been noted, different people will respond in their own way to reminiscence-based activity, reflecting something of the person they are.

It follows that arranging any activity, especially a reminiscence-based activity, must first be preceded by a detailed assessment not only of the needs of the individuals to be involved but also by an understanding of what is motivating and affecting the person organizing the activity and/ or caring for those who will participate. To complete our understanding of how activities can most effectively be organized for people, we must also appraise the settings in which the activity will take place.

In order to help identify the many and varied sources of need that will have to be taken into consideration when organizing reminiscence-based activities, we have classified them under our three headings and shall consider each in turn.

- Client: pertaining to the abilities, motivation and predisposition of participants.
- Carer: pertaining to the hopes, expectations and motives of those who serve or care for the participants, usually other staff.
- Context: pertaining to the physical and care philosophy elements of the environments in which the reminiscence-based activities take place and the various pressures that those environments are likely to be under.

Client factors

Detailed assessment is the key to ensuring that all the needs that are apposite in a given situation are understood and taken into account. Sources of information for assessment are extremely diverse, ranging from direct observation, biochemical and physiological data to subjective reports from both the individuals concerned and those who care for them.

The way information required to help in the assessment of needs is collected will also vary. For instance, it may involve simply talking to the person to determine what their desires, perceptions and motivations are. However, this kind of assessment may need to be combined with observation of behaviour, systematic recording of that behaviour on charts, records or graphs, interviews and detailed reports from those involved with the person and/or the use of more formal psychometric tests (see Holden and Woods, 1995, for example).

The precise method of assessment that is appropriate will depend on the kind of individuals involved. In all cases, however, in order not to compromise the important aim that the individual's integrity and self-esteem are to be sustained, it is important that during the assessment the person should never feel devalued, judged or undermined. Even with the most difficult of people, it is important that they feel respected, valued and affirmed as, not only is this fundamental to the reminiscence-orientated approach, but also such an attitude will make cooperation and involvement in any activity planned much more likely.

We now examine those factors which centre on the person (or persons) who are targeted for reminiscence. These are factors which stem from the person's own past or predisposition:

1   Physical and sensory wellbeing
2   Cognitive abilities
3   Individual background past/character
4   Personality characteristics
5   Emotional state
6   Motivation
7   Life adjustment

Physical/sensory wellbeing

The particular vulnerability of older people to physical illness and the widespread effects of any illness on their physical and mental functioning is well known (e.g. Hunt, 1979). However, the importance of poor eyesight or hearing should not be underestimated. Whilst it is not within the scope of this book to examine such factors in any detail, it is obvious that physical or sensory health should not be allowed to prevent anyone from participating in any reminiscence activity. It is quite possible, and in many cases quite simple, to compensate for such deficits, yet these can so easily be overlooked.

A comprehensive assessment of physical and sensory performance will rely on those who know the person best and/or who are in a position to monitor them over a period of time, keeping a lookout for changes in behaviour and other signs and symptoms which might be indicative of physical ill-health. Among the kind of factors that influence ability to be involved in reminiscence or any other similar activity are such conditions as a chest or urinary tract infection, constipation, toxic levels of drugs or alcohol which cause temporary confusion; diabetes and cardiac problems which can cause both temporary and more long-term damage; and sensory difficulties – difficulties with sight or hearing – that can give rise to behaviours that look like confusion, as when there are wild guesses because a person did not hear the question, which 'proves' they have dementia. With older people this is particularly important because of their increased susceptibility to illness and the fact that any physical imbalance in their body is likely to have far wider effects than for younger people. Thus, a dose of flu might inconvenience a younger person by making them feel drowsy and stuffed up, and giving them a headache and cough to contend with. The older person is more likely to be knocked off their feet, suffer from short-term confusional episodes and be completely disorientated. Immediate treatment of any physical or sensory disability usually alleviates not only the primary cause but also any secondary effects and so will obviously decrease any difficulties that might be produced.

Cognitive abilities

These are the factors concerned with the nature and level of an individual's mental state and functioning. The level of cognitive functioning should always be considered where a person has suffered brain damage or experienced educational and/or developmental difficulties. Cognitive ability also affects how well equipped an individual might be to carry out normal, everyday tasks or functions. In everyday life problems may go unnoticed because the person may have strategies for coping with routine, well-learned tasks or be able to avoid carrying out tasks for which they are not mentally equipped. However where a person is being asked to undertake a specific task, requiring specific cognitive skills, the consequences of any problems may become more obvious or express themselves in a reluctance by the individual to become involved in the activity.

There are cognitive skills involved in taking part in reminiscence work, so we do not want to expose a person to a failure experience. If we know their level of cognitive ability, we can then most usually create a setting whose demands are appropriate to that level.

There are a whole range of conditions that result in limited cognitive functioning. These include problems arising during the course of natural development, involvement in road traffic accidents, other types of head injuries, heart attacks and strokes, and the consequences of suffering from a dementing illness (see below). It is also important to recognize that these various conditions may give rise to quite subtle and specific deficits in cognitive functioning. They may be deficits in specific areas of memory functioning or an inability to recognize quite specific things, as well as more generalized dysfunctioning of such areas of the brain as the frontal or temporal lobes as illustrated in Table 6. (Una Holden's 1995 text is a useful account of such difficulties.)

The condition most often thought of as accounting for problems of cognitive functioning in older people is, of course, senile dementia. Not only is this inaccurate – the most frequent causes are physical conditions – but the term 'dementia' itself is often used in a misleading way. Quite literally, to talk of 'dementia' or to refer to a 'dementing illness' merely describes a progressive deterioration in cognitive functioning. When used in this way, it refers only to a *set of symptoms*, such as forgetfulness, disorientation or non-rational speech, which are the result of some underlying *cause*. As we have already indicated, this underlying *cause* may be one that is treatable, and so although a person may be described as 'dementing', their dementia may not be incurable or, indeed, inevitable.

It is only when these reversible causes of dementia have been investigated and ruled out that a diagnosis of 'Alzheimer's' or 'multi-infarct dementia' should be made. These are the two most important and commonest forms of organic brain damage. In these conditions, it is assumed that the person is experiencing progressive loss of mental functioning associated with identifiable loss of organic brain cell function. Progressive loss of function in this case seems to be inevitable.

On the face of it this sounds rather depressing and hopeless. However, it needs to be emphasized that Alzheimer's disease, which is the

Table 6 *Possible cognitive deficits which may impair the individual's ability to participate in reminiscence-based activities*

Deficit	How you can recognize it
Short-term memory	Person needs repeated reminders to do things, asks repeated questions.
Recall memory	Person will only remember something if given a cue or clue
Agnosias (inability to recognize objects/sounds)	Person fails to react to something unless its meaning/purpose is demonstrated to them
Apraxias (inability to put together sequences of movements)	Person needs help in activities of daily living or dressing
Receptive dysphasia	Person has difficulty in understanding what is said to them
Expressive dysphasia	Person has difficulty in finding the right words in conversation
Frontal lobe problems	Person will only do things when asked or gets stuck once started, and socially disinhibited behaviour

most common form of dementia, has been identified as occurring in only 5 per cent of people age 65 and over, and only 1 in 4 of people who are 85 and over suffer from the illness.

Alzheimer's disease is characterized by a gradual loss of global mental functioning, usually beginning with memory. Less common forms of dementia, such as multi-infarct or arteriosclerotic dementia, are said to show small step-like decreases in mental functioning interspersed with periods of stability. Other types of organic dementia are Creutzfeldt-Jakob disease and Lewy Body dementia.

Diagnosis of the cause of some deficits in mental functioning can often require specialist help. However, the diversity of causes of problems in mental ability indicates just how important it is that assessment of mental functioning does take place. At the very least, some informal assessment of mental functioning and ability will be necessary if success in reminiscence activity is to be maximized. Non-specific assessments of intellectual functioning may be sufficient where no obvious impairment is detected but if a person seems to be reluctant or have difficulty in engaging in the possibility of reminiscence then more detailed assessment may be useful. Sometimes it is helpful to try a single, pilot session and see how the persons gets on.

What is important to note is that, even where deficits in mental functioning are identified, providing that when a reminiscence activity is planned they are taken into account appropriately, they will not necessarily stop a person from participating in that activity. Indeed, much of what you will find written later in this book will testify to the different ways in which reminiscence activities have been adapted to account for the varying degrees of mental ability encountered with a whole range of different groups of older people. Whilst reminiscence activity may not cure mental disability, it can certainly provide a means of exercising the abilities the person retains.

Individual background/life history

The basis on which reminiscence work is founded is the recognition that each of us is different by virtue of the experiences that have been part of our lives. Obviously, knowing something about a person's life history can help us understand why people respond in a particular way in different circumstances. Such information will be particularly useful if we are trying to determine why some people respond more positively to reminiscence activity than others. For older people in particular, problems arise when current lifestyle and/or the expectations placed upon them become incompatible with their past.

Finally, if we want to make the contents of a group relevant to a person, we need to know about their life.

A more detailed account of how the background, past lifestyle and character of a person can be systematically assessed and taken into account in planning reminiscence activities can be found in our *Groupwork with the Elderly* (Bender, Norris and Bauckham, 1987).

Personality characteristics

One of the themes that will emerge as we pursue our consideration of the enormous variety of situations and people with which reminiscence-based activity can be seen to be appropriate is that such activity may either have to be adapted in particular ways for some groups of people or may be less suited in some circumstances compared to others. A major influence in considering suitability is going to be the kind of person who is being engaged in the activity. An obvious example is whether the individual is extrovert or shy. The latter does not preclude reminiscence work, but it may well have to be in a less public, one-to-one setting if the introverted person is to be involved; or the group leader may have to pay more attention to helping the members feel relaxed.

It may also be necessary to take into account more subtle personality traits. These are the kinds of qualities or characteristics of the individual which may only be gleaned from the sort of background information mentioned in the previous section. For instance, if a person comes from a background of a high status occupation she may not take kindly to being placed in a situation where she feels out of control of the situation. Reminiscence activity for this person is most likely to be facilitated when involvement is negotiated on their terms – a suggestion that the participation of that particular person in the activity would be an especial privilege, for instance, or that they might have an especially important contribution to make.

Emotional state

Peter Coleman's work indicating the different ways people respond to reminiscence work reminds us that not only will reminiscing affect how people feel about themselves, but also, how people feel will affect whether they want to reminisce. The 'disengagement theory' put forward by Cumming and Henry (1961) suggested that as people grow older they need to withdraw from their involvement in all that is around them in order that they can adjust successfully to old age. In contrast, 'activity theory' (Havighurst, 1968) argues that continued involvement in various activities is crucial if a person is to be satisfied in their old age. What this debate highlights is that there is a fine balance between recognizing, on the one hand, that because of a person's mood or disposition they may or may not be inclined or appropriately included in a reminiscence activity and, on the other hand, the fact that encouraging them to be involved in reminiscence activities may actually improve their mood. So, it is obviously important that a person's emotional state is taken into account when considering what kind of reminiscence activity may be appropriate for them. It is important to know the emotional 'frame' the member is likely to bring to the group in order to prepare a strategy of how to relate to it.

Motivation

Whilst lack of motivation may be a symptom of some of the other factors already mentioned, it is important to consider what the perceived role of undertaking a reminiscence activity will be in the eyes of the person who is being recruited for involvement. No matter how nicely they are asked, it may be that *from their perspective* the activity may be seen as an unwarranted and unsolicited intrusion into their life, as previously highlighted by Coleman's work. Again, respect for the individual is of paramount importance in reminiscence work, so to zealously pursue recruitment at all costs is nearly always inappropriate.

Life adjustment/coping style

There has been plenty of work – pioneered by workers such as McMahon and Rhudick in the USA and followed up by Peter Coleman in this country – to indicate that the way in which people reminisce, or indeed don't, relates to their coping strategies as they get older. So it appears that those who have a positive attitude towards growing older and an ability to develop and change in old age are much more likely to be willing to reflect on their past and to view it in a positive and realistic manner. Conversely, the reminiscences of those who have experienced unresolved conflicts in their past, if they occur at all, are much more likely to be characterized by guilt, exaggerated self-importance and anxiety. The implications of such observations emphasize again the importance of being aware that different individuals will perceive the value of reminiscence in different ways, and these need to be taken into account if reminiscence-based activities are to have their full, positive impact.

Carer factors

The second heading under which we can consider the factors that will influence the outcome of encouraging reminiscence-based activities we have termed 'carer' factors. These refer to the influences which are centred not on the individual client/patient/participant but on those with whom they come into contact. This may mean professional carers, such as nursing or residential care staff, but it can equally refer to others who form part of the person's social environment, including family, friends, acquaintances and others in their peer group.

Carer factors influencing the effectiveness of reminiscence may be listed as:

1 Physical and sensory wellbeing
2 Individual background
3 Personality characteristics
4 Emotional state
5 Cognitive abilities
6 Motivation
7 Life adjustment
8 Hopes and expectations
9 Willingness and cooperation
10 Staff training

Many of the factors under this heading parallel those already listed under the 'client' heading, which is hardly surprising given that neither 'clients' nor 'staff' should be regarded as alien beings in relation to one another. For instance, a group leader who is listening to members' accounts of severe physical punishment inflicted on them when they were children will react at least partly in terms of *their* own upbringing and the ways *their* parents punished them, thus showing that they are just as open and vulnerable to their past as the group members are themselves.

For this reason, we will not laboriously go over each factor. Rather, we will highlight a few clusters.

Hopes and expectations

Although it might be argued that the primary motivation for another person to be involved in the care of an individual is to ensure that the needs of that individual are met, we must still be mindful that their own needs must also be taken into account. Sometimes these needs may be in conflict with those of the individuals upon whom care is being focused and if the person being cared for is vulnerable or frail it is likely that carer needs or wishes will predominate. For instance, supposing a member of staff leading a reminiscence group is motivated by the desire to jolly the members on. If a time comes when members of the group seem to be facing difficult memories, it might be a temptation for the staff member to gloss over what might be shared in the interests of 'not upsetting the resident'. Similarly, although it might seem harsh when written down in black and white, the fact of the matter is that for some staff members, there is a vested interest in perceiving those whom they care for as being in some way disabled or dysfunctional. It follows that their hopes and expectations for the clients are likely to be limited. If a reminiscence-based activity challenges their perception of what the other individual should be like, then this is likely to exert a negative influence on their handling of such an activity.

Willingness and cooperation

Related to the above issue is how well motivated other staff who come into contact with the group members are to engage in and/or encourage reminiscence-based activities. Motivation has an effect on the encouragement of reminiscence at both ends of the motivation spectrum. On the one hand, poor motivation is, at best, likely to result in impoverished reminiscence work. Staff may come to a reminiscence activity with the belief either that it is a waste of time or simply another additional load for them to bear in an already busy schedule. Such beliefs will, of course, affect the attitude with which that member of staff will contribute and be committed to making a reminiscence-based activity work. On the other hand, too much enthusiasm on the part of the leader is likely to mean important cues and opportunities may be missed at the expense of the individuals involved.

Training

The issue of whether someone who engages in encouraging reminiscence-based activities needs to be trained, qualified or boast some particular background or experience is often raised. The balance to be addressed in this context is between ensuring the right skills are available to be applied and not creating an exclusivity about who can or cannot appropriately be involved in reminiscence work. The solution to attaining the right balance must lie in a careful consideration of what the aims of the reminiscence work being attempted might be. Explicitly 'therapeutic' reminiscence work which is directed towards facilitating psychological resolution or development clearly requires the appropriate professional training and ongoing supervision. By contrast, reminiscence as a means of encouraging social stimulation is something in which many people are engaged even without being aware that this is what they are doing. Using reminiscence for this purpose requires less training. The possibility that training may help to refine skills and capitalize on opportunities present should not be dismissed, however. We shall return to this important issue later in the book.

Context factors

Our third heading embodies all those influences that stem from the physical or social environment in which reminiscence-based activities are to take place and which will impinge on those activities. These influences are often embodied in the management practices of an establishment or expressed directly in the attitude of managers, proprietors and senior staff of the facilities in which reminiscence activities are likely to take place. The reason why it is particularly important to identify these influences is because they can be quite subtle, unspoken and not always palatable in terms of the values a particular care environment might wish to believe it holds. Such influences are especially difficult to confront when what is declared by policy, aims or mission statements fails to materialize in terms of what is practised. These factors nevertheless can exert a very profound influence on to what degree any activity is encouraged or passively tolerated, or indeed, whether it is consciously or subconsciously sabotaged! It should be noted however, that merely identifying the problem is not enough and considerable careful attention has to be paid to how issues that challenge the ethos of a particular environment can be successfully handled. (Bender, Levens and Goodson's *Welcoming Your Clients* (1995) addresses these issues at length.) Among the issues that might have to be addressed are:

1 Respect
2 Feasibility
3 Resources
4 Space
5 Timing

Respect

To respect someone is to treat them as an individual whose beliefs and feelings are to be valued and, if at all possible, furthered. The dictionary says 'to pay due heed to, to appreciate fully, to be mindful of and not belittle or treat with contempt'.

We consider respect more in terms of *context* rather than in terms of the individual carer. This might seem surprising. It might be thought that respect should be considered a carer factor. After all, surely respect is an attitude that one person has towards another person? This is quite correct, but respect for others is not instinctive. We learn it from the way others behave towards different classes of people. Of course, we do bring our attitudes from our previous life and experience to our work; but these are weak effects compared to the attitudes of staff to the clients in their particular unit. The culture of the workplace is a far stronger determinant of what happens than any one individual worker's beliefs or wishes. We quickly get to see how other staff behave towards them; and so we quickly learn the culture – the atmosphere of the unit – when we start work. So, to respect or not respect clients is a group process and, because often not clearly or openly stated, hard to put a finger on.

Reminiscence work and respect are closely related. Respect is crucially about valuing the individual, reminiscence work is about valuing what the individual has to tell you about their past. Thus effective reminiscence work is one type of respecting and it is very difficult to do or feel good about doing it in any unit that does not pay respect to the individual client.

Feasibility

Every (care) environment has its own ethos, both declared and in reality, as well as its own rules and regulations. Some of these will be explicit such as 'No smoking in bedrooms' whilst others will be implicit, for instance, in the philosophy of care which places a low/high value on tender loving care and minimum demands on the residents. It is therefore important to ensure that any activity which is proposed takes especial account of these implicit values, particularly if they are likely to challenge the prevailing ethos of that environment. Reminiscence-based activity can encourage each member to express their individuality, so that if it takes place in an environment where routine and conformity dominate the daily routine, conflict and resistance may well arise. This may be expressed explicitly by the attitudes of those who have charge of that environment or it may be implicitly noticed through the hesitation and reluctance observed from those invited to take part in the activity themselves.

Resources

Any activity requires resources – resources and motivation from those who are to participate in the activity; ability and motivation from those who are to organize the activity; and resources from the environment in which the activity is to take place. The environmental resources which need to be identified may simply be in terms of availability of the necessary physical space in which the activity is to take place (see our *Groupwork with the Elderly* and also the next following section). Usually, these environmental resources also include resources such as stimulus materials, the appropriate hard and soft ware to utilize them, as well as people, space in the timetable and finances.

Good planning is an essential part of organizing and implementing any activity and so it is vital that these considerations are negotiated and resolved right from the outset.

Space

The provision of not only physical but psychological space in which reminiscence-based activities can take place is so important that it deserves emphasizing. It almost goes without saying that in order to ensure that such an activity can attract the attention it deserves, there must be a well-defined place in which it can happen. However it is also important to ensure that such a place is free from distraction, disruption or other factors which will inhibit the activity. For example, holding a discussion-based activity in a corridor will permit constant intrusions on privacy, and slide shows need to take place in a suitably darkened area where they can be clearly visible. If intimacy and disclosure are to be encouraged then the environment must be enveloping, warm and comfortable – gymnasia tend not to be the best places to hold psychotherapy groups!

Timing

Even the slot in the daily routine given over to an activity may have an influence on how successful that activity is likely to be. If there is a siesta hour after a midday meal, such a time slot will therefore be less conducive to activity that will require concentration and effort. Choosing a time which immediately precedes or, especially, which follows other physically or emotionally demanding activities should be avoided. Obviously how these things will affect an individual will vary from person to person but they must nevertheless be carefully considered if the optimum conditions for reminiscence-based activity to be successful are to occur. It is also likely that an environment has a rhythm affecting all its members to a degree.

Overview of assessing sources of need

Thus far we have been examining the various influences which it may be important to consider in ensuring the maximum chances of success for reminiscence-based activities. What our overview indicates is that, before such activities are undertaken a comprehensive assessment of need must be carried out. What we have endeavoured to illustrate is that the source of that need is not necessarily confined to the individual participant in the reminiscence activity. If reminiscence work is to be successful, it is vital that those who plan it take into account the various forces at work.

The starting point must be the needs of the client. This principle applies with any activity but it is especially important in the context of reminiscence-based activities because a central part of what they are designed to achieve lies in ensuring that the needs of the individual are not only recognized but respected, and providing a vehicle for their expression.

Reminiscence activity, as we have said, may also be established as much to meet staff or carer need as the needs of any of the individuals who might become participants. What is important from the outset is that the organizers recognize just whose needs are being met and therefore what objectives are likely to be achieved. All too frequently reminiscence activities set up under the guise of meeting a need for a group of patients/clients/ residents etc. in reality have more to do with staff enthusiasm than meeting appropriate client need.

Likewise in many professional care settings an organization feels it *ought* to be engaged in certain types of activity. If these activities bear no relationship to meeting the needs of the individuals for whom they are to be established, then their validity is to be questioned.

The following is a simple list of questions which might help determine the need for reminiscence-based activities:

Client issues

1 Do the people to be involved in the activity enjoy talking about their past?
2 When they talk about their past, are their reminiscences characterized by anxiety, guilt, hesitation or reluctance?
3 Are there any features of their cognitive functioning or sensory abilities or emotional state which need to be taken into account for them to gain the full benefits of reminiscence?
4 Are the people who are to be involved on the whole well motivated towards the activity?
5 Do they make excuses for not being involved? Why?
6 Are any of the people naturally shy or introverted?

Carer issues

1 Under whose initiative is the reminiscence activity being established?
2 Have those involved received any training for the activity and the objectives which are being established?
3 Are those involved fully committed to their own participation?
4 Has a thorough and objective assessment of client need been carried out?

Context issues

1 Is there an appropriate location in which the activity can be held?
2 Is the activity planned to happen at a time which will maximize the opportunity for full participation?
3 Has the activity got the support and cooperation of management and those whose responsibility it is to ensure the necessary resources – people, time, materials, finance etc. – will be made available?
4 Are the aims of the activity compatible with those of the context in which the activity will take place?

Conclusion

The recognition that not only service provision but also organization of activity and therapeutic endeavour must be needs-led has become pretty well established. What this book seeks to do is highlight the fact that the source of need may vary or be a combination of that which stems from factors associated with those for whom activities are organized (clients), those who are organizing the activities (carers) and the environment and/or context in which the activity takes place (context). In the following chapters we shall examine, in detail, how a variety of needs can be identified, separated out and met through reminiscence-based activities. In so doing, it is our hope that future applications of such activities will be more carefully planned to ensure they fit a suitable defined purpose, whether for the client, the carers or the context.

Reminiscence-based work boasts as one of its major achievements the re-establishment of the importance of the individual and their background in the care they receive. It is our hope that by examining the different ways in which reminiscence activities can be used, the way those activities themselves are planned and run will take account of individual needs – both of clients and staff – and thereby promote individuality and be even more effective.

Bibliography for Part One

Bender, M., Norris, A. and Bauckham, P. (1987) *Groupwork with the Elderly*, Winslow Press.
Bender, M., Levens, V. and Goodson, C. (1995) *Welcoming Your Clients*, Winslow Press.
Bornat, J. (ed.) (1994) *Reminiscence Reviewed*, Open University Press.
Butler, R. (1963) 'The Life Review: an interpretation of reminiscences in the aged', *Psychiatry*, 26, pp. 65–76.
Coleman, P.G. (1974) 'Measuring reminiscence characteristics from conversation as adaptive features of old age', *International Journal of Aging and Human Development*, 5, pp. 281–94.

Coleman, P. (1986) *Ageing and Reminiscence Processes*, Wiley.

Cumming, E. and Henry, W. (1961) *Growing Old: a Process of Disengagement*, Basic Books.

DHSS (1979) *Reminiscence Aids*, DHSS.

Erikson, E. (1950) *Childhood and Society*, Norton, republished (1965) Penguin.

Freud, S. (1900) *The Interpretation of Dreams*, Hogarth Press.

Freud, S. (1904) *The Psychopathology of Everyday Life*, Hogarth Press.

Gibson, F. (1994) *Reminiscence and Recall*, Age Concern.

Havighurst, R. (1968) 'Personality and patterns of ageing', *Gerontologist*, 8, pp. 20–3.

Holden, U. (1995) *Ageing, Neuropsychology and the 'New' Dementias*, Chapman and Hall.

Holden, U. and Woods, R. (1995) *Reality Orientation*, Churchill Livingstone.

Hunt, A. (1979) 'Some aspects of the health of elderly people in England', *Health Trends*, 1, pp. 21–3.

McMahon, A. and Rhudick, P. (1964) 'Reminiscing: adaptational significance in the aged', *Archives of General Psychiatry*, 10, pp. 292–298, republished in Levin, S. and Kahana, R. (eds) (1967) *Psychodynamic Studies on Ageing: Creativity, Reminiscing and Dying*, International Universities Press.

Norris, A. and Abu El Eileh, M. (1982) 'Reminiscence groups', *Nursing Times*, 78, pp. 1368 1369.

Piaget, J. (1950) *The Psychology of Intelligence*, Routledge and Kegan Paul.

Thornton, S. and Brotchie, J. (1987) 'Reminiscence: a critical view of the literature', *British Journal of Clinical Psychology*, 26, pp. 93–111.

Note: The Help the Aged tape–slide pack is now marketed by Winslow Press, Telford Road, Bicester, Oxon OX6 0TS.

PART TWO

REMINISCENCE WORK THAT HELPS CLIENTS

We now proceed to look at 16 purposes of reminiscence that relate to the needs of clients.

Each chapter will first give the rationale for each reminiscence activity. There will then be an outline of the goals implied in that purpose and an identification of what the group leader's tasks will be in helping to achieve these goals. There will be practical advice on how these tasks can be or have been carried out and examples given of the particular purpose in action. Finally, before reaching some conclusions on the importance of a particular purpose for reminiscence and offering some useful reading lists, there will be one detailed account of how a purpose has been worked out in practice.

To make each chapter more user-friendly and comparable, we employed an identical set of headings for each:

- The rationale for the purpose: our first task is to 'spread out' each purpose so that the reader will feel familiar and at ease with the thinking behind the use of reminiscence for this purpose. Where did the idea of using it in this way come from? What were the authors of the idea trying to get at?
- The goals implied in that purpose.
- The tasks – be they individual or in a group – that such a purpose entails.
- How those tasks might be carried out.
- Examples of work for the purpose.
- One detailed account of the purpose in action usually drawn from our own experience, to provide a more detailed, 'warts and all' account.
- Conclusions.
- Useful reading and resources.

Purpose One

REMINISCENCE TO ENCOURAGE SPONTANEOUS CONVERSATION BETWEEN CLIENTS

Rationale

Basically, we are social beings, disposed to hold social dialogue with others – to be friendly. So most people prefer to live in a community, and to seek the company of others. Any one community has its own distinct cultural patterns and institutions, sharing common aims and interests. Here we can relate to others, live and interact, whether it be in formal or informal ways. The extent of our involvement, how much we engage in social discourse, and seek companionship or communal activities, depends upon who we are, as individuals, on our personality, our makeup. That is not to say people do not want their own space, but few are born social isolates. However, through circumstances we can become one.

Observing people coming together or living together, we automatically think that an opportunity has been provided for friendliness and conviviality. When we are young and have the confidence of youth, or success and self-reliance as our careers and life progress, or the self-possession and assurance that maturity brings, this may be so. However, life is cruel and this confidence can be taken from us, be this through personal circumstances or illness, never more so than in old age. A personal tragedy or a debilitating illness may affect us at any time. However, *may* is the operative word. Old age is there waiting for all of us. How it will affect each one of us and how each of us will cope with it is entirely different. Many live productive fulfilling years, but this may well depend upon the network of relatives, friends or significant others who are still living or able to interact with us. If this network diminishes through illness, death or the older person's own frailty and inability to travel freely in order to maintain these links, then the person becomes insular. They end up with fewer companions, and become physically and psychologically isolated.

An older person who enters a care setting such as a day centre, residential home or hospital, may have lived for some considerable time alone before becoming known to any of the support services. During this period, in some cases, eyesight and/or hearing may have failed and with loss of ability to read the daily papers or listen to the radio or television, communication may all but cease. Then not only has the older person coming into care been starved of companionship, but they have also been starved of stimuli with which to initiate conversation, should someone enter their life. The ability to converse requires nourishment; without it we dry up and become dull and barren.

The aim therefore when using reminiscence for the purpose of **spontaneous conversation between elderly clients** is to assist in helping to initiate conversation, client to client, encouraging bonds and forming relationships by using the common ground of their past. We can encourage social growth by providing stimulus material in the daily living situation on which our clients can focus. This material should be familiar and relevant to those who live in or visit the care establishment. Most older people want to talk to someone, they have just forgotten how, and need something to get their conversations started.

Inviting elderly clients to join a reminiscence group has been shown to promote social dialogue between staff and clients, and with positive staff running a group, between client and client. The situation is, of course, to some extent contrived and stage managed by staff. While not wishing to devalue such work, we would point out that its purpose is somewhat different. The essence of Purpose One, on the other hand, is to provide an environment that provokes and encourages *spontaneous* conversation *without* the direct intervention or presence of staff. An added bonus is that this important goal, once the positive situation has been created, is low in its demands on staff time.

Goals implied in the purpose

1 To trigger spontaneous conversation between clients.
2 To assist in the forming of friendship.
3 To increase self-esteem.
4 To aid independence.
5 To support the empowerment of older people.
6 To provide a familiar, stimulating and enjoyable environment.
7 To reinforce a sense of security.

The task

The core task is to facilitate conversation between clients who have come together in a residential or day centre setting. To achieve this end without the physical presence/or assistance of a staff member you will need to provide something tangible with which to open dialogue. This energizer can be visual, auditory or tactile. The responsibility for this task does not only lie with a group leader but with any staff member who has been authorized and encouraged to effect the change and is confident enough to accept the challenge of change, not only to the environment but also the change in their client group. This is because, as people form bonds and unite, they may become more self-assured, gaining in strength and self-reliance, and able to speak out. The process is empowering and they will become more assertive and demanding of their rights.

How to achieve this task

There are many items that can be used to assist in aiding spontaneous conversation between clients:

- Pictures on the wall depicting scenes familiar to your client group
- Old newspapers/magazines (placed on a table in reach of your clients)
- Objects from the past – (a flat iron or curling tongs etc., left on a table or unit in reach of your clients. Items should be non-breakable and not likely to damage bones if dropped)
- Displays on notice boards/room dividers with a theme, i.e. local dance halls – pictures, programmes, adverts, tickets
- Choice of menu offering meals that were commonplace (i.e. oxtail stew, jellied eel and mushy peas – depending on the culture/sub-culture)
- Furnishings (an old mangle placed in a corridor or a collection of related objects)
- Music from their adult days
- Video/films
- Coinage from yesteryear
- Outings to places that were familiar to the client group

In practice anything that can be safely left in places where your clients meet, for them to see or touch or hear, that is from times and places they are familiar with, should help facilitate conversation – but don't leave it there to accumulate dust; change it when you suspect it has lost its value (been talked out). The same rule applies to most of the above listed items. So 'review' each item from time to time to see if it has kept its 'trigger' value.

It may be difficult to change pictures that are part of the furnishing of the establishment. However, should you be about to purchase such items, chose pictures of a similar size in order that they can be easily interchanged in other rooms or corridors. If the organization for whom you work has more than one establishment catering to the needs of your specific client group, you may be able to interchange items from unit to unit.

When hanging pictures, there is one golden rule. Place them at an appropriate height for the eye-level of your client group and not for effect (or for staff eye-level). If one area is mainly used for sitting and/or wheelchair users, adjust the picture height accordingly.

The size of pictures is also important. A group of four small pictures may look stylish but will do little for those with failing sight. Also if the subject matter is detailed this may add to the problem. For example, a small picture of a busy street viewed in passing or from a distance from a sitting position will be of little consequence. A single subject will prove more effective, i.e. a picture of a tram or horse-drawn tradesman's vehicle.

Since your aim is to try to get the clients to talk to and listen to each other, you need actively to prevent the noise pollution so common in units for older adults – the television that is always on, even when no one is in the room, canned music, blaring tannoys for the staff and so forth. This is particularly important because hearing loss is common among older people, which much reduces their ability to separate two competing sources of sound (for example, another person's speech and the television). Switching off the sources of noise will make the achievement of informal communication all the more evident and striking.

Examples of work for this purpose

The literature offers examples of work to create a reminiscence-eliciting environment. John Adams, a nurse on a physical medical ward for older adults, converted part of the ward using furniture and objects dating from the patients' earlier days; and there have been various accounts of rooms being converted into the style of the 1930s. This is fine, but with such measures you are not taking the usefulness of reminiscence into the communal areas where the clients are. Rather, you are moving them into a special area, to do something different. What we want to achieve, with this purpose, is to increase the quantity and quality of relationships in the living areas.

This can be done in one of two ways: (1) you can increase the stimulus-value of the environment, so that people can see things they want to talk about with others; (2) you can change the frequency with which people meet; this is especially likely to be beneficial if they have shared a group experience together. The example which follows uses the second method.

Having run a reminiscence group for the purpose of group cohesion, we monitored the interaction between clients once they had left the room where the activity had taken place. After a great deal of hard work, the group had been successful in that residents were relating to each other in sharing a common ground. On leaving the reminiscence session, however, they were each returning to their own space within the lounge, seated around the periphery staring ahead or falling asleep. Conversation between clients was all but nil. It was suggested that the group members be seated together in the dining room in order to see if this would effect change. This was a major challenge which the officer-in-charge took up. It was not easy to accomplish, as many residents and staff were opposed to any alterations in the seating arrangements. (We were told we would endanger the lives of those with special diets, although none of the residents involved was on a special diet.) Following negotiations with residents and determination on the part of the officer, change took place.

Initially a member of staff joined the residents at lunch and encouraged conversation on one of the themes that had been highlighted during the earlier reminiscence session, frequently addressing the residents by name, which was also the practice in the group. As a result, members started to interact. More topical subjects were introduced, but this did not have the same effect, as often only those who were able to read the daily papers or watch television were interested, leaving others at a loss. That is not to say that older people with some cognitive damage cannot learn from conversation about the present. They were, in fact, being drawn into the conversation by using the past as comparison. However, a member of staff was required as a facilitator, as to use this technique requires a measure of skill and the people in our group were frail and needed a bit of help. It was also recognized that some simply did not care. If other members were not conversing they hardly noticed, speaking only to those who were sociable. It had, in all probability, been a long time since they had conversed socially with others, so concern for those who did not respond was of little importance. Eventually staff involvement withdrew and the group were observed from a distance. Once the reminiscence group had come to a close, conversation at the dining table reduced considerably, although members continued to address each other by name, commenting on the meal of the day or asking 'Pass the salt, Fred.'

What we learned from this was that residents who had been part of the reminiscence group had bonded and were more willing to accept the change, i.e. the new seating arrangements in the dining room. In contrast, the changes promoted complaint from those who had not been involved. It was also felt that all would *not* accept similar movement in the lounge, where each had their individual chair, be it by the window or door or near the television.

Another positive outcome was that members now called each other by name and did talk during meal time, albeit on a surface level. Some also sought each other's company on social occasions. This was further supported by a photo recognition test, where photographs were taken of the six members of the group and six other residents who had not been involved in the group. On being shown all 12 photographs, the group members recognized each member of the reminiscence group by name, whereas the other six people who had not been members were physically described, for example, 'that tall chappy, she's in a wheel-chair, sits by the door' and so on. On the other hand, the comparison group in general recognized many, again describing their physical appearance or where they sat, but only two out of the six correctly named another resident. What further came to light, more by default, was that during the showing of the photographs residents had been shown a picture of themselves, and out of the 12 residents, only 5 recognized themselves. Contributory factors to this were felt to be:

- Failing eyesight prior to entering the care system, such that the elderly people had not really seen themselves for some time.
- Spectacles were rarely cleaned or were of inappropriate strength or fitting.
- Mirrors in their own home were in general positioned over the fireplace and were not appropriate for their present physical stature.
- They perhaps did not recognize/accept their own body image and the changes that age brings. When faced with their photograph, therefore, this, sadly, was someone they did not know.

Following this revelation, it was proposed that with the refurbishment of the interior of the home large mirrors should be placed at an appropriate height for the residents. Interestingly, this seemed to effect very little change, as many of the older residents did not wish to see what age brings and chose not to look at themselves.

In addition, new pictures were purchased to replace familiar prints of the painting of the crying child, the green faced oriental lady, the galloping horses and the poster urging you to enjoy the ski slopes of St Moritz. With prior thought, and some searching, large black and white copies of photographs of scenes of everyday life of yesteryear were purchased. (Nowadays you can get them in many shops.)

The effect of the pictures was quite astounding. Anything new in a home can be a major event for those whose daily routine has become dull and unstimulating. Residents began talking to each other, laughing as they discussed the picture of the boys playing street cricket against a lampost and the turban-clad young mothers chatting over a backyard fence. The reproduction of the Sunlight Soap advertisement evoked memories of wash days, with discussion on mangles, pegs, starch, scrubbing boards and the lines of washing often drying in the kitchen on rainy days. Any reminiscence group leader will not find this unusual, as presenting material from the past does stimulate and encourage interaction between clients as they share familiar experiences. However, this was not a reminiscence group but six women and two men meeting within a small lounge. There were no group leaders but a residential social worker who was dispensing the daily medication and listening in a slightly puzzled way to this excited buzz as the residents shared their memories. Not for one instant would we wish to suggest group leaders are redundant, for there is room for all types of reminiscence, but this was unplanned, unmanned, with no rules and it was working. It had aroused spontaneous conversation between residents who were exchanging memories with people with whom they now lived, who previously they had rarely if ever spoken to. The pictures continued to energize the group for some time, restoring residents' self-esteem and acting as a tonic. There were exchanges of dialogue on the theme of the pictures between residents, staff and residents, relatives and residents and even relatives and staff. Eventually the excitement they had stirred subsided as they became part of the home. However, the ice had been broken in the sharing of a common bond, the past, and some residents continued to converse with others and to pass the time of day and feel at ease and welcome in the environment they were coming to terms with as their home. Not all residents used these opportunities, but the majority did.

We would like to say that we learned from this experience (which we did) and changed the pictures on a regular basis. Sadly, in this instance that was not so. Change takes time and also finance. (Incidentally, choosing new pictures or music can be used as an opportunity to involve the clients in some decision-making with practical results; as well as giving purpose to outings to such places as libraries, record libraries, second-hand record shops, junk shops.)

What was interesting was that not all homes chose pictures of yesteryear. Some staff, sadly, could not resist the temptation to impose their own ideas of good taste!

We started this section by distinguishing between making communal areas reminiscence-rich, and creating a special reminiscence space – an interacting museum, if you like. We have been concerned in this purpose with the former use, but in no way would we deny the usefulness of the interactive museum. Indeed, some time later when space was available and after many years of collecting objects of days gone by, senior management in the London Borough of Newham gave support to establishing a Reminiscence Centre. The home in question had been adapted to small group living and the large dining room had become somewhat obsolete. A talented recreational team set about designing a kitchen and lounge reminiscent of the 1930s and 1940s. There was an official opening where residents of the home, relatives and friends were invited.

It was far more successful than had been anticipated. Not only were residents reminiscing as they laughingly pointed to the tin bath hanging on the wall; they ran their fingers over the scrubbing board and smelt the carbolic soap, recapturing memories of when they were young housewives and mothers. Their sons and daughters were also reminiscing as they showed their children the wind-up gramophone which crackled out an old Al Bowley song. The opening of the Reminiscence Centre had a knock-on effect, as objects, photographs, records and containers, even items of furniture from the past were given or loaned to the centre by those who had been at the opening. (A similar project has been undertaken at Palmer Community Hospital, Jarrow, South Tyneside, where a redundant treatment room was decorated and furnished as a late Victorian parlour.)

Interiors of houses depicting the lifestyle of days gone by can be visited in many parts of the country and will evoke memories stimulating dialogue between those involved. However, rarely does the situation occur when three generations of one family get together for such an occasion, as happened at the opening of the Reminiscence Centre. What occurred at this event gives support to many of the purposes outlined throughout this book. There was an energizing of a group of people, spontaneous conversation was aroused as the elderly people spoke one to another. Once again sons and daughters had something to say to their frail elderly parents, grandparents to grandchildren, and virtual strangers were now engaged in convivial conversation.

Conclusions

We have shown how the creation of an interactive reminiscence museum can give elderly people a boost into reliving the past, especially those for whom words are no longer so evocative, but objects and sounds do still evoke. The museum is thus a great place for reminiscence groups.

Creating a gentle reminiscence environment pays homage to the lives of your clients, and we have emphasized, has the purpose of encouraging spontaneous conversation.

In a more genteel age, in the so-called 'polite circles', unusual items were often used to decorate the home in order to provoke conversation; indeed, these were known as 'conversation pieces'. The pace at which we live in today's society leaves little time to seek or bother about such niceties. With age we have the time but not the energy. Staff can support and encourage social growth in older people by providing a stimulus that may elicit spontaneous conversation without their direct intervention. The process can be further strengthened by asking the clients to decide which objects they would like to see or have around; and in certain settings asking them if they would either bring them in from home or find them on stalls, and in second-hand shops. (If the objects are theirs, make sure this is logged somewhere, and that the object has the owner's name on it.) Involving the clients will increase their participation and feelings of giving to the unit. And it will give them more to talk about – where they got the object, its history etc. – further adding to the stock of conversation.

Don't rest on your laurels once you have some pictures or objects in the unit. Stay alert and keep monitoring. Novelty does wear off. Moreover, simply replacing one photograph of the old days with yet another will probably create little interest. It is important to work on stimulating interest and the community of memories in a *variety* of ways, through a *number* of senses. You can also vary the time frame occasionally, with 'Then and Now' comparisons or plans for future building on well-known sites, as long as the plans are visually attractive (and a visit to the planning display might be enjoyed by clients).

Remember that as time passes so the era of childhood of your clients moves forward. When we started reminiscence work in the early 1980s, clients' dates of birth were frequently before the turn of the century – and the First World War a vivid memory. Indeed, members of Peter Coleman's research sample (1986) had fought in the war. Nowadays the older person's childhood is likely to have been in the two decades before the Second World War, so make sure you match the clients' actual experiences and your chosen objects. (Don't give them a mish-mash of Bing Crosby and flapper outfits!)

To converse with someone sounds such a simple thing to do but it is a skill requiring regular exercizing in order to be retained. We as carers can assist in supporting those who have, through lack of use, lost the skill to talk informally with others. The presence of material from the past viewed as part of everyday life but displayed in an eye-catching way can act as a catalyst, encouraging social dialogue in sharing a common ground; and your clients will usually find talking a socially pleasurable experience, gaining in confidence and self-esteem. Your work will be rewarded by enthusiastic remarks and questions from relatives and visitors. Your unit can become a much pleasanter place for you to work in and be part of.

Useful reading and resources

The reader may want to try to get some idea for themselves as to why people reminisce. The book to read is Peter Coleman's *Ageing and Reminiscence Processes* (Wiley, 1986). Marianne Lo Gerfo (*International Journal of Ageing and Human Development*, 1980–81, 12 (1), pp. 39–48), suggests that reminiscence may be informal, evaluative or obsessive. Deirdre Boden and Denise Bielby (*Human Development*, 1983, 26, pp. 308–319) analyse transcripts and suggest reminiscing for older people is about achieving a shared sense of meaning.

In a related manner, Rhonda Parker proposes that reminiscence allows the individual to see continuity across their life span (*The Gerontologist*,

1995, 35 (4), pp. 515–525). Finally Paul Wong and Lisa Watt suggest six functions of reminiscence (*Psychology and Ageing*, 1991, 6 (2), pp. 272–279).

On the practical side, John Adams describes how a geriatric ward was made more reminiscence-eliciting (*The Oral History Journal*, 1984, 12 (2), pp. 54–59).

Sources of archival material will be mentioned throughout this book. The following may be useful:

The National Sound Archive – 'the world's largest sound archives, with over a million items of recorded sound' – welcome visitors to have reference to material, but it cannot be taken away. It is part of the British Library at 29 Exhibition Road, London SW7 2AS (tel. 0171 412 7440).

A visit to the Imperial War Museum, Lambeth Road, London SE1 6HZ, may give you ideas.

A visit to the Robert Opie Collection, Museum of Advertising and Packaging, Gloucester Docks, Gloucester GL1 2EH (tel. 01452 302309) will reveal a goldmine of 1950s memorabilia with replicas for sale (and give you a great day out).

Purpose Two

REMINISCENCE TO ENCOURAGE INFORMAL CONVERSATION BETWEEN STAFF AND CLIENTS

Rationale

This purpose has many similarities to those of Purpose One. However, the purpose in reminiscence to encourage informal conversation between staff and clients is, for staff, more task-orientated. Staff members have but one chance to create a first impression, and throughout this chapter suggestions are given in order that you can make it a positive one.

Another key difference is that Purpose One is likely to be more relevant to older adults – they have more history to share. Purpose Two is a vital one for staff to achieve with clients *whatever* their age and disability, because we cannot be of help to people if they don't trust us, or if they don't think we see them as individuals. Since even 5-year-olds have a clear idea of their life history and their interests, reminiscence can help us build a bridge, independent of the client's age or problem (or lack of problem).

The majority of people working in a caring profession do care about the wellbeing of the clients for whom they are working; and try to provide a welcoming and accepting home, or place away from their own home where they will spend some considerable time. Wanting to feel comfortable and accepted into whatever setting you are living or working in applies both to ourselves and our clients. Initially this is achieved by speaking to someone – informal chit-chat, 'breaking the ice'. The dialogue we use to open up a conversation when meeting a new colleague, at a social gathering or over lunch, will probably do little to break the ice with the client group for whom we are working. Our clients may well not want to be where or how they are. Therefore when meeting a client in a residential or day care setting for the first time, whether we use open-ended questions or not may be of little consequence until a measure of trust has been established. Questions, however well meant, relating to where they lived, how many children lived in the house and what their husband/father did for a living, may be seen as just more red tape and misinterpreted as prying, resulting in you being seen as yet another figure of authority; and this can be a two-sided sword, as we as staff are human too, we have feelings of anxiety and of not wanting to be rebuffed.

How do we bridge the gap with the people for whom we care when we enter a new unit or post, or a new client is admitted to our unit? To decrease the risk of being rejected we need good interpersonal skills and an open and relaxed manner when talking on subjects we know will be familiar to our clients. We need to ensure that our questions are not too probing or don't sound like an interrogation, and that, until a relationship has developed, they remain at the surface level (or more exactly, at the level the client wishes the interaction to be at).

Goals implied in the purpose

1   To help establish the staff/client relationship.
2   To help our clients feel at ease and welcome in the unit.
3   To assist in the forming of an accepting relationship built on mutual respect.
4   To develop trust.
5   To aid staff in developing a greater knowledge and understanding of their clients.
6   To forge and strengthen bonds within the unit.
7   To encourage empowerment.

The task

The rejecting of people who are in some way different from us is not uncommon. Think of the low status of the disabled, the old and the mentally infirm, or children placed in care. This may be further compounded if the person in question is black. Whether the reason is because they are different, or people even fear them, rejection is something they may well have experienced many times. Therefore when a relative stranger attempts to befriend them, not just 'care' for them, a measure of mistrust should not be of surprise to us. The essence of this task, then, is to initiate and open up a dialogue between staff and client that underpins a commitment to a positive staff/client relationship.

How to achieve this task

Whatever client group you are working with, you should have some knowledge of their way of life prior to entering the unit. Inviting our client, by using *informal conversation*, to participate on a one-to-one basis in discussing a topic that is familiar to them and non-threatening greatly assists the ice-breaking. As in Purpose One, providing something in the everyday living situation on which to focus and use as a conversation starter is both helpful to staff and client in getting the ball rolling. Again, you can use everyday objects that are familiar to the clients, in addition to music, reading material, the menu, pictures of buildings and people. Make sure it really is their experience, not a stereotypic picture – people from the West Indies may be amused by a poster of islanders drinking rum on a tropical beach at sunset, but are hardly likely to conclude that you know a lot about their culture!

With elderly people you may wish to display artefacts of everyday life of yesteryear, or provide visual displays on corridor walls and in the main living and dining areas. Should you be working with a client group that may require assistance in the bathroom, it has been found that pictures displayed on bathroom walls have proved extremely advantageous in opening up dialogue and reducing feelings of discomfort and awkwardness. For almost all people to be without clothes gives rise to feelings of vulnerability; we feel exposed, looking for something to hide our nakedness. For our client group, requiring help in this most personal area, these feelings must be intensified. Therefore to be involved in informal conversation provides something to hide behind, or can at least take the client's mind off their vulnerability. Some of the most positive relationships have been established in the bathroom setting during this one-to-one interaction. Informal conversation generated through reminiscence allows trust to be forged far sooner.

Hanging pictures of stars of stage and screen near to the record player, CD or music centre has proved extremely fruitful. These can be focused on, discussing who they liked and whether they had ever seen them. The who–where–why–when sequence then comes into play. Afterwards you could see if there is a tape or record of that particular person and asking whether they would like to hear it played will give you another opportunity later on that day or week to approach your client on an informal level. It also lets them know that you were listening and paying attention to them.

Framed pictures are very nice but they can prove costly. A visually pleasing, but nevertheless effective, method of displaying photographs or pictures is to buy large inexpensive frames (jumble sales or boot sales are ideal hunting grounds), remove the glass and replace it with stiff pale coloured card or sugar paper on which you can stick your pictures with Blue-tac. This is an ideal backcloth to display whatever subject is a topic for discussion and pictures can be easily interchanged. (Sticking pictures directly on to newly decorated walls will not please management.)

Don't become too concerned about reminiscence being related to the distant past. Yesterday will often do nicely. With the young, it may well be easier and more useful to focus on fashion, sports personalities, cars, interests and hobbies, stars of films and television or pop music. Recognizing the rapid speed at which these change, you may find you are considerably dated in your choice. This should not deter you, as you will no doubt be quickly corrected and informed that they are 'naff', or whatever the in-word for 'rubbish' is. Nevertheless, as long as you take your 'ancient' status in good humour, dialogue has been opened and from that stance you can work, building on the conversation by enquiring who or what kind of music they like. If you have never heard of their particular choice say so, and ask if they have a picture, tape or CD of them and could you hear it some time? To talk of a particular piece of music that was in the charts last month requires us to recall and therefore reminisce and may, in so doing, start a conversation about what we were doing, where and with whom. With the young people 'face' is always very important in their interactions, especially with adults, so what they say is not always what they privately think. Often the seemingly hard, uncaring, disinterested persona is but a mask. Therefore the use of and the interpretation of non-verbal communication/body language can be extremely important, even if you would be unwise to comment on your observation.

So far, we have considered relationships between staff working in units for various types of clients. Of course, much work is done in clients' homes – think of home care. Here Purpose Two is equally – if not more – relevant. Staff have to show interest if they want to get on with the client and they are going to have to do it by themselves, since they do not have the protection and support of colleagues, as staff working in a unit do. But they do have one big advantage: staff within a unit often are working in a visually deprived and unstimulating environment, but a person's home usually has most of the objects and pictures with which to piece together their life story, if they choose to tell it to you! Your job is to form the relationship – again without being nosy or critical – so that they do want to share those experiences. Training-wise we are talking 'listening skills', although many home care workers seem to be born listeners. So the purpose stays the same and as important as ever, but the ways of achieving it change.

Examples of work for this purpose

During August 1977 there was a new admission, a young boy called Billy, to the children's home where I was working. I was introducing him to the layout of the home, other children and staff. He responded to no one, just shrugged his shoulders acting in a couldn't-care-less manner. On entering his room he turned on a small transistor radio he had brought with him which blared out yet another Elvis Presley song, as during that week Elvis had died. Trying to keep the conversation informal and thinking I would curry favour with him by discussing a pop music legend, I said how much everyone would miss Elvis and his music. He glared at me, picked up the radio and threw it across the room yelling 'F——— Elvis Presley that's all she ever plays and I'm glad he's f—————— dead.' I tried to say I was sorry, and that I thought he might have liked him, but he never heard me, he just went on with a tirade of abusive language from which I gathered he was speaking of his mother. I didn't attempt to analyse his behaviour, as at the time I was simply an unqualified member of staff trying to calm a 9-year-old boy who I knew had been both physically and emotionally damaged, but I found the outburst somewhat alarming. However, having vented his anger, he then yelled at me 'Go on, go and tell 'em what I said.' I said there was nothing to tell but I now knew that he didn't like Elvis Presley! He stared at me for a minute and then grinned. During his abusive outburst Billy had disclosed episodes of a traumatic home life, which gave me a far greater knowledge of him than I gleaned from his file. Billy's period in care was extremely volatile, but, from this rocky beginning, we developed a good professional friendship, initiated and stimulated by a song.

A detailed example of this purpose in action

For an elderly person, taking up a permanent place in a residential home is a painful transition. For most it is not from choice but from recognizing that they can no longer live within their own home without being in danger. So they have had to admit that they can no longer cope with daily living and managing their own life. Confidence and self-worth may well be at their lowest ebb when entering the care establishment which is to become their home. Staff are, in the main, assiduous in their efforts to make this as comfortable and pain-free a period as possible.

Maud had been admitted directly from her own home as an emergency admission. From the pitiful conditions she had been found in and her own self-neglect, it was felt that in all probability she would not return home. When an admission is unplanned there is little or no time to read and discover the background of the person who has been placed in your charge. However, the neighbour who had informed the services of this 'poor old lady' understood that at one time she had been a teacher. From her appearance you certainly wouldn't have guessed. She was sitting quietly drinking tea, foul smelling, her hair matted and in an extremely sorry state. She was nervous and frightened, continually twisting and untwisting the belt to her coat. I knelt down next to her introducing myself, and asking her name. She responded by telling me that she was quite alright and that there had been a little problem at home with the water, the pipes had frozen. I asked if she would like something to eat. She informed me that the kind lady who had come to her house had bought her fish and chips. Having finished her tea, I

asked if she would like to go along to see her room, where she would
sleep that night. She agreed, stressing that once the pipes were repaired
she would be going back to her own home. I assisted her as she walked
with some uncertainty down the corridor, talking and trying to make
her feel at ease, while she somewhat apologetically told me that she was
quite capable of walking on her own but was just a bit stiff as she hadn't
been out much lately.

As we came to her room, Jenny, the care assistant who had been
allocated as Maud's key worker, arrived. It is wonderful to observe
someone carrying out a job that they obviously love and have an innate
skill in doing. While this frail old lady was proudly holding onto the last
remnants of her self-esteem, Jenny proceeded, using empathy, tact and
loving care, to coax and assist Maud out of her wet and dirty clothes.
Maud had obviously been in them for some considerable time. In
addition, she had a continence problem (the reason for this was not at
this time known). Having assisted Maud into a dressing gown Jenny
gently asked if she would like a bath. Maud declined, 'No, not today.'
Responses to Jenny's light chatter were minimal – things were happening to her and about her. Jenny asked if she would like to see where
everything was, the television room, the library or quiet room, toilets etc.
I did not observe all that happened next but am reporting here what
Jenny fed back to me later. Maud asked if she could be shown where the
toilets were. From there Jenny showed her into the room adjoining them
saying 'and next door is the bathroom'. On the walls of the bathroom
were large photographs of everyday life of yesteryear relating to
washing and drying cloths, ironing and in particular one 3 ft picture of a
young child standing in a tin bath. Maud made comment, saying that it
was the sort of bath her mother used. From there Jenny kept the
conversation going, asking how the water was heated and what soap
was used. Also Jenny used comparisons with then and now, talking of
her own grandmother and the problems she had had as she got older in
getting in and out of the bath. Maud asked how had she managed, and
Jenny casually replied 'I helped her.' Maud seemed taken aback saying
that not even her husband had seen her without clothes, let alone a
young girl like Jenny. Jenny pointed out that she was 43 years old and
that sometimes we all need a little help, stressing how much her 'nan'
had hated not having a regular bath.

Whenever possible Jenny assisted Maud throughout the day and in
the evening, thus strengthening the relationship. Two days later Maud
asked for a bath. I understand that during the bathing session the
pictures on the walls were used to facilitate conversation. Not only did
this help ease the situation which Maud initially found embarrassing,
but Jenny was now getting to know and understand Maud's life with
ever-growing appreciation. Maud related how, as young children, their
mother sometimes bathed them, sitting them on the edge of the copper
dangling their feet in the water as it was heated for washing clothes.

We were later to learn that Maud had been a music teacher. She did return home, but was later once again readmitted to residential care on a permanent basis.

Conclusions

If our clients are in their own homes, then we can use the abundance of material that they decorate their home with to open conversation. If our clients are in formal settings – such as clubs, day or residential care – the use of informal dialogue allows us to adopt a more relaxed stance. The naturalness and simplicity of the conversation allows for familiarity to develop without the formality which is often the cornerstone of such establishments. The topics discussed may seem non-personal and inconsequential, but from this initial 'chat' we can open up a meaningful and purposeful relationship, resulting in a greater knowledge and understanding of the person for whom we are caring. Using items, pictures and music from the past as energizers to initiate informal conversation not only assists us in carrying out our job but provides something for both client and staff to focus upon and for the relationship to grow from.

Useful reading and resources

Bill Bytheway's *Ageism* (Open University Press, 1995) is a good introduction to the topic.

Richard Nelson-Jones' *Human Relationship Skills* (Cassell, 1990) deals with listening skills and other works by him will also be helpful.

M. Bender, V. Levens and C. Goodson's *Welcoming Your Clients* (Winslow Press, 1995) looks at similar skills, less in the counselling mode, but in institutional settings.

As background reading, Ian Morton and Christine Bleathman's articles 'Does it matter whether it's Tuesday or Friday?' in the *Nursing Times*, 1988, 84 (6), pp. 25–28 is one of our favourite pieces of background reading. It points out that what matters when you work with people who are confused is your relationship with them and your understanding of their meaning.

S.B. Merriam's 'The structure of simple reminiscence', *The Gerontologist*, 1989, 29 (6), pp. 761–767 analyses transcripts of reminiscing and suggests that the process consists of four elements: selection, immersion, withdrawal and closure. The article may help staff move along this process when talking to clients.

Purpose Three

REMINISCENCE AS FUN

Rationale

Having run numerous reminiscence groups for a variety of reasons, and sometimes, in retrospect, a confusion of reasons, what was becoming increasingly evident was that it could be fun. People were really enjoying themselves in the sessions. This was not just because they were recalling past events and having staff actively listen to the group or individuals. It was that members were smiling, laughing and actually having fun; people were feeling good about what they discussed. It was, in essence, a tonic. The effect of this was that a far more lively group of people left the reminiscence activity than had arrived. It was observed that numerous memories, first told in a group, were retold to other residents, staff and visitors. Not all members found the stories amusing but those who had been actively involved in the group did and carried this good humour through each re-telling of the event.

Most of us at times like to forget our problems. When we are continually involved in a heavy workload, even the daily news, can make us dispirited. So we may choose to have our spirits lifted and seek more light-hearted reading, visual material or company. The individual or group we are working with may not have that choice. The reasons vary from poor or failing eyesight or hearing, to an inability to read or to not having the choice or power to make change.

In the main, fun comes from sharing an experience with another person – rarely is it a solitary pursuit. We can have very pleasant and enjoyable periods alone engaging in something we enjoy. However, to laugh and have fun in the main is brought about by listening or watching someone relate or act out an amusing episode or by actively involving ourselves with other people in something light-hearted.

On re-evaluating earlier groups, we recognized that the subject matter was important in determining the mood of the group. One must be aware that when recalling past events you cannot always be aware where pain and trauma may be hidden. For example, when discussing food as a 'waste not want not' subject in contrast with today's modern throw-away society, it was accepted by an East London group that I was running that stale bread was used for bread pudding and was part of the indigenous population's diet. The group were discussing how it was prepared – a subject which seemed of no real consequence – when I noticed that Gladys was sitting in her wheelchair crying silently. When I asked if we had upset her and she replied that bread pudding was 'just about my George's favourite food'. I attempted to change the topic, but she then said 'No, it's OK' and sat quietly listening and smiling.

Goals implied in the purpose

Fun reminiscence is a practical activity involving elderly people. It can help to achieve the following effects:

1 Enjoyment – lifting of one's spirits.
2 Lifts depressed moods, creating a feeling of wellbeing, but –
3 Encourages the experiencing of a wide range of feelings.
4 Reinforces security and group membership.
5 Builds confidence.
6 Energizes.
7 Increases communication between participants; and if they've really enjoyed it, between participants and other people in the unit who didn't attend the session, but may decide not to miss out on the next one!

The task

The group leader's role in Purpose Three is to be a facilitator/co-ordinator as reminiscence for fun is, in essence, a leisure involvement. An outgoing personality/lively style is an asset but not essential; but a smiling face can be contagious. As reminiscence for fun has a more open approach, your co-worker(s) (more than one if possible) can be a volunteer from a local school, a relative, or a domestic. The session can be programmed or near-spontaneous depending upon availability of group facilitators.

How to achieve this task

As with all groups, be prepared. An inefficient quiz master stumbling for ideas and names is a sure recipe for disaster. Frail elderly people with memory impairment have limited concentration, so hold their concentration, minimize disability by involving them, allowing them to hold pictures or prompts. The poorly sighted can be helped by using stimuli related to sound, such as 'who said?' or 'who sang?'. Do not place them at a disadvantage by using visual material. Incorporate physical movement. This can heighten more confused members' involvement in the activity. For example, consider the old parlour game Musical Chairs. Obviously, running around between chairs while the music plays is inappropriate, but we can adapt it. The group should be seated within reach of another member and while the music plays a large sponge ball, bean bag or wooden or plastic baton is passed from one to another. One of the facilitators stops the music and whoever is holding the ball is asked a question from one of the chosen quiz subjects at a level that is appropriate to their cognitive ability.

Resources for fun reminiscence can cost very little, but it does require preparation time in collecting information and material beforehand. Should funds be available there are many resources for this activity that can be purchased (the majority through Winslow Press or Nottingham Rehab.):

- *The Reminiscence Quiz Book* (Mike Sherman, Winslow Press).
- Down Memory Lane – board game
- Life Stories – board game
- Winslow Press Quiz Boxes
- Sounds Nostalgic
- Radio Theme Tunes from the 40s and 50s
- Famous Faces
- Musical Quiz
- Bygone Faces – jigsaws

BBC CDs and tapes can also be very effective stimuli.

In general, the following create a feeling of wellbeing and good humour and can be used as a springboard to initiating reminiscence for fun:

- A visit to the theatre
- A visit to the cinema
- Roller skating
- A day at the seaside
- Childhood games:
    Hopscotch
    Skipping
    Knockdown ginger
    Four stones
- Ball games

- Dinners of days gone by:
    Fish and chips
    Meat pudding
    Oxtail stew etc.

This list relates to activities that were found useful working in the East End of London. Do make sure the materials used or the activities you suggest are relevant to the lives of *your* clients. Once you get into reminiscence for fun you may find you can adapt your own ideas and create quizzes and games to suit your specific client group, relating to their age, culture, special interests or gender.

Examples of work for this purpose

A group run for the purpose of fun can encompass far more participants than a formal reminiscence group (seven members), as this example shows.

On arriving at a residential home for elderly people to run the weekly reminiscence group I was informed that staffing levels were low due to sickness and it would not be possible to release a staff member to co-lead the group. Residents were seated around the lounge. Those residents who were part of the regular group were extremely disappointed as they had come to expect their weekly reminiscence sessions.

The topic for that week was to have been 'Social Life'. My past experience was that this tends to be a light subject that is well received. I had brought with me a large pack of photographs of famous faces of stage and screen to use as reminders/prompts. However, I could not ask 19 residents of varying frailties how they had spent their leisure time, so a more encompassing approach was required. Following a pooling of suggestions with the member of staff on the floor, we improvised. We asked the residents if they would like to join in a quiz on stars of stage and screen. Some responded positively, others made little or no comment.

The photographs were large and we proceeded by handing a photograph to a resident, asking if they could name the person. If the answer was correct we asked another resident to name a film they had been in or who their famous partner was, e.g. Fred Astaire – Ginger Rogers; Stan Laurel – Oliver Hardy. We gave prompts and clues, asking for catch phrases of famous people, or trying it the other way around: 'Who said "Hello Playmates"?' Answer: Arthur Askey. If the photograph was of a singer they were asked to name a song they sang, or to sing or say a line from the song. Should there be no response then the question was offered to the whole group. The result was an hour that went all too fast – all had participated if not verbally then with their body language, joining in the chorus of songs or laughingly watching others take off Mae West or Greta Garbo. Questions were aimed to minimize or avoid failure: for example if the question was 'In which hand did Charlie Chaplin carry his cane?' someone had to get it correct. When it came to close the group residents were asking for more, and when would we do it again?

It had been light-hearted, unplanned and a success. Why? We had been asking questions which had a high probability of being answered correctly. We had wanted them to succeed and in succeeding they had felt good and ready to try the water again. It had not been painful. They had not failed or been let down by age. The essence of the 'Quiz Time' session as we were later to call it, was its underpinning by reminiscence, those long-stored memories of times past and, as already stressed, hopefully good times.

When working with older people who have memory impairment or dementia, staff must be aware that there are individuals who may have insight into their problem. Therefore in tailoring the difficulty of questions to an individual's frailty do not make the mistake of making them childish. *Simplify* the approach, but keep the subject matter *adult*. This rule also applies to adults with learning difficulties. So often a snapped 'I'm not a baby' is heard in response to over-simplified subject matter.

Reminiscence for fun using this 'Stars of Stage and Screen' technique can involve many client groups:

- Children, even with learning difficulties.
- The elderly with sensory impairment.
- The elderly with physical frailty.
- The elderly with mental frailty.
- Adults with learning difficulties.

Staff must do their homework and recognize where the individual's store of knowledge lies (the relevant time and period), collect pictures, memorabilia, or songs around which questions can be directed. Depending upon the client group, these will vary from Vesta Tilly, Vera Lynn, Morecambe and Wise, Elvis Presley, Tom Cruise and Take That to whoever is/was high profile during the person's teenage and young adult years.

Another tried and tested idea for fun reminiscence is the game Hangman. The materials required are simply a large board/paper on which to write, chalk/marker pen and Blue-tac if using paper. (The plain side of old wallpaper is ideal.)

Staff choose a name (say the topic is famous people) and dash out the exact number of letters, e.g. ---- ------- for Judy Garland, on the paper. Then in turn each member of the group is asked whether they want a letter or clue. For a clue you may say 'entertainer', 'female' or 'singer' for example. If a letter is called out which is not part of the particular name, then staff draw one of the 16 stages of the hangman:

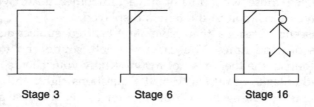

| Stage 3 | Stage 6 | Stage 16 |

The group tries to guess successfully who the celebrity is before the hangman is completed.

When working with older people a range of reminiscence topics can be used for Hangman. For example, items from the kitchen:

- The kitchener
- Hobbing foot
- The mangle/wringer
- Black lead
- Flat iron

giving clues such as: 'a cleaning aid', 'made of iron', 'it has moveable parts'. Other topics might include:

- Items from the parlour
- Items from the bedroom
- Shops in our town/village
- Political figures
- Films
- Songs
- Sports personalities

It's easy and it's fun with limited cost. However, there is one golden rule, as with Quiz Time, **know your group**. Not all elderly people completed their education. Many left school to gain employment and to help support the family, or to go into the services; for some their schools got bombed out during the war. Learning difficulties and poor literacy are not always obvious. Do not assume that because someone has brought up a family they can read. You may have to broach the subject tactfully with their family to discover that 'Mum never could read', and this is not for everyone to know. If an elderly person can go through their life managing money, running a house or holding down a job without disclosing this, then hidden it should remain.

To cope with this problem of possible poor literacy you should avoid written questions or answers. With Hangman, do not ask people which letter will fill the gaps. Rather offer a choice of letters to each member or let them choose from a box of letters of the alphabet. In this way they will maintain their self-esteem. The clues will cue people into the subject. Even those who do not have difficulties make wild guesses which have no relation to the letters displayed.

Reminiscence sessions that have light-hearted subject-matter evoke memories of good times. You can use smell, sound and touch to aid recall as long as the theme is not heavy. Know your clients, know their past, get the 'level' of difficulty of the questions right, and you'll have the residents pounding down the corridor to get the best places for a reminiscence as fun session.

One final hint. When running a fun session quit while you're winning and before the group members get tired. Active disappointment that there isn't more means they'll be back to get more next week.

Conclusions

We have already suggested in Part One of this book that goals for reminiscence should be needs-led. Certainly, Purpose Three is very relevant for physically and/or mentally frail individuals who may also suffer sensory impairment. Cultural pressures, individual circumstances and perspectives do play a decisive role in inducing an elderly person to abandon their previous life's interests and activities. With advanced age and increased isolation it is recognized that old people experience loss of role as spouse, parent or breadwinner, have fewer social contacts, and often take on the ascribed role of being unproductive, useless and a burden.

But reminiscence for fun is definitely applicable across our 5 to 95 age span, because sadly, feelings of rejection occur across that age span too. Those who are rejected come to reject themselves and have low self-esteem and in turn experience depressed mood. A well-run reminiscence for fun group can achieve its goals creating feelings of good humour and wellbeing; and that wellbeing can be a springboard to greater involvement with other people and in life generally.

Useful reading and resources

Reminiscence as fun may seem simple but probably requires the same level of skill as more complicated procedures to keep in touch with the group and how it is feeling. A tough but worthwhile read is Dorothy Stock Whittaker's *Using Groups to Help People* (Routledge, 1985). Easier to read is our manual *Groupwork With the Elderly* (M. Bender, A. Norris and P. Bauckham, Winslow Press, 1987).

Other sources of materials that may be of use are given at the end of the next chapter.

Purpose Four

REMINISCENCE TO PROMOTE EMOTIONAL AND SOCIAL STIMULATION

Rationale

Reminiscence for stimulation is similar to reminiscence for fun but it is, in fact, more purpose- or task-orientated. Reminiscence for fun has a more open-ended approach – if it works, use it. However, when used as a means of stimulation we must look more closely at client need, whether they be depressed, dispirited or have chosen to disengage.

Cummings and Henry, the proponents of 'disengagement theory', argued that as people grow old, they gradually slide into the role of an 'older person' and their rate and variety of social involvement decreases until death. However, critics quickly suggested that there are serious limitations to disengagement theory. They asked whether older people do actively withdraw or disengage from society, or is it rather that society isolates them? One could argue that the factors influencing this process are cultural pressures rather than the individual circumstances of the older person.

Again, when looking at what causes an elderly person to abandon previous interests and activities, consideration must be taken of an individual's self-concept and levels of physical and mental infirmity. Age has taken its toll, leaving the scars of sensory and physical impairment and also the burden of multiple losses. Older people who once moved freely now need help to move. Fingers have stiffened and hands that were once flexible and strong can no longer create or carry out basic everyday tasks. All these factors make 'engaging' a more exhausting business; and the losses of functions and friends may well result in grieving, with a lowered desire to interact.

Finally, in addition to all these factors, there is the effect of widespread cultural stereotyping and labelling of older people, in the media and in society generally, reinforcing what older people can no longer do, underlining the often used words – 'deterioration', 'disability' and 'helplessness'. Of the many examples, the complete lack of older adults as newscasters, and the continued debate about 'the cost of health care for the elderly' are only two. These negative attitudes are often internalized by older adults, resulting in many cases of *involuntary* disengagement.

The aim, therefore, of reminiscence, when used with people for the purpose of stimulation, is primarily to re-awaken an interest in life.

Goals implied in the purpose

In running a group for the purpose of social and emotional stimulation we aim to:

1 Stimulate and awaken or re-awaken the older person's interest in life.
2 Encourage social interaction.
3 Reaffirm the older person's self-esteem.
4 Increase self-confidence.
5 Develop friendships.
6 Establish trust.
7 Develop staff/client relationships.

The task

The prime task of the group leader is to involve the older person and to increase their sense of alertness and aliveness. Through this involvement the older person becomes part of the group and thus a feeling of belonging is created, of being part of the setting in which they live. As self-worth and confidence increase the group leader can encourage and support the older person to participate and involve themselves in other activities that are taking place; and to take part in the decision-making processes regarding the group's activities.

It is vital that the initial involvement is a positive experience, reinforcing that what the older person has to say is valued. The group leader must create a setting of security and trust in which the older person feels safe in the knowledge that they are with a (professional) friend who will not let them make a fool of themselves. In order that the older person can feel confident enough to contribute to the discussion, the theme or subject of the reminiscence group should be well known to the client.

For us all, the responses we receive from others reinforce that what we say is of interest and that we are being listened to. In any group of older people we cannot say with any certainty how they will react to each other, but we hope they will listen and eventually interact, and we can assist this in the way in which we run our group (see our *Groupwork with the Elderly*). Of paramount importance are the group leader's responses, both verbal and non-verbal, which will encourage the client to take that first step and say 'I remember' or 'I did that'. Once there is an opening the group leader must not lose it, but use 'how, where, why, when', encouraging the client to share his/her experiences with the other members of the group.

How to achieve this task

Before the group

1 Discuss fully with the officer in charge that the objective of your group is social stimulation, outlining the aims and who you would like to involve.
2 Forward planning is essential, looking at what *to* discuss, and what *not* to use as lead topics.
3 Because you must be prepared for refusals, your 'shortlist' of potential members should be larger than the number of members you want in the group. Work down your list until you have got the required number.
4 Ensure you can maintain a weekly commitment to the group, as consistency is essential when working with withdrawn elderly people.
5 Establish a trusting relationship individually with your intended members before inviting them to join the group.
6 When inviting an older person into a group for the purpose of social stimulation, it is *essential you ascertain that the subject is familiar to them, prior* to introducing them to the group, as this will underpin the success of the group. If they feel isolated by or alienated from the subject matter in the first session, you may never get them to try again. Remember this is not a life review group but a group discussing specific subjects on days gone by with which they are familiar.
7 When selecting members to join the group it will prove helpful if the majority have socialized together to some extent *outside* the group in order that some interaction can be anticipated.

Establishing the group

In the setting in which you work, you should first identify those who have disengaged or appear to be lone or lonely figures. There are often many in most units for older adults.

In order to ascertain who is slipping through the 'social involvement net' list all the activities that take place in your establishment over a period of one month, both internal and external, noting who participates.

This can be simplified by using an Activities Register such as the one in our *Groupwork with the Elderly*. In this way you will identify those who do not involve themselves. You must then establish whether this is by choice or whether their needs are not being addressed.

To achieve success with loners, it is far better to mix two loners and four more sociable types, so that they can integrate relatively easily. This is preferable to the daunting task of trying to establish dialogue with six people all of whom have lost the art of conversing or have not much interest in doing so.

Remember many elderly people have lost almost complete confidence in themselves and will not voluntarily join in a social event or activity. Befriending, persuading and cajoling are therefore of great importance when trying to motivate an older person to join a group. Appeals to help you, coupled with a sincere 'Give it a session or two and if you're not enjoying it, feel free to stop coming' can be effective. Having persuaded your clients to come along to the first session of a group 'talking about the old days', where tea and a biscuit are provided, the next hurdle is to hold onto them. The subject matter should act as the catalyst. You must therefore ensure that *your homework has been carried out*, and that is to get a working knowledge of each person's life history – their history and geography (see the Biographical Profile on pp. 78–104). From these combined life histories, make your best guess as to what topics would be of interest to the group members to reminisce about and discuss. The aim is to get them involved, and to assess whether you are achieving this you need feedback. This comes in seeing the group interact, but remember, more signalling is done non-verbally than verbally. Read the signs, observe your clients, watch out for the nod of the head, the quiet smile or the slight movement that indicates they are listening to what others are saying. You will know you are succeeding when they come back for more.

Once a group has gone three or four sessions, bringing in new members can be disruptive for the existing members and difficult for the new ones, as they have missed so much of the group process. If vacancies arise before the third session, seek group permission to introduce new members. If they are hesitant, it may be because they know more about the person than you do! Also, it is better to introduce new members in twos. To be the only new member in an established group is a nerve-racking experience, while introducing more than two new members at a time risks splitting the group into sub-groups – of the old members and the new.

'Doing the homework'

Having decided who you feel would benefit from social involvement, you must then look at their past. Establish:

- the year they were born and major world events they have lived through (their time frame);
- where they went to school (childhood);
- where they have lived during their life (geographical area);
- their partners (relationships);
- whether there were children (family);
- their work or profession (lifestyle);
- their religion (beliefs);
- their interests or hobbies.

You can start seeking this information in their file, although unfortunately there often may not be much detail there. Approaching the family may also pay dividends. Make sure you tell the member what you are doing and why. They might well enjoy visiting their relative(s) (or vice-versa) and helping you do your research. If the person has a social worker, he or she may know more about their client than they have put in the referral letter, so contact may be worthwhile.

Another option is their GP. Recognizing the pressures most local doctors work under, a letter may be the best option, outlining the purpose of your enquiries. A helpful receptionist may be able to give you a lead from which to work. In making your approach you can point out the value of your work, in that in all probability it will benefit the person's health, in that socially active people are less depressed, often requiring less medication. With restored self-worth and given a purpose to move, even incontinence can improve considerably and has been known to cease.

We reproduce here the Biographical Profile proforma we use for people using accommodation, such as respite care. You will see it is detailed, for which we make no apologies.

Introduction: Guidelines for undertaking a Biographical Profile

The Biographical Profile is an essential tool to allow for the creation of relevant services and treatments for the individual client. This provision can only be achieved if the way the client is *now* is understood in terms of their *biography*.

1 The task should not be started until a relationship of trust has been created, specifically between yourself and the client; and, more generally, the client feels secure and trusting of the unit or the service.

2 The task may take two hours or more so will require more than one session.

3 The *same* person should complete the whole profile.

4 This will normally be the key nurse/care manager, i.e. a central figure in the design and monitoring of treatment.

5 You must understand the purpose of completing the profile and should explain and discuss the purpose before beginning the profile.

6 Since one of the purposes of the profile is to allow you to get to know the client, most of what the client says is relevant in forming a larger picture, so don't be too task-orientated. Conduct the interview at a leisurely pace, displaying a high level of interest.

7 The person's behaviour may have changed greatly in the past few months. For some of the questions, therefore, you will need to ask:
   • what were they like before that period?
   • what have they been like in the past few months?

8 Where the person themselves cannot answer the question, find out the name of the person who knows them best and say you would like to see the two of them together to get a picture of their life.

9 Fear of failure and the avoidance of situations where failure might arise is a feature of people with dementia, and also with depression. Remember to allow a relationship to form before attempting to fill in a Biographical Profile. Even then, you may need to be clear as to the great importance the Biographical Profile has in improving treatment. Just as if someone needed an X-ray, you would be firm as to that need, so should you be equally firm about the importance of getting a full Biographical Profile.

10 The order of the sections is not cast in stone. So, for example, if you think questions about accommodation might raise anxieties that you are trying to get the person into a nursing home, you might choose to defer asking this section. (So that you don't then miss any sections out, there is a checklist of sections that lets you tick them off when you have completed them.)

11 Finally, this is a semi-structured interview. The spaces we have allowed may be and often will be quite inadequate for what the client wants to say. So you may do better to copy the questions onto a pad as you go along. Don't let our requirements for economy of space affect your work in the slightest.

Biographical profile of

Date of birth:

Age:

Completed by: . . . .

Date: . . . .

	Page:	Date completed:	Signature:

CONTENTS

General Introduction of the Biographical Profile to the Client

You need to explain:

1 You're not being nosy for the sake of it
2 You do want a pretty complete picture of their life and their likes and dislikes so that you can tailor the service to their individuality
3 And likewise, if thinking about individual or group activity, tailoring it to client's needs and wishes
4 There's no rush
5 And no rights or wrongs
6 You'll need to inform them as to who has access to this profile [confidentiality]

FORM OF ADDRESS

May I start by asking you how you like to be called? _____

1   Present Living Arrangements

Who do you live with? _____

_____

_____

_____

And in what type of accommodation? [Check for how the accommodation space is split]

_____

_____

How long have you lived there?_____

_____

Who else lives in the place? [List] _____

_____

_____

And how do you get on with the other people in the house?

List [from previous question]

Name/Relation   How well you get on with?

_____

_____

_____

_____

_____

_____

_____

_____

_____

2 Sleeping and Waking

I'd like to ask about how you get off to sleep

a) Actual   b) Your ideal – how you'd like it to be

AT NIGHT

What would be your usual and ideal amount of sleep per night?

_____

_____

What time do you go to bed? _____

_____

What sort of things do you do before bed? (supper, reading, hot water
bottle etc.) _____

_____

Do you take any medication to help you sleep? _____

_____

What time do you fall asleep? _____

_____

Do you do anything to help you get off to sleep? (habits, rituals)

_____

_____

What position do you like to sleep in? _____

_____

What do you wear? (pyjamas, bedsocks, fleece rug) _____

_____

Do/did you sleep well? (Find out how often and why they wake up; about nightmares, cramps etc.) _____

_____

_____

_____

At what time do you wake up?_____

_____

3   Food and Drink – Likes and Dislikes

I would like to ask you questions about your eating and drinking habits.

1   Tell me about your normal eating and drinking patterns (when? what?).

On waking: _____

_____

During morning (breakfast, snacks): _____

_____

Lunch: _____

_____

Afternoon/evening (tea, dinner, supper): _____

_____

2   Do you have any particular likes or dislikes? (e.g. spicy food, chocolate, etc.) _____

_____

What are your favourite snacks? _____

_____

How do you like your tea/coffee? (milk/sugar) _____

_____

3   What size portions do you like? _____

_____

_____

4   Have you any food allergies? _____

_____

5   Is there any medical problem regarding diet? (e.g., diabetes/fat-free)

_____

_____

_____

6   Do you have any difficulty swallowing or chewing? _____

_____

7   Have you ever suffered from any eating disorder? _____

_____

8   Are there any specific cultural preferences? (e.g., religious/vegetarian)

_____

_____

4   Structure of the Day

We would like to know what sort of things you did during a typical day over the last year/before your illness.

You have told me you would wake at about _____ o'clock. What happened next?

Morning (washing, dressing, breakfast etc.): _____

_____

_____

_____

Lunch (who makes it? where eaten?): _____

_____

_____

Afternoon: _____

_____

_____

_____

Evening: _____

_____

_____

Resting during day

Is there a time of day when you feel brightest/worst? _____

_____

How much rest do you like during the day? Any catnaps? When?_____

_____

_____

In bed or a chair? _____

_____

Who visits you during the day? [Go over the days of the week] _____

_____

_____

_____

_____

Do you go and visit anybody regularly? _____

_____

_____

_____

Do you listen to or watch any radio/TV programmes regularly? _____

_____

_____

_____

_____

Do you take part in any activity or social group regularly? _____

_____

_____

_____

_____

Page 9

5 Hobbies

I would like to ask you for (more) information about hobbies and interests.

When you were young (say age 8–21), what sort of hobbies and interests did you have?

_____

_____

_____

As a young adult, perhaps courting, what sort of things did you enjoy doing?

_____

_____

_____

What about during the (1939–45) War? _____

_____

_____

And after the War? What about your interests and hobbies? _____

_____

_____

[If they brought up children] What other interests did you have (besides the children)?

_____

_____

_____

What did you do after the children left home? Did you take up new interests? Renew old ones?

_____

_____

_____

After you retired, did you take up any new hobbies? _____

_____

_____

ALSO:

[If there was a partner] What activities did you enjoy together?_____

_____

_____

Did (either of) you get involved in local community activities? _____

_____

_____

Did you join any clubs? _____

_____

_____

You mention a number of interests [Go over each hobby and interest]
Please tell me a little more about . . .

1 _____

_____

_____

2 _____

_____

_____

3 _____

_____

_____

6 Activities/Hobbies Chart

On the Activities/Hobbies Chart, record any regular events:

- activities, such as cleaning the house or shopping
- hobbies
- visits to places of recreation/clubs
- outings – walks/lunch out

and the frequency with which it happens (once a week/fortnight/month).

Activities/Hobbies Chart

	Morning	Afternoon	Evening
MONDAY			
TUESDAY			
WEDNESDAY			
THURSDAY			
FRIDAY			
SATURDAY			
SUNDAY			

7 People You See

On the Socializing Chart fill in the details of the following:

- Who do you go and see with any regularity?
- Who visits you?

Like the Activities/Hobbies Chart, record the frequency and where you meet (your home/club/their home).

Socializing Chart

	Morning	Afternoon	Evening
MONDAY			
TUESDAY			
WEDNESDAY			
THURSDAY			
FRIDAY			
SATURDAY			
SUNDAY			

Page 14

When you have filled in the Socializing Chart, list all the people who matter to you but whom you do not see regularly (for example, family or friends you see once a year).

Name	Relationship	Frequency

8 Family Tree

Ask for a family tree to include details of the individual's primary family, e.g. mother, father, grandparents, brothers and sisters, and secondary family, e.g. spouse, children, grandchildren.

Ask for:

- Names
- Dates of birth and death (approximate will do)
- Where they lived
- Their occupation

Work on it together during the session, so that they understand what you want. Then you can give it to them as 'homework', especially if the people at home can help them fill it in.

9   Client Biographical Profile

Original surname, if female _____

Brought up: (list places lived till age 18) _____

_____

_____

_____

_____

Mother and father

1   Where did they live when you were younger? _____

_____

_____

_____

2   Employment of parents _____

_____

_____

_____

_____

_____

Important others when growing up: _____

_____

_____

_____

_____

Schooling

What schools? _____

_____

_____

What subjects did you enjoy? _____

_____

How did you get on at school? _____

_____

Did you do further study/obtain qualifications? _____

_____

_____

What did you feel about school at the time, and later on in life? _____

_____

Employment history

Could you tell me about your employment history? _____

_____

_____

_____

_____

_____

Main occupation? _____

_____

_____

Where you worked?	**Job**	**Where**
_____		_____
_____		_____
_____		_____

When did you retire? Why? _____

_____

What did you feel about retirement at the time, and later on in life?

_____

_____

Spouse

Spouse(s): [Find out how many times they have been married. Then ask the questions in this section for each spouse]

1   When and where did you meet your husband/wife/important partners?

_____

_____

_____

2   Where were you married? _____

_____

3   If spouse deceased:

When did they die? _____

May I ask from what? _____

Were they ill for long? _____

4   If widowed:

Have you found someone to be close to since? _____

_____

Page 19

Children: [Ask about miscarriages]*

1   Dates of birth (and death, if appropriate)*

_____

_____

_____

2   For each child:

Name	Where live now?	Main employment

Client's close friends and important relatives, when adult

_____

_____

_____

_____

Religion (and how relevant): _____

_____

_____

_____

* Obviously these questions require sensitivity and the ability to handle answers/
  reactions competently.

Important values/beliefs: _____
_____
_____
_____

Places of special significance: _____
_____
_____
_____

Date came to present location (if incomer): _____
_____
_____

Page 21

10   The War

This section, more than any other, should be taken at a slow, unhurried pace.

1   Can you tell me about your War? _____

_____

_____

_____

_____

2   What did you do during the War? _____

_____

_____

_____

_____

3   Did you see active service? What was it like? _____

_____

_____

_____

_____

4   Did you see or experience the bombing of Plymouth (or appropriate location)? What was it like?

_____

_____

_____

_____

5   What were your worst experiences during the War? _____

_____

_____

_____

_____

6   Looking back, how did the War affect or change your life? _____

_____

_____

_____

_____

[If too young to have lived through the War]

As you were told about it, how did the Second World War affect your parents? How did their experience affect the way they treated you?

_____

_____

_____

_____

_____

_____

_____

11   Additional Information

Have I left important aspects or events of your life out? _____

_____

_____

_____

_____

_____

_____

Since we first started working on this profile, is there anything you want to change or add to?

_____

_____

_____

_____

_____

_____

_____

_____

_____

Page 24

May I ask how you found doing the Biographical Profile? _____

_____

_____

_____

_____

_____

_____

_____

_____

_____

Give information (repeat if necessary) on what happens to the information.

Thank the client for their cooperation.

Using the information

Having done the profile, before you start your group you should be able run through in your mind the major events in the life of each member. You may find that you now know them better than you know the lives of your parents or partner!

If your client's experience of a reminiscence group is to be positive, then at least for the first few sessions the subject matter must be familiar to them. To guide their reminiscences into an area they can each enter you need to know about the following areas for *each* individual member.

AGE – WORLD EVENTS   Discussion of world events can lead you into the 1914–18 war or onto the first man on the moon. This is where knowing each of your member's age becomes so important. People don't usually have vivid memories much before 6 years of age. For example, a discussion of the First World War means that the members shouldn't be born after 1910. Start thinking in terms of 'age cohorts' – people born at the same time will experience the same major events. So a person born 1908 is part of a quite different age cohort from one born in 1918, although we might mistakenly lump both of them together as 'very old'.

BUT don't despair if you suggest a topic that doesn't have much relevance to the members. Once the group is established, if the atmosphere in the group is good, they may well enjoy pointing this out to you!

WHERE THEY LIVED – GEOGRAPHICAL AREAS   Knowing where someone lived allows you to look at what happened in a specific area – local disasters, royal visits, local industries, famous or infamous people who lived in the vicinity. In addition, you can discuss the shops in the main high street, the name of the roads, local public houses (watch out for changes in pub names which can get confusing), significant landmarks, local parks, the train station and even the number of a bus. Allowing the conversation to dwell on familiar ground will mean your client can feel safe should they wish to enter the conversation.

MARITAL STATUS – RELATIONSHIPS   In general, we usually know when working with women whether or not they were married by the presence of the word Miss or Mrs affixed to their name. With men, however, there is no certainty as to their marital status. Should there be some doubt, because there is no evidence of a wife's presence in someone's life, this does not mean you should assume that the older person you are working with never married or had a serious relationship. Young men and women during the war years paid a high price in losing their loved ones. Some husbands lost their wife early in married life during the bombing of mainland Britain and, conversely, wives lost husbands fighting in the services. In fact do not assume anything about a client, especially with regard to their sexual orientation. To say you are gay or that someone is gay is fairly commonplace in today's society, but, until the 1960s homosexuality was a criminal offence. This stigma may remain with the older person and they have every right to keep private whatever they wish. Seek out information that will be of use to you in helping to socialize with a client but do not pry into personal areas. It's an odd thing but true that if you are respectful (but interested) and don't pry, people are more willing to self-disclose than if you go after them with leading questions.

Having established that the majority of your members were married, then discussions on weddings, setting up a home, shopping, food of the day, household items, the family unit, clothes, holidays, days out, marital expectations – who does what and so on – can be introduced. Should you have any misgivings, then leave this subject until you feel your clients are secure in the group.

Finally, leave enough 'space' for important relationships after bereavements. Widows do not often marry again but they may well develop important friendships, often platonic, with neighbours, which are very important and have a similar role. Because they have no formal role/ name in our society, they are not considered important; but as a group develops, the members may well appreciate the opportunity to talk about these friendships.

CHILDREN – FAMILY   As with the previous subject, do not assume, cruising mindlessly along a highway of your stereotypes about older adults. Childbirth out of wedlock did occur in the past, and we are not discussing legal status but establishing whether there were children in the member's life, including nephews, nieces and neighbours' children. This can lead to a very productive discussion, from pregnancy and childbirth, sickness, health care, medication, doctors, hospitals, to schooling, holidays, pocket money, Christmas.

Alternatively, the discussion may be centred around the group member's own childhood and the above subjects could still be discussed.

One note of caution. There may well be miscarriages, stillbirths or early child deaths in the personal experiences of your member. Your homework should have forewarned you about some of these tragedies. Some you will not know about. So think what you'll do if a member describes a harrowing experience.

OCCUPATION – LIFESTYLE   The occupation of the older person you are working with will have had a profound effect upon their lifestyle. Whether you go to work in a cloth cap or bowler hat has a major effect on people's lives; and in the era you are discussing it was even more important than today. Management or factory fodder? Upper, middle or lower/working class were the classes people were placed into. Discussion around for whom they worked and what the end product was can be fruitful and enjoyable: the environment in which they worked, the hours, the wages, the management or the work force and the feelings regarding these; what they wore; transport, how they got to work; lunch, be it a wrapped sandwich, a visit to the canteen, or restaurant. Much will depend upon what they did for a living.

RELIGION – BELIEFS Religion can play a very important part in some people's lives. They may have strong beliefs and have attended church regularly. Religion can go hand in hand with culture. For such a person, discussion on religious festivals, superstitions or taboos and their effect on the family unit may prove positive.

Be careful to make no assumptions about which religion, if any, they belonged to or how important it was to them. 'I suppose we all went to Church on Sunday' is *not* the way to open up the topic!

Again, be sensitive to those who have either temporarily or permanently lost faith in God after a traumatic event.

INTERESTS AND HOBBIES These can prove a light-hearted but positive way of introducing an older person into a reminiscence group – sport, entertainment, collecting, reading, gardening, cooking, woodwork, handicrafts, pets and so on. Each covers a wide area that can be supported with pictures, objects and sounds to stimulate the memory.

These are the major content themes, but you will, of course, add one or two, take away one or two, to maximize the relevance for *your* group. On the whole, these themes seem able to draw interest and live experience from a very wide range of group members. One of the first reminiscence groups reported in the literature, in 1982, was run by clinical psychologist Andrew Norris, charge nurse Mohammed Abu El Eileh and OT aide Cynthia Stroud on a psychogeriatric ward at Stone House Hospital, Dartford, and written up by the first two for the *Nursing Times*. The suggested 12 session topics were:

1 Getting to know you
2 Schooling
3 Work
4 Family
5 Hobbies
6 Happiest and saddest events of their lives
7 Leisure activities
8 Holidays
9 The War
10 Slides of the 1930s

11   Innovations and progress
12   Famous events – Coronation, D-Day etc.

and a Goodbye/Evaluation session. This would still be a good set of themes to start with today.

Examples of work for this purpose

Since this is probably the commonest use of reminiscence, examples of it in action abound. Certainly Paulette Bauckham and Mike Bender nearly achieved their aim of having a reminiscence group running in every one of the ten social services residential homes in the London Borough of Newham. The groups were either run by one of them with two staff, or, as those staff members received some training from them and showed their competence, the staff would run the groups by themselves with supervision. Faith Gibson, in Ulster, has also encouraged a great number of groups in residential and day units.

The range of people that can be stimulated is great. Certainly, it is our therapeutic prescription for isolated people, who actually only meet and talk to people on the days they come to a centre – the 'social hypo-thermics'. But because it uses long-term memory, this approach is a good morale booster for those with difficulty recalling recent events. Modified appropriately, it allows the sensorily handicapped to com-municate. (We will expand on such use in the chapter on using reminiscence to create group cohesion.) It also minimizes feelings of being deviant, of being a marginal member of society, because it stresses *shared* experience of important events and *belonging* to an age cohort. So, it is good for people who do feel they are marginal men and women, such as people who have been in the psychiatric system a long time, or people with learning difficulties.

There are often advantages in holding a reminiscence group away from the unit/place where the members usually meet. Examples of such groups would be using a room in the local history museum. One of us helped run a very successful group in the re-created late nineteenth century kitchen of the Cornworthy Museum, in Kingsbridge, Devon. Although the kitchen's utensils illustrate a period two or three decades before the members' own childhood, many of the cooking and cleaning utensils had been in use when they were young and so were highly evocative for them. For the men who had worked on the local farms, the farming implements had the power to transport them back to the time before the War. Again, bussing residents of homes to Newham's Remi-niscence Centre gave them novelty and expectation; and the centre itself, described in Purpose Eighteen (reminiscence to train staff in groupwork skills), was of course also highly evocative. So once they arrived, they quickly wanted to make good use of the experience.

Just to show how reminiscence can work for people who are not old, we will briefly describe a project undertaken by a Community Services Volunteer student aimed at gathering memories of people in their fifties and then using the material to provide an enjoyable and stimulating evening for other 50-year-olds.

I joined forces with Paul Stevens, Community Services Volunteer organizer, and a CSV, Gary; and we decided to look at Leisure in the Fifties in East and West Ham.

The idea of using the 1950s was so that Gary could use his parents and their generation to gather information. He then linked up with Howard Bloch, Local Studies Librarian with Newham Libraries, who was very helpful. By going through local newspapers and other sources, he quickly developed a picture library which we got made into slides. I have to admit to being impressed by the wealth of detail his researches revealed – not just the very full picture of the great variety of leisure pursuits (this was pre-TV days), but the way that these pursuits were undertaken, the social groupings, the rituals, the celebrations and so on.

In order to see how this material would appeal, we organized a small gathering with Muriel Johns, then matron of a local authority residential home and half a dozen of her friends, all East Enders of the appropriate age group. We asked her to organize a traditional East End meal – cockles and whelks and jellied eels – to create the appropriate atmosphere. (I have a feeling that reminiscence can be strengthened accompanied by rituals since they lend solemnity and togetherness.)

The evening was a great success and it was nice to see Gary witnessing the results of his hard work. The food obviously was enjoyed. The slides were analysed in great and joyous detail by the group as to the date and location of the pictures and sparked off many reminiscences. We eventually had to stop them to get home.

(We didn't take the idea further, although now we knew how to go about it and had made contacts, it could easily have been developed further. Gary got himself an apprenticeship, and the CSV unit in Newham was closed by central government.)

A detailed account of this purpose in action

We had been working in a residential home in an inner London borough and had introduced reminiscence work into it. We were then requested to run a second group. It was suggested we focus on residents with differing physical frailties which had restricted their social involvement. It was specifically requested that we include a man named Stan in those plans. Stan had been in residential care for over a year and his level of involvement was limited to remaining on the periphery of the lounge during social occasions in the home. Although invited to join in various activities, barely lifting his head, he would respond with a low grunt of 'No'. Stan had diabetes. His sight had progressively deteriorated and now he could no longer see. His verbal exchanges with fellow residents were nil.

The other members put forward for the group did, to some degree, interact with staff and other residents in the home. It was recognized that Stan was a solitary person with little self-worth. Following a discussion with the officer in charge and Stan's key worker, Pearl, it was agreed that Pearl would be one of the group leaders. She had been acting as key worker to Stan since his admission to the home and their relationship was felt to be good. Staff felt she was the only one he really related to. As Stan had been known to Social Services for some time, we had some knowledge of his background prior to the onset of his sensory impairment. He had no extended family, but an old friend did visit occasionally. Pearl agreed to study Stan's file for anything which might assist with the planning of the group. In the meantime she would continue forging a positive relationship/friendship with him.

An Activity Register had been kept for one month, and following a planning meeting we looked at who the other four members of the group should be. We felt that any more than five members for this particular group might prove difficult when taking Stan's blindness into account. The criterion for admission to the group was that all the members required social stimulation to some degree as their physical frailties had reduced their confidence, placing limitations on what they felt they could participate in. Besides Stan, it was also thought that Ellen would require careful nurturing in order to put something positive into her life again and restore self-worth. Ellen had been admitted to residential care following a stroke. She was wheelchair-bound and was coming to terms with her disability and gradually adjusting and integrating into the lifestyle of her new home when there had been a major setback. Her daughter had died and her family had kept this from her until after the burial. They had, considering how debilitating her stroke had been, and with the best intention, felt this would be too much for her. Once the home became aware of the situation, she had been told (by a member of her family). Eighteen months had passed, staff had tried to counsel her but she appeared to have cut herself off from the life of the home. Jenny, Ellen's key worker, informed us that she did take her to visit her daughter's grave and that she now spoke freely of her daughter. However, during the months of her grieving, she had disassociated herself from other residents in the home and was quite a solitary figure. Although never refusing to participate in social events, she showed little emotion. With much coaxing, staff would get her permission to push her wheelchair to the edge of the lounge and there it would remain until the activity had finished, Ellen sitting with her head bowed and apparently uninterested.

PLANNING   Having looked closely at the backgrounds of the proposed five members, we were then in a position to choose and shape the topics we might discuss and their sequence. We knew Stan had no extended family, Ellen had lost a daughter and another member, Rose, had a daughter who did not visit her. These pieces of information led us to decide that we would not introduce the subject of children until the group was well established. All our members were from the East End of London. If not born there, they had lived a major part of their lives there. Therefore geographical area was placed on the agenda alongside occupations, as all male members and female members' husbands had been manual workers.

Religion, at this point in time, was a no-go area as Ellen often said there was no God (perhaps as a result of unresolved grief) and it was not felt to be a subject to introduce to this particular group (unless or until they raised it). All the members of our group had been married, therefore 'relationships' was felt to be a usable topic, as were interests and hobbies. We could use world events after the mid-twenties, as our youngest member Clara, was born in 1919.

Four of the group arrived promptly for our first session, and although it was some time before Stan arrived, arrive he did! Pearl was holding his arm as he thrashed about with his cane, hitting out at the wall, chairs, tables or whatever was in his path as he walked awkwardly down the corridor. Cursing loudly as he entered the room he was assisted to a chair. Bill, the other man in our group, thought this was extremely funny but the women looked frightened. It had been explained to them that we were being joined by a man who had lost his sight, but his appearance had been something of a shock to them, not only for his noisy and ungainly entrance but Stan was at least 6 foot 2 inches tall. We sat there trying to establish calm for a group that looked totally bewildered and a bit frightened. The staff group leader had good relationships with the members, and so was able to reassure them, and sharing a cup of tea also helped.

We opened with a discussion on entertainment in the area in days gone by. Initially it was slow going, but as discussion developed it gained momentum. We had been to the local studies library so photographs were at the ready to be used as cues and prompts. The local cinemas were the favourite form of entertainment, especially the Coronation, Manor Park, where stage entertainers had preceded the film. Favourite film stars were discussed and members tried to recall various names of films. Our hour was nearly up and neither Stan nor Ellen had spoken until Clara said 'Whereabouts was the Coronation, was it near East Ham Station?' and Stan responded, saying 'No, it was up past the Ruskin [pub] near the Broadway.' The session came to a close. It had not been easy (first sessions rarely are); the pace had been slow, but everyone except Ellen had been involved.

At the group leaders' debriefing it was decided that Stan should be brought to the next session before the other members, to avoid the negative impact his late arrival had made.

During the course of the week, photographs of various celebrities of stage and screen were posted on the walls alongside pictures of local cinemas and theatres. Pearl was describing these to Stan as the members of the group arrived. As tea was prepared, the pictures were handed to the group. Rose announced that she had seen Rudolph Valentino in *The Sheikh*. We went from silent movie stars to the first talking movie with Al Jolson. No one could remember its name, but it was a good session. Neither Stan nor Ellen had spoken during the session. However, their body language indicated that they were listening and taking an interest.

During the group leader's debriefing Pearl said that when she had returned Stan to the lounge he had said 'It was *The Jazz Singer*, that was the first talkie.'

Note the importance here of pre-group briefings and post-group debriefings to keep the leaders on the ball, staying 'tuned' to the members. It is this fine-tuning and depth of understanding that helps a group move and develop.

We tried to introduce local shops into the discussion during the third session but Clara took us back to entertainment by announcing that, when her sister visited last week, she had asked her the name of the first talking movie. It was *The Jazz Singer* with Al Jolson. Pearl informed the group that Stan had also said this. No one seemed to take much notice but Stan had lifted his head. Talk went on to local dance halls and music of the day, Bill and Rose sang some of the old songs and we were about to tactfully stop them by taking them on to another subject, as we did not want the group to develop into a sing-a-long, when Jenny nodded toward Ellen, who had joined in the singing.

During the debriefing we all agreed that things were moving, albeit slowly. It was felt entertainment would not last a third week, although the group definitely liked the theme.

At the beginning of the next session, it became clear that Clara was obviously discussing the group with her family, as she told us that her sister had said there had been dances held over some of the pubs. To this Stan growled out 'They did at the Ruskin.' Jenny asked if it was his local and he replied 'No, but I worked there as barman for years.' **We were in**. Bill joined in saying he drank there, Rose said she liked the Black Lion and the talk went on to almost every public house in East Ham and Manor Park.

At the debriefing, it appeared we had all noticed how Ellen, although not speaking, was watching Pearl assist Stan when offering his cup of tea, ensuring the handle was the right way around and that a table was nearby and directing him verbally.

At the next pre-session briefing Jenny told us that one of Ellen's sons had asked her who Stan was, as his mother had been talking of him. Each session grew and interaction developed; the theme remained on the local area, discussing the local factories, notably how many sweet factories were in the East End (Bill informed us that his wife worked in Trebors during the evening and brought home cheap broken sweets for their children). Stan no longer hung his head but held it high, switching it from side to side, catching what others were saying.

What they had done for a living was a topic that evoked a lively debate. Bill had been a baker's roundsman, telling tales of his old horse that pulled the bread cart and how it used to take his sandwiches from his pocket. Clara told of her husband's job in the fruit market, working in all weathers. He had brought home cheap fruit. Rose said she had worked in the Co-op for years and her husband worked in the docks. Ellen was thawing out as she said 'So did my Sid. He worked down the Royals.'

The group was working. It went from strength to strength. It was by no means an easy group and initially the subject matter had to be well thought out and planned. But it gained its own direction and subjects discussed from one session would point to the next.

Bill died before the group closed, which caused some distress, but the members talked about it and had a small collection for some flowers. Rose and Clara joined other activities in the home and Stan was a positive member of the quiz group and extremely verbal at residents meetings. Ellen never did join in any activity but she had formed a close friendship with Stan. Following the group they were placed next to each other in the dining room where she assisted and directed him at mealtimes.

Conclusions

Stimulation through the process of reminiscing can prove an extremely effective tool. This does not only apply to the dispirited and depressed. There are times when we all need something to motivate us to arouse the senses. Reminiscing can act as a stimulus capable of creating a response in people. We do not necessarily mean to make them spring into action but to trigger a spark that can initiate conversation and open up dialogue to support us in sharing a common ground. I am sure many of us have been in an uncomfortable group situation, mentally searching for words that will break the ice and relax the situation, not wanting to be the outsider but wishing to feel part of the group or unit. With prior knowledge of what is common ground, then how much easier would it have been? We do not all possess that outgoing personality that can initiate conversation at the drop of a hat, and if we did, age has a way of taking that from us. How formidable this must be for those older people entering the care system, with cumulative losses of home, family, health, body image, status and self-esteem. We as staff can facilitate in restoring their self-worth by assisting them to establish bonds and reaffirm self-esteem by running a well-thought out reminiscence group so that people can see that they are from the same 'community of memories'. It is very rewarding to the group leader to see the ice broken, seeing friendships forming outside the group, seeing increased social participation – to see increased hope and purpose.

Useful reading and resources

E. Cumming and W.E. Henry explained their theory about people disengaging as they get older in *Growing Old: The Process of Disengagement* (Basic Books, 1961). Though generally considered an inadequate explanation, it was one of the first, modern attempts by social scientists to ask 'What is the nature of a good old age?'

A variety of such approaches are discussed by Peter Coleman in a chapter entitled 'Identity management in later life' in *Handbook of the Clinical Psychology of Ageing*, edited by Robert Woods (Wiley, 1996, pp. 93–113). Disengagement and alternative formulations are also discussed in Eleanor O'Leary's *Counselling Older Adults: Perspectives, Approaches and Research* (Chapman and Hall, 1996).

Faith Gibson has written up her pioneering work in a chapter in Joanna Bornat's edited volume *Reminiscence Reviewed* (Open University, 1993) (which also includes a chapter by Mike Bender, describing a number of groups relevant to the present purpose). Also, see her chapter 'The use of the past' in Alan Chapman and Mary Marshall's *Dementia: New Skills for Social Workers* (Jessica Kingsley, 1996). Her manual *Reminiscence and Recall: a Guide to Good Practice* is published by Age Concern.

A good source book of ideas to stimulate discussion and reminiscence is Caroline Osborn's *The Reminiscence Handbook: Ideas for Creative Activities with Older People* (Age Exchange, 1993).

A short Biographical Profile can be found in *Getting to Know Me* by Eric Midwinter (Third Age Press, 1996).

The following books and packs can be purchased through the various addresses listed. However, your local library will in all probability have a wealth of information, both written and visual, that can be loaned giving information on the main sources of employment in your specific area, theatres, cinemas, skating rinks, public houses, dance halls, schools, markets and shops, in addition to back copies of local newspapers. Once you have a name you can make contact direct; people may then be able to furnish you with pictures of their building and/or the work force. Objects are a wonderful stimulus, so beg, borrow and search out memorabilia; try jumble sales, boot sales and charity shops, approach family, friends and clients' relatives. Good luck and happy hunting!

Further reading/ideas and material that will assist when running a group for the purpose of stimulation are:

World events
Banner Headlines (large posters of major events between 1936 and 1981); Winslow Press, Telford Road, Bicester, Oxon OX6 0TS.
The Wartime Scrapbook (book of photographs of food, fashion and comic postcards); The Robert Opie Collection, Museum of Advertising and Packaging, Gloucester Dock, Gloucester GL1 2EH.
Keeping the Wheels Turning (video with material on the activities of women and children whose lives were affected in various ways during the 1939–1945 war); Winslow Press, address as above.

General
Faces of Britain (a picture of Britain 1800–1919; a book of photographs depicting City Life – Country Life – Working Life – War Years – Family Life – Childhood Days – Beside the Seaside – Taking it Easy – Sporting Moments); N. Hindmarch Keen, Bookmart Ltd, Desford Road, Enderby, Leicester L49 5AD.

Running a home
Famous Brands Poster Pack (large posters reflecting on food and cleaning products), Winslow Press, address as above.
Can We Afford the Doctor? (will give staff insights into health and social welfare that can be raised in group discussion); The Age Exchange Reminiscence Centre, 11 Blackheath Village, London SE3 9LA.
Winter Warmers (six in a bed, stone hot water bottles, winter recipes and cures: this book will give staff information on winters of yesteryear); The Age Exchange Reminiscence Centre, address as above.
The Robert Opie Collection of Advertising and Packaging (postcards and posters of products of days gone by can be purchased); address as above.

Childhood
All Our Christmases (reading material with ideas on subjects for group discussion on Christmases past); The Age Exchange Reminiscence Centre, address as above.
The Reminiscence Toy Box (a collection of toys from yesteryear); Winslow Press, address as above.
Good Morning Children (schooldays 1920s and 1930s, reading and photographs to support the childhood theme); The Age Exchange Reminiscence Centre, address as above.

Professions
My First Job (memories and photographs from pensioners who started work between 1912 and 1940); The Age Exchange Reminiscence Centre, address as above.

Interests/leisure

Sounds Nostalgic audio-cassette tapes (voices from the 1940s and 1950s, featuring politicians, broadcasters, the royal family, showbusiness personalities); Winslow Press, address as above.

The Time of Our Lives (memories and photographs of leisure time 1920s to 1930s); The Age Exchange Reminiscence Centre, address as above.

Famous Faces (cue cards: personalities from the world of sport, show-business, politics); Winslow Press, address as above.

Reading material

Groupwork with the Elderly (practical manual on running successful groups); Mike Bender, Andrew Norris and Paulette Bauckham, Winslow Press, address as above.

Purpose Five

REMINISCENCE TO PROMOTE EMOTIONAL AND SOCIAL STIMULATION WITH PEOPLE WHO ARE SEVERELY DISORIENTATED

Rationale

Purpose Five extends groupwork to make it relevant to those considered to be suffering from severe confusion/dementia. Reminiscence groupwork is often not considered as relevant in units serving people with dementia, because 'they would not attend;' 'they'd wander' and/or 'they will be disruptive'. But we want people to attend groups if possible; or to be more specific, we want people to be able to receive stimulation, support, warmth in either individual or group formats, if possible. We do not want to deprive them unnecessarily of the benefits of groupwork. So, in this chapter, we will discuss:

1   how to prevent unnecessary exclusions;
2   how we can modify reminiscence groups to make them interesting and relevant for people with dementia.

The purpose of the groupwork will stay the same as in the previous chapter – to provide emotional and social stimulation – and again we look at the use of a group formed to help people re-socialize and re-engage. Certainly the medium of a group is preferable to individual work to achieve these goals. This is because a group has its own dynamic, its own energy over and above a given purpose or task. Independent of *why* a person is in a group, they are meeting people and talking to them, and, we can hope, they may begin to feel they belong, and feel valued.

Thinking about exclusion

SENSORY HANDICAP   There are people whose sensory handicap is so severe it makes their participation difficult. Here we are obviously thinking of severe loss of sight or hearing.

In the case of hearing loss, every unit should have a loop system. This greatly improves accessibility for those whose hearing is impaired. (We describe a group for the hard-of-hearing in Purpose Seven: Reminiscence to create group cohesion.) Also, we have found that a sighted majority can 'carry' a blind person within a group. The other members 'take them under their wing' and, for example, explain what's on a slide. The acts of caring, including and communicating – in short, acts of altruism – are considered by Irving Yalom as key contributors to improved mental health in a group, so these are psychologically important activities in themselves.

In the present context, we are suggesting that sensory handicap need not exclude people from a group, as long as the handicap is taken on board and helped.

Unfortunately, there will be units without a loop system, units where the staff don't have the skills to incorporate members without sight. Then one-to-one work will be necessary, *as a short-term measure*, until the resources needed are installed and/or staff are trained in groupwork skills.

SEVERE COGNITIVE LOSS   There is another group of people who might not seem suitable for a group. These are the very cognitively damaged, so damaged that they have lost speech or at best can only use short sentences.

It is all too easy for clients to be scapegoated as 'difficult' and for staff to agree that he, or less often she, could not possibly successfully take part in a group. The first thing to say about such a judgement is that it is self-fulfilling. Now condemned to boredom and under-stimulation by the staff's decision, it is very likely that the person will engage in attention-seeking/attention-creating behaviour. The second thing to note is that the statement 'Mr Smith is disruptive, no matter which staff he is with' is quite often incorrect. While certainly, he may 'play up' with those staff members who do not value or respect him (or anyone else with dementia), with more caring staff who transmit respect, he might well be fine. So, the blanket 'he'll disrupt any group' may well be untrue, and has, as its function, the protection of incompetent staff.

The person who is thought likely to be disruptive needs to be given a chance, and one way we can test out this disruptiveness is by running a pilot session. Most groups start without any piloting, but after all, industry doesn't work that way. A firm mocks up a product and then tests it to see if people want it. Although in this book we have generally written as though groups will be started without pilot work, a pilot session or two is a very useful way of ironing out difficulties *before* you're committed to eight or ten or however many sessions. It is particularly useful in the present context of working with people with severe disabilities as such work is very exhausting, particularly so if the group's not working. Also, your ability to predict what will work, what will light that spark, is lowered.

For both these reasons, pilot work for the ideas discussed in this chapter may well pay extra dividends. The important point to note, however, is that the first sessions of any group are anxiety-making for all – members and leaders. This anxiety can lead to increased disruptive behaviour initially. Remember it often takes two or three sessions for a group to settle down and its anxiety to decrease. Try to keep the 'disruptive' person in the group for those two or three sessions if possible. What you are looking for is whether this behaviour can be controlled – whether the person can sit down/not sing/not grab. If they can, then they should be kept in for the rest of the group.

Seating can be very important in the early stages. An overactive person may drive one member crazy but just be a source of tolerant amusement to another. You can increase leader control by sitting next to a potentially disruptive member. So a seating plan should be on your agenda before each session; and the degree of its success discussed after each session until you feel that you've got it as good as it can be. This means, of course, that the group must understand and learn that you are in charge of the seating plan. Try to avoid letting people sit down and then having to move them. Better is to have large cards with each member's name on. This is a very strong stimulus to sit in that seat. Even people with severe cognitive damage recognize their name and respond appropriately. Also, even if they can no longer fully recognize their written name, guiding a person to a seat with their name on it is usually a non-troublesome business.

Finally, don't make a big issue of it, or feel guilty if you do ultimately have to exclude. Other staff should know in advance that you're trying to get Mr/Mrs X into your group, and that it may not work. Your criterion is simply: is this person seriously decreasing the usefulness of the group to the other members and their satisfaction? If he or she is, they must stop attending. If disruption is too bad during the session, then you must get them out in a non-demeaning way: 'Mrs X, I don't think you're enjoying the session, so why don't we see what's going on that you'll enjoy more?' Once outside the group, hand over responsibility for that person to another staff member; and then return to the session.

So, we can take risks because membership in the early stages in the life of a group is not set in stone; and we want to take risks because the use of a group is to be preferred over individual work with potentially disruptive members. One-to-one work provides little social control and actually gives the message 'you're uncontrollable'. In a group, the desire not to upset others and to take part can be quite a strong motivation even for a very damaged client; it is certainly harder to do than stopping work with one member of staff.

Remember people living with severe dementia are rarely malicious. Those who disrupt have learnt inappropriate ways of gaining attention. They can often learn to trust the group and get a huge amount out of it. Seeing such a change is very rewarding. Consider carefully then that being severely cognitively damaged does not necessarily imply a person cannot enjoy taking part in a group. Indeed, because of their isolation in their disability, the experience of sharing may be extremely important. So, reminiscence workers should strive to create relevant group experiences while at the same time, assessing what the damaged person wants and needs. They can then make an informed decision as to what kind of activities would be most appropriate, and whether these should be undertaken one-to-one or in a group setting.

There will be some overlap between this chapter and the next, which is on individual work. This is because the ways of behaving and communicating with people who are either physically or cognitively frail are not very different whether you are in a one-to-one or a group situation.

Goals implied in the purpose

1　To provide the most appropriate means of communicating with and demonstrating you care to people with severe damage to their physical/sensory or cognitive systems.
2　To skilfully use non-verbal means to **communicate** and elicit response. Success in such attempts may only be recognized by the client's non-verbal behaviour because their ability to verbalize is severely damaged.
3　To use non-verbal means to **elicit memories**. Verbal prompts will not elicit much response once the systems of speech and particularly thought are severely damaged, so alternative prompts, be they tactile or auditory or smell, are needed.
4　Again at a non-verbal level, to help people with severe system damage to interact with other people and **enjoy that interaction**.
5　Thus, generally, to stimulate, engage and give pleasure to people with severe cognitive damage.

The tasks

The group leader's tasks are:

1　To have a strong sense of the importance of working and communicating with very damaged people.

2   To be able to give of yourself, to transmit attention and respect.
3   To find quiet times and quiet places to communicate.
4   To maximize the clarity and warmth of your non-verbal behaviour.
5   To utilize a small group format, with no more than four members
    and leader: member of ratio 1:2 or even better 1:1½.

To elaborate on these tasks, there is an irony about working with very damaged people in that you yourself need to be very sensitive, very attentive and to make sure that the conditions in which you communicate with the person are as conducive to ease of communication as possible. At the same time society has little interest in such people and your work is not going to bring you any credit, nor be financially rewarded. By contrast, a psychotherapist, working with someone who only needs a little time and space to help sort out their problem can charge high fees and is a prestigious figure in society. If you want to work with this kind of client then, you will need a strong sense of inner purpose and of conviction of its usefulness.

Secondly, you will be giving a lot of yourself, transmitting your energy, your care for another human being. This may sound rather spiritual and perhaps it is, in the sense that what you are doing can't be explained or justified by any material values.

Thirdly, because they have little energy to focus on what you are saying or doing, you must find a quiet place and a quiet time to maximize the opportunity for communication.

Importantly, you also need to work on making your non-verbal and vocal behaviours as non-threatening and as warm as possible. For a person living with major system damage the world is a very scary place. They may also be afraid – probably correctly – that they will soon die, and the fright increases again. So you need to provide (and communicate) solidity and security through slow, careful movements, slow, but clear speech with longer pauses than you would use with non-damaged people, minimizing your physical impact by sitting with your eyes at the person's level and giving the impression that you have all the time in the world to relate to that person, that there is absolutely no hurry. (These ideas are elaborated in our book *Welcoming Your Clients*.)

We can all improve our non-verbal communication, for example, by going on training courses, by asking colleagues for feedback and by having the time and the opportunity to discuss difficult situations, both before they occur and when they have occurred, with colleagues we trust.

How to achieve these tasks

The absolute essential with people with severe disorientation is that you know their biography. As we shall see in the chapter on assessment, understanding their past illuminates their present. Many of the things they do stop looking like being deranged behaviour due to brain damage and start making sense in terms of their life history. The person who gets up at 5 o'clock may well not be confused but just doing the same as they did all their working life.

Also, of course, you can't plan groups without biographical information. Such information – the Biographical Profile – should be gathered when you first meet the person, and if the person can't give it, arrange a series of meetings with that person and a relative or friend who has known them for many years. (It's important that the client is there. This increases involvement and ownership of the creation of the Biographical Profile and decreases distrust/paranoia.) The personal information you gather can then be converted into a very useful aid by associating it with a list of major historical events, such as the one we offer here.

MAJOR PUBLIC AND PERSONAL EVENTS IN THE LIFE OF:			
Date	**Major public events**	**Major personal events**
1900	Boer War	
1911 June 22nd	Coronation of George V	
1914 Aug. 4th	Britain declares war on Germany	
1915 July 15th	200,000 Welsh miners strike for more pay	
1916 Aug. 19th	German warships bombard the English coast	
1918 Nov. 18th	Fighting ceases on the Western front	
1919	Lady Astor becomes Britain's first female MP	
1926	The General Strike	
1928	All adult British women can vote	
1929	The Wall Street Crash triggers the Great Depression	
1933	Nazis move to power in Germany, Hitler became the Fuhrer	

Date	Major public events	Major personal events
1935	Stanley Baldwin becomes PM	
1936	King George V died	
1937	King Edward VIII abdicated	
1939	World War II begins	
1940	Winston Churchill forms a coalition government	
1941	The Japanese attack Pearl Harbour	
1942	Montgomery defeats Rommel in the battle of El Alamein	
1944 June 6th	D-Day	
1945 May 8th	VE Day. War ended in Europe	
1947	The marriage of Princess Elizabeth to Philip	
1948	The National Health Service formed	
1952	George VI dies Elizabeth II succeeds	
1953	Hillary and Tensing climb Everest; Coronation of Queen Elizabeth II	
1957	Sputnik T launched in USSR	
1960	The end of National Service	
1961 Jan.	J.F. Kennedy sworn in as youngest US President	
1962 Aug.	Marilyn Munroe dies	
1963	Beeching axes railways	
1963 Nov.	J.F. Kennedy assassinated	

Date	Major public events	Major personal events
1964	Beginning of US involvement in Vietnam war	
1965	Churchill dies	
1966	England win World Cup – beat Germany	
1966 Oct.	Aberfan disaster	
1968	Martin Luther King assassinated; Tony Hancock dies; Bobby Kennedy assassinated	
1969	Concorde maiden flight	
1970	General DeGaulle dies	
1972	Three-day week; power strikes; blackouts lasting 9 hours	
1974	President Nixon resigns	
1977	Space shuttle maiden flight; Queen's Jubilee; Elvis dies	
1979	Margaret Thatcher wins General Election	
1980	Alfred Hitchcock dies; John Lennon shot dead	
1981	Ronald Reagan assassination attempt; Brixton riots; Prince Charles and Diana's wedding	
1982	Falklands war	

Information collected by: . . . .

Date: . . . .

Table 7   *Types of stimuli for situations where verbal communication is not available*

Medium or modality	Examples
Visual representational	Photo, slides
Smell/taste	Smell kits
	Types of food
Visual direct	Looking at objects of autobiographical meaning
	Painting
Music	Familiar tunes, records from times past
	Making music
Tactile	Touching physical objects
	Manipulating materials to get sensory experience, e.g. planting bulbs
	Feeling a piece of silk
	Painting
	Massage

We now turn to consider how to modify the methods of reminiscence groupwork to make them relevant for people with dementia. The major requirement is *to move away from verbal stimuli* and replace them with auditory and physical stimuli. Table 7 shows the various types of stimuli you might consider.

The next level of prompting is photographs and music. Remember the *Recall* pack is about and for people of East London so some of that material probably won't be relevant to your clients. Check out all stimulus material beforehand.

Songs are more likely to elicit memories than photos. This is partly because photos or slides need a reasonable level of eyesight, but also because music seems able to evoke stronger, more emotion-laden memories.

If photos or slides are not achieving results, you need more powerful stimuli and to use relevant objects. (Even if slides and music are being effective, having objects available gives you more scope and variety.) Staying with the war, gas masks, ration books, large, blown-up propaganda posters (for the Land Army, or an exhortation regarding unappetizing food) may all elicit hesitant but definite memories.

Just as music seems to get through where words cannot, so smells can do the same. Kits are available (Winslow sell one) but it's cheaper and more enjoyable to make your own. You can only use one or two, very different smells in any one session. Again, be sure the smells you choose relate to the life experience of your members.

If you are working with this kind of group, you need quite a lot of carefully chosen material to illustrate the theme of the session – early childhood, schooldays, entertainment, fashion etc. So give yourself plenty of time to gather the material together from all the kinds of sources we've mentioned before – flea markets, jumble sales, boot sales or relatives, who may be quite happy to lend materials. Planning the

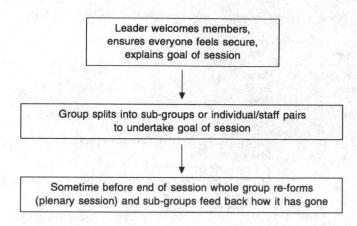

Figure 1   *Sequence of a session where a group sub-divides*

content of each session is time-consuming. Allow at least six weeks from the beginning of serious planning to the first session. This is by no means excessive and it will be time well spent.

Sometimes you will find it useful to work individually within a group setting, but remember to begin and end as a group. Get the group together, and settled, and explain the task; individual clients and staff then work together for a prearranged length of time, after which the leader re-forms the group and everyone feeds back how they've been getting on (Figure 1).

So far we have used the 'standard' reminiscence format. All we have done is make the stimulus material more immediate and more powerful. Additionally, we have changed our expectation so that the group will be paced more slowly and we will be encouraging members more; and, if necessary and only when necessary, guessing what they want to say and checking we are right.

Examples of work for this purpose

We have devised three 'levels' of reminiscence for people with dementia:

- Reminiscence using non-verbal material
- Unison groups
- Sensory stimulation

Reminiscence using non-verbal material

We have already discussed the use of non-verbal material to encourage reminiscence with people who do have some speech. In a wide variety of settings we have found such groups to be highly effective in gaining members' attention and eliciting reminiscences, albeit simply expressed. Obviously we use a leader : member ratio of 1 : 2 or better to energize such groups.

We compared the level of member involvement or attention during reminiscence sessions with their involvement in what was going on in the ward at the same time of day as the session after the group ended. During the group, the members had been involved 64 per cent of the time; on the ward, they were involved only 39 per cent of the time. When we ran a similar group in another unit, again with people with severe dementia, the comparative figures were 72 per cent and 29 per cent. We found these kind of differences each time we ran reminiscence groups on units for people with severe dementia.

With a group in a day centre we used another research method and we showed that members were able to know more about each other at the end of the group than at the beginning. Given that people with dementia are assumed to have great difficulty in learning, this was an important gain.

Unison groups

These are a mixture of a little reality orientation and a lot of reminiscence using long-term memory. The idea is to look at the seasonal activities that take place during the life of the group, and other calendar events – such as the FA Cup Final or a village festival, if these are relevant to the members – and by providing the relevant material, create an enjoyable and stimulating experience for the group members. The idea of the Unison group will be more fully described in the next section.

We can use the basic concept of Unison – relating to the seasons – to create therapeutic outings. In the summer we can go to the beach, or have a trip to a beauty spot; in autumn, go into the forest and see the array of colours; in winter, sit in a café and watch the weather outside. For somewhat more able members, we may combine the outing with a follow-up creative activity session. Thus after a trip to the beach we might make a necklace of shells; or following a trip to the forest make a collage of variously coloured leaves.

We have described such work here in relation to dementia because that is our experience, but it would be equally applicable to many other client and non-client groups. Inner city children and people with learning difficulties might well find such activity stimulating and enjoyable.

Sensory stimulation

A sensory stimulation group is yet another type of activity that can be used either individually or as a group. Here, the material is *completely* non-verbal. One example of such work is to create a 'Feelie Wheel'. The wheel is just a piece of plastic or hose and to it the group members attach a wide variety of materials – lace, wool, knitting, felt etc. etc. – the list is as long as your imagination. The materials should be interesting and/or pleasurable to touch, and, hopefully, at least some of the materials should stir memories. The presentation of the materials should be accompanied by a verbal explanation: 'This is a scouring pad. You used to use it to clean pots and pans. Feel its rough surface?'

It may seem that attaching such materials to toilet roll centres (or some other form of attachment) to create a wheel cannot take long; in fact, with our group it took 12 half-hour sessions. Such work – indeed all the activity suggested in this chapter – requires a high leader:member ratio. Certainly no more than 1 (leader) to 2 members. Even then, at this level of disability, a free-floating additional staff member may be very useful. With severe disability, members cannot self-motivate or self-stimulate. So, when not given attention, they soon 'switch off'. The Feelie Wheel is also a good activity for individual work, requiring a little bit of work at a slow pace in each session.

The need for relevant material – whatever the level of disability – was neatly illustrated. At the time we ran this particular group the wards were single sex. For the first few sessions, the men were offered the same materials as the women's group; but unlike the staff working with the women's group, the staff reported the sessions as very flat. Only when we got material relevant to the world of men and manual work (many had worked in Plymouth Dockyard) – pipes (both kinds), bolts, hinges, screws – did the male group take off. When, in the last session, we had a triumphal meeting of the two groups and a joining of the two halves of the Feelie Wheel, the join between the work of the two groups was all too evident! (As a postscript, it is nice to recall that when the ward closed and moved, there weren't many mementoes of the old hospital in the new building, but the staff took the Feelie Wheel with them.)

Once again, we could show the benefit to the members from participation in the group. In the male group, members were paying attention, on average, 51 per cent of the time compared with 14 per cent after the group ended and they were sitting on the ward. For the female group, the equivalent figures were 77 per cent and 41 per cent.

A detailed example of this purpose in action

By the early 1990s, it was clear that reminiscence groups that expected spontaneous conversations between members who came from continuing care wards/units were not going to work. Stronger, more basic and non-verbal stimuli were needed to evoke memories. It was also apparent that to expect members to verbalize what had been evoked was unrealistic; group members were in more restricted, more silent, more limited worlds. Working with very damaged patients on long-stay wards, I therefore began thinking about what could achieve that fleeting moment of recognition and also give them group sessions that because they were connecting, they could actively enjoy.

I based the idea of Unison groups on the changes of seasons. The seasons seem a very basic, primeval movement affecting mankind: primitive as they are based on the sun, but inexorably affecting us – whether we're indoors sheltering by a fire or outdoors enjoying the heat. So, because the seasons affect us at such a basic level, I thought it might be possible to use them to get through to those with severe dementia living on long-stay ('continuing care') wards.

Working with nurses and occupational therapists, a programme was drawn up for 12 sessions. The time of the year was September to December. Each session could either relate to a calendar event (e.g. Guy Fawkes Night, November 5; Remembrance Day, November 11; Christmas Day) or the changing of the seasons (e.g. a trip to Dartmoor to see it in its autumnal colours).

The sessions need not be elaborate, but they must have a theme that can be used to communicate with the members: 'This week we'll be going onto Dartmoor to see the colours of autumn'; 'Next Sunday is Remembrance Sunday, so we'll go to see the War Memorial'; and if at all possible, should have a practical aspect – the use of hands, as with compost running through one's fingers when planting hyacinths in pots for Christmas.

Certainly one session of that first group, for which Julian Davies, Daphne Wallis and Lena Cole were the group leaders, with me, stands out – blackberry picking in the grounds of the hospital. It was not dramatic or difficult to organize – just wheeling those with severe mobility problems, or a hand/arm for the more mobile, because the blackberry patch was only about 150 yards from the door leading off from the corridor. Some could reach the blackberries, one watched while we picked them and ate them as fast as we picked! Suddenly, these people came alive; they had purpose, or interest.

That small event taught me the importance of outings. Not only do they make people come alive, but suddenly, just for that time, they are no longer patients. There is a scene in the film of Ken Kesey's novel *One Flew Over the Cuckoo's Nest* where a group of long-stay psychiatric patients are taken sea-fishing for the day. As the camera pans slowly over the faces of the fishermen-for-a-day you are asked to see how normal they look. Although Kesey is mainly describing people diagnosed as 'schizophrenic', the same analogy occurs in those with a diagnosis of 'dementia'.

However, the importance of outings as outings should not detract from the need for a seasonal theme to provide a purpose and a focus. This can help make an enjoyable outing even more stimulating.

(Remember with outings to take at least one extra staff member. It can take two staff to fight their way with a wheelchair into public toilets, which might leave the rest of the group unsupervised; so plan well ahead as to staff resources when that particular Unison group session is to be an outing; and also because you'll need much longer (increased time resource) to get anywhere. We like an outing every second or fourth session.)

Here is part of an account written by Kate Mort, Staff Nurse at Lamellion Hospital in Cornwall, on a Unison group run on a continuing care ward for physically frail people by three staff. It was published in the Trust's house magazine, thus bringing the notion that valuable work occurs on long-stay wards to a larger audience.

> The sessions are designed to capture the flavour of the changing seasons, to bring back memories, to celebrate birthdays, visit places of interest, to reawake the physical senses. If a group member dies this is acknowledged by the group. So far the group has made an Advent Calendar, prepared individual Christmas cards for their families, co-operated in the making of a spring collage. One morning they made fruit buns and were able to eat them with the coffee. An outing was organized in the hospital minibus to a nearby garden centre to buy pots, bulbs and fibre in preparation for the following week when the group planted up the pots. One very popular session was designed to celebrate Shrove Tuesday. The group members were able to sample pancakes prepared earlier by Gwen (OT aide). They recalled old Pancake Day traditions, squeezed and sniffed lemons. Another happy session was led by Kate who had prepared a map of Cornwall as well as a smaller one of Britain (for one member from the north of England). On to these maps each member was able to put the name of his or her place of birth. For each place a coloured picture had been found to illustrate it. These sparked off lots of happy memories. The group members were helped to do the writing themselves and to stick on the pictures. . . .
>
> Plans for the near future include making Easter cards, decorating hard-boiled eggs, and a visit to the local church to hear the organist play Easter hymns.

A group as successful as Unison will shine out like a beacon in the drab light of a long-stay unit for people with dementia. Therefore, it is sensible for the unit, which is devoting staff resources to it, to get some credit. Certainly, it should make sure that management and other potentially useful allies know. By means of a pamphlet – relatively easy in these days of word processors – the relatives can be informed of the group. In a ward or in a nursing home relatives often feel very bad that they had to give up caring for the person. Seeing the person enjoy the group and being informed about it can help them feel better. In day care settings, because the member often cannot recall what they did in the unit by the time they get home, a good opportunity for communication is lost. If the relative gets a pamphlet explaining the purpose of the group, and a timetable of what will happen when, then an important channel of communication is opened up between relative and attender, and also between relative and day unit.

The benefits of Unison groups in helping people with severe dementia enjoy themselves and participate with others were so obvious from the outset that such groups have been run ever since, and in a variety of settings. The only change I have made is to see the theme of the Unison session as an opportunity to build interest around it during the week – talking about the theme before the group and after – and also encouraging practical work to be completed outside a session. The session should run for its allotted time and no longer, but if the work/project isn't finished, time can be made available during the week when a group leader and the member can finish off. The pleasure of the work and of its completion can thus run on (but remember that the product of the extra sessions should be brought back to the next group session).

The seasons, if we stop to feel, are powerful controllers of our behaviour, and elderly people who have developed dementia in the past few years previously had many, many years of experiencing this. So they can still relate to the slow but very definite rhythms. Good staff can and will create environments and experiences where the rhythm can be heard clearly. Then the results are surprising and gratifying.

Conclusions

This chapter has been about relating and communicating with very damaged people. You will have noticed we advocate a staff ratio of either 1:1½ or, at least, 1:2. This may seem high, but high or low *only* makes sense if you know the context. For example, even 1:1 is a very low ratio for an emergency life-saving operation. With dementia, if you don't provide the energy and the attention many of the people will stop attending, simply stop doing, as if their power supply had been switched off.

These forms of reminiscence are based on early memories and on non-verbal or on motor memories such as stirring a pudding mixture, and on the slow changes of time and the seasons, and of community. 'No man is an island', and perhaps we can best summarize the aim of this kind of work as creating an island where the group members can feel safe and good and relate to the sea of time.

Useful reading and resources

Irving Yalom describes what he thinks are the essential ingredients in effective group therapy in his classic text *The Theory and Practice of Group Psychotherapy* (4th edition, Basic Books, 1995).

Welcoming and the communication of respect is the theme and purpose of *Welcoming Your Clients* by Mike Bender, Val Levens and Charles Goodson (Winslow Press, 1995).

Smell kits can be purchased from Winslow Press, Telford Road, Bicester, Oxon OX6 0TS.

Unison groups are described in Mike Bender's article 'Orientation by seasons', *Nursing Times*, 2 May 1995, pp. 64–65. He has written more recently about reminiscence for people with dementia in *Reminiscence in Dementia Care*, edited by Pam Schweitzer (Age Exchange, 1998). The whole of this book is very relevant to Purpose Five.

Feelie Wheel groups were written up by Kay Mowle-Clark, Mike Bender and Karen Brown in 'Discovering the magic circle', *Therapy Weekly*, 3 December 1992, p. 8.

Ken Kesey's novel *One Flew Over the Cuckoo's Nest* was first published in 1962 and is available in many editions, such as Pan. It is often considered a fictional equivalent of Erving Goffman's sociological analysis of institutions *Asylums*, which was published at much the same time, in 1961. Again, this is available in many editions, such as Penguin.

Purpose Six

INDIVIDUAL REMINISCENCE WORK

Rationale

In the previous chapter we talked of intensive reminiscence groupwork for people who are not usually considered suitable for groups. Essentially, we suggested changing the nature of the group to make it suitable for them. These modified techniques can also be used in individual work. The reader of this chapter should therefore make sure that they have also read and digested the ideas and methods of the previous chapter.

Our position and experience is that much of the restlessness, inattentiveness and disruptiveness that is shown by a *few* people with dementia is due to their feeling unsafe and fearing failure. If we can structure the task and create an atmosphere of calm and security, most will, within a few sessions, learn to enjoy and participate in the group. That will still leave a few – and it's *only* a few – who cannot handle the rules of a group, that is, letting other people get on with what they're doing. They interfere or disrupt; they get up and wander, or shout for no apparent reason. Such people should not be deprived of stimulation, but it will need to be on a one-to-one basis.

But by far the commonest need for individual reminiscence work will come from *physically*, not cognitively, frail people. Being physically ill is a lonely and isolating business and if we can get the person up and dressed, and to a group, albeit in a wheelchair if necessary, we should do so. In this way, we take them out of 'the bed-ridden' category and back into the human race. We may well want to use, at least initially, some of the ideas of reminiscence as fun (Purpose Three) to start things moving, but to get something out of a group you have to put something in; you have to have some energy. If you're very frail or ill, you haven't got this energy; and then we need to think of reminiscence on an individual basis.

We also need to be aware that very frail people are likely to die soon. So we are often working in the area of 'palliative care', and here there may be relevant ideas we can borrow from hospice care; in reminiscence terms, we would think of Erikson's last stage of 'Ego-integrity versus Despair'. In religious terms, the person may well think of 'meeting their maker', having to explain past acts, and the possibility of making amends.

Goals implied in the purpose

1 To maximize the comfort of the individual.
2 To maximize the dignity of the individual.
3 To help them with any unfinished business, either through talking to them, or by arranging for other people, such as relatives, to come to them.
4 To provide a satisfying experience.

The tasks

The worker's tasks when using reminiscence for this purpose are:

1 To be available when needed.
2 To be calm and be calming.
3 To make the person as comfortable as possible.
4 To be able to access other staff and techniques to maximize that comfort.
5 To understand the philosophy of reminiscence in order to apply it flexibly.
6 To use reminiscence techniques to fulfil, as appropriate, the variety of needs the client may present.
7 To value and look after their own mental health, through seeking regular supervision, preferably off-line, and helping to create good peer support within the unit.

How to achieve these tasks

A useful place to start when trying to make sense of the needs of a physically ill person is Maslow's hierarchy of needs, with which you may already be familiar (Figure 2). Maslow said all human beings have various, different types of need, ranging from the need for such basics as food, water and air, up to the need to develop an identity. You will see from Figure 2 that Maslow put the need for *shelter* as a most basic need; *safety* next and *affection* at the next level. All of which means that, when you are face to face with someone who is ill or very frail or very damaged, it would be inappropriate to rush in with an activity. Maybe what they want most is someone who can sit quietly and talk calmly and

```
┌─────────────────────────────────────────┐
│                    7                      │
│              Aesthetic Needs,             │
│              Self-actualization           │
│           Realization of potential,       │
│           personal autonomy, order,       │
│        beauty, privacy, truth, spiritual goals │
│                                           │
│                                           │
│                    6                      │
│              Cognitive Needs              │
│          Knowledge, understanding         │
│         exploration, comprehension,       │
│          stimulation, personal mastery    │
│                                           │
│                                           │
│                    5                      │
│               Creative Needs              │
│           Self-expression, usefulness,    │
│             creativity, production        │
│                                           │
│                                           │
│                    4                      │
│               Esteem Needs                │
│        Dignity, respect, deserved praise, │
│         self-esteem, individuality, sexual │
│       identity, personal identity, recognition │
│                                           │
│                                           │
│                    3                      │
│        Belongingness and Love Needs       │
│       Affiliation, affection, companionship, │
│        relationships, comfort, communication, │
│            giving and receiving love      │
│                                           │
│                                           │
│                    2                      │
│               Safety Needs                │
│       Freedom from fear and threat of injury, │
│     need to depend on someone, to orientate oneself, │
│        for order, for security, for an ordered world │
│                                           │
│                                           │
│                    1                      │
│             Physiological Needs           │
│       Water, food, sunlight, shelter, oxygen, sex │
└─────────────────────────────────────────┘
```

Figure 2 *Maslow's hierarchy of needs*

reassure them that, for a little bit of the time they've got left, their world, with this person (you) around, is safe for the moment. So, don't rush in and *do* something *to* that person. Rather, start by *being with* that person. Ignore, if you can, pressure to look busy and professional, because to do so is to be unprofessional.

Once the person feels secure, or feels a little better, they might enjoy some stimulation, some mental activity. To provide this, you need to know what would be *appropriate to that individual*. To know what is appropriate you must get hold of the relevant information to make up the life history of that person. Of course, now that they are ill or frail, to get that information from the person themself becomes difficult or even impossible. A well-run day care or residential unit will gather the information needed for a biographical profile at the time of admission, if not from the client themself, then from a relative or friend. A well-run community service, going into people's homes, will, similarly, attempt to get as much background material as possible.

Once you have reached an understanding of the person's life, you will know the major events in that life: *where* they took place – the geography of that life – and *when* they took place – the chronology or history of that life; you will know of their interests and hobbies. Armed with this information, you can then try to gather together photographs or objects or music that relate to that person's life and which they might enjoy and be stimulated by. Much of this material will be in their home, or, if they have not got one, with their relatives. If this is not possible, then you may have to use less individual material.

You have to find a quiet time. If the person is bed-bound this may be when everyone else is in the day room. If there is no such time, you may need to move the person to a quiet room. Having achieved these necessary conditions, you should present one item at a time to the person, giving it to them, asking them if it reminds them of any time in their life, anything they did. Your words are an accompaniment to the physical presentation of the object. They synchronize the spoken with the physical reality.

Hopefully, and certainly not always, you will note some response and you can ask the person what it has reminded them of. If they cannot tell you, you might want to make a hesitant guess, and wait for them to tell you – verbally or non-verbally – whether you guessed right.

The sessions should be short. Twenty minutes may be quite long enough. Always stop while the person is still enjoying the activity and long before you have tired them. The sessions should be leisurely and enjoyable, a shared pleasure.

Such sessions may be quite frequent, but make sure at the beginning of each session that the person feels up to it. Sometimes just holding their hand for a few minutes or some gentle massage may be much more appreciated. So, check out how the person is at the beginning of each session.

To give a bit more detail, let us say we are working with an old person who is physically frail, and relatively immobile but, as long as they're not tired and not rushed, is lucid and unconfused. Such people are to be found in a wide variety of types of health, social service, residential and nursing units.

With such a severe loss of physical wellbeing, it is quite likely that such a person will not live long. As such, according to Butler (see Purpose Fifteen on life review), there will be some urgency to get their life in order.

It may well be the case that they have photographs of themselves and their family in a box or boxes, maybe not in the home but stored with a relative. It may be possible to get hold of those photos and, acting as the person's hands, put them in order in an album, writing a few words for each on who, when and where. A few postcards or pictures of the places that have featured in their life can be fun to find, and add some explanatory background to the life. By doing something like this the person can be helped to create a record that their children can show their grandchildren – a legacy.

At the same time, however, we need to be very aware of any expressions by the person of wanting 'to put their house in order'. Sometimes, these will be explanations to you of why what had to be had to be; or of mistakes they made. Sometimes, it may be things they want to do or people they'd like to be in touch with. Then, you need to discuss how that might be achieved.

One has to judge, in each case, the possible role of relatives. Initially, this activity should most definitely and most clearly be just between the staff member and the client. *Confidentiality must be offered and maintained.* Only in this way can the person use the sessions to explore what might have been, regrets, aspects of their life that make them guilty and so on. If you allow a relative to sit in, you limit such possibilities. On the other hand, there may be things they want to say to their daughter, or to their son, and the medium of creating a family album can allow that recon- ciliation and exploration to happen; and for them to share a good experience in the time left. So, don't automatically include relatives. Get the activity started by yourself and then the client will most likely tell you whether he or she wants a relative present. Give the power to the client.

Examples of work for this purpose

We have suggested that some of the methods discussed in some detail in the previous chapter can be easily modified for individual work, whether this be for the cognitively and/or the physically frail. The method offered would be appropriate to the needs and abilities of each, separate, individual. For those 'minds imprisoned in a failing body' verbal methods of reminiscence may be the method of choice. With more cognitively frail people, the methods might include Unison and sensory stimulation. If the person is mobile, then an outing to a place they are familiar with (which we know from their biographical profile) and which is appropriate for the time of year, should be very enjoyable. If they wish, they can invite a friend. Even if they cannot tell you the name of a friend, offering them one or two names and seeing whether they nod or grimace should give you a clue. Having identified what seems to be the most suitable candidate, you can double check with 'So, we'll take − − − − −. OK with you?' One of the joys of a trip out is that you often see greatly improved practical skills, such as talking and eating, and also improved social skills.

Another useful way of relating is to find out the person's favourite music and sit together and listen to it.

Age Exchange hire out Reminiscence Boxes, each with 'at least 25 objects and photographs' on various themes such as 'Childhood games' or 'In the kitchen'. There are boxes for the Caribbean, the Indian Subcontinent and Ireland. In Dorset, a group have set up a Dorset Memory Box Library. Each memory box has '20–30 items of ephemera 1900–1950'. There is a charge for use of these. You could easily make your own, especially if you work in a team and enjoy car boot sales.

The Kensington and Chelsea Community History Group have started a project whereby volunteers get referrals from the social services of older housebound people. The volunteers receive training in reminiscence work and talk to the people about their past lives. Besides being enjoyable and stimulating at the time, the volunteer and older person can contribute to a newsletter that comes out four times a year, called *Memories Shared*. In the first issue, there are two fine quotes: 'It would be such a waste to lose the past of ordinary people . . . it is all too good to lose', and 'God gave us memory so that we might have roses in December.'

A detailed account of this purpose in action

I became aware that one of the physical wards I was working on had two distinct populations. Half the beds were taken by people in the rehabilitation stream; they would leave the hospital, either to go home or to a residential or nursing home. The other half were occupied by people who would die in that bed in that hospital. The staff were very caring but were not providing enough stimulation and hadn't addressed the fact that, in this half of the ward, they had a hospice. Neither had they addressed this in terms of the patients' needs or their own needs, for example accepting their grief at losing a friend when a patient died.

Once it was agreed that this half of the ward was about palliative and terminal care, the staff were quickly able to focus on the necessary tasks. With regard to physical comfort, some got a brief training in hand and foot massage, which the patients found very pleasurable and relaxing.

I provided back-up and ran a staff support group where staff could talk about their feelings about their work – frustrations, pleasures, grief and so on. One of my most useful acts was to give the project a name. We called the staff who were working on the project and their patients the Sundance Group, with the implication that perhaps it was the patients' last dance in the sun and it was our business to create a suitable setting. A nurse, artistically talented, drew a Mexican sun as a logo. This identity was a good label with which to gain publicity and resources.

Because of their frailty, reminiscence work could only be done with a small number for whom it was provided, but most could enjoy a sensory stimulation group. We also moved towards a '30 Minute Club'. It was relatively easy to ascertain which staff members got on best with which patients and allocate accordingly. Then, each week a half hour session was created for sitting together and talking one-to-one. The key workers undertook a biographical profile from whatever source was useful – the patient, their notes or their relative – and that knowledge would inform the session. So one or two worked on life books, others went over what music they would like to hear, outings that could be arranged, individual sensory stimulation work, such as making a simple collage and so on.

Another feature involving reminiscence ideas was an early evening 'Music and Conversation Club'. Very little happens after tea in hospitals: the occupational therapists and physiotherapists go home, and the nursing staff numbers are reduced, but there are still long hours before bed. We knew what music people liked from their biographical profiles. We could get tapes and records from the library. We encouraged more mobile patients to go up to the library to choose their own music and get the choices of those who couldn't get out. Then once a week, for an hour or so, their musical choices would be played. There were a couple of staff present and the members of the club could just sit and enjoy the music or talk quietly to one another or to the staff. The music, of course, evoked memories which led to conversations. At some point, tea and biscuits were served. In all these ways, building strong individual relationships with patients helped them to contribute to the stimulation and well-being of others on the ward.

An unexpected bonus came from the relatives. They felt very good about what was happening to their loved ones, and with a bit of encouragement from us, they put on old-fashioned teas with nicely laundered white linen table-clothes and silver cutlery and doillies in a nearby hall. Everyone – patients and staff – wanted to visit this Lyons Tea House!

You will see that this is not directly a reminiscence project; its main aims were helping patients feel comfortable and valued. But reminiscence ideas were involved in the 30 Minute Club, because the biographical profiles helped start conversations; and again were used in the Music and Conversation Club and the creation of a 1950s atmosphere with the cakes and tea. (The idea of a 'reminiscence philosophy' is discussed in its own section, p. 283.)

Of course, all these efforts couldn't and wouldn't have happened without the very active support and encouragement of the ward sister. How far we could have gone is anyone's guess – it felt as if the sky was the limit. Unfortunately this project was never developed to its fullest potential as management and staff changes forced the termination of the Sundance group. But the patients who had been part of it and their relatives had been given a much improved service and that experience couldn't be taken away from them.

Conclusions

One-to-one work is called for where a person is so cognitively frail or so physically frail that they cannot participate in a group. That said, if their needs would be better met in a group context, then, every effort should be made to adopt a group format to their needs. But there will be people and times where individual work is appropriate. (We have not mentioned therapeutic reminiscence where working one-to-one may be preferable because the material is too personal, at least initially, for a group. This will be discussed later.) More generally, we have shown here how methods used in groups for severely disabled people can be relatively easily modified for individual work.

One-to-one work is as staff-intensive as it is 'time-consuming'. Therefore, before undertaking such work, the active support and informed understanding of the relevant manager or managers must be achieved.

We hope we've shown how reminiscence ideas can inform the whole regime of activities for frail people. Again, we would remind readers we are talking 5 to 95. There are many sources of frailty, besides those related to old age. Cognitively, many of these ideas are appropriate to people with learning difficulties. Physically, there are many people, of all ages, whose condition will need weeks or months in a medical or rehabilitation setting. The individual approach to using reminiscence ideas and developing new methods has tremendous potential.

Useful reading and resources

Maslow's ideas are outlined in many books, such as Mike Bender, Christa Lloyd and Alison Cooper's *The Quality of Dying* (Winslow Press, 1990). The original text is Abraham Maslow, *Towards a Psychology of Being* (2nd edition, Van Nostrand, 1968).

There are a large number of books on grief and grief counselling. Colin Murray Parkes' *Bereavement* (Penguin, 1986), and J. William Worden's *Grief Counselling and Grief Therapy* (Routledge, 1991) are classics in the field.

For less formal conversations, we found Ted Menten's *Gentle Closings* (Running Press, Philadelphia, Pennsylvania, 1991), and Robert Buckman's *I Don't Know What to Say: How to Help and Support Someone Who Is Dying* (Macmillan, 1988) useful.

Age Exchange Reminiscence Boxes can be hired from Age Exchange, The Reminiscence Centre, 11 Blackheath Village, London SE3 9LA (tel. 0181 318 9105).

The Dorset Memory Box Library works out of Westhaven Hospital, Radipole Lane, Weymouth DT4 0QE.

The Kensington and Chelsea Community History Group's address is 240b Lancaster Road, London W10 (tel. 0171 792 2282).

Purpose Seven

REMINISCENCE TO CREATE GROUP COHESION

No man is an Island, entire of itself; every man is a piece of the Continent, a part of the main . . . And therefore never send to know for whom the bell tolls; it tolls for thee.

John Donne, *Devotions*

Rationale

The use of reminiscence for cohesion does not appear in the original claims for reminiscence, where its merits for life review, for stimulation and for energizing were highlighted. But as people began running reminiscence groups, they started rediscovering some of the principles and 'laws' of groups and groupwork. This area of study is part of social psychology, but there is not much contact between academic social psychologists and field workers. One of the interesting properties of a group is that, over time, its members develop a loyalty to it and towards the other members. The group becomes a reality for them, one facet of their lives, around which they structure their time and energy.

The idea of 'group cohesion' has been around social science for a long time. To some extent its origins can be found in the years following the Second World War. As the superpowers moved away from conventional arms to nuclear weapons, small numbers of troops, widely scattered, found themselves entrusted with control of these weapons in conditions of great secrecy to avoid detection by the enemy. Perhaps the most striking example is the nuclear submarine, somewhere under the polar icecap. Those in high command realized it was vital that these small groups of people living together stayed sane, or they could start World War Three – the scenario of the film *Dr Strangelove*. The military therefore devoted research money from their vast budgets to social scientists. Key figures in this field were Kurt Lewin, Leon Festinger and Stanley Schacter, but there were many other research workers. Their job was to advise on how to keep a group atmosphere sweet and its members working effectively together. In short, how to make a group cohesive.

The realization that groups had this power to mould, to cohere, to enthuse, was 'rediscovered' by workers in quite different settings, such as reminiscence groupwork. Finally, in terms of background, it is worth saying that group therapy uses group cohesion to help people sort out their emotional problems. Achieving loyalty to a group has the effect that members stay in the group and get feedback from other members about themselves. The classic text here is Irving Yalom's *The Theory and Practice of Group Psychotherapy*.

So what is group cohesion? We will make a stab at defining it by saying it means:

1 Members feel loyalty towards the group.
2 Members share common goals and resources.
3 The group has goals which the individual member would be unable to achieve (or only with great difficulty) but which together they stand a chance of achieving.

One word of caution before we proceed. Because you need cohesion for a group to be successful, group cohesion tends to be seen as 'a good thing'. It usually is, but there are two very important 'buts'. First, group cohesion can be for good or for ill. 'Not in my back yard' might be such an example. Of course, it can help a group fight off a proposed road through a site of outstanding beauty, or it can be used to stop desperately needed houses being built. You can't always predict the goals the group will aim for. A difficult example for community development workers in the 1970s was that they would work to get underprivileged council tenants empowered, only to find they used their newly found power to be viciously race prejudiced. Secondly, bear in mind that groups can, over time, get over-cohesive. They don't want to take in newcomers in case they rock the boat, but without the views of new people to challenge the established ways, the group dies as a creative environment.

Remember that the group leader is both leader and member. They too can find the group comforting and comfortable, especially in times of stress, when the knowledge of a safe haven for an hour a week may be all too reassuring. So, remember what we say: that groups can be for good or for ill; can espouse unethical goals as well as life-enhancing ones; can start healthy and get sick; and these warnings *include you*. Monitor the health of your group continually. Outside observation and advice can be very useful in giving you feedback as to the group's state of health.

Groups don't stand still: they are always changing, even if that change is not perceptible, which is one reason for needing supervision. The supervisor can see much more easily than the leaders what a group is doing – whether it is stationary, taking off, slowing down, or stale.

Goals implied in the purpose

We want each member to:

1 Feel they belong to the group.
2 Feel that they, as a person, independent of what they do, or social class or race or gender etc., are valued by the group and its members.
3 Feel they have something to contribute to the group.
4 Feel their contribution to the group is respected.
5 In time and with time, feel that the group belongs more to them than to the leaders or to the unit.
6 Come to see how the group can be productive of ends or products they value.
7 Help in the achievement of those ends.

The tasks

These seven goals may seem a bit abstract. Trying to flesh them out, we seek to achieve the following.

- The members are to be welcomed by the group leaders, and *feel* welcomed, from the first session.
- The group is made a safe and friendly place to be so that the members look forward to coming to it.
- We must ensure that there are no character assassinations or hurtful criticisms.
- At the same time we want to encourage positive feedback, so that each member knows they are valued while being open to constructive suggestion.
- When a member speaks, the leaders must be interested, and encourage the other members to be also.
- With time and increasing cohesion, the members are asked what they want the group to achieve and are helped and resourced to reach those goals.
- As the group becomes more cohesive we must aim to fade out, offering the appropriate level of support.

The core task of the group leader working to achieve group cohesion is bitter sweet. It is the task of, in the long run, making oneself less central to the group, even to the point of leaving it to get on with its own life.

This is essentially a three-stage process. First, as with all groupwork, the task is to create a group climate in which the members feel secure, which they enjoy and which they look forward to. Secondly, we want to

indicate early on the value we put on the achievements of communication between members, and of giving and sharing between members.
This leads to the third stage of decision-making by the members. The
value you set on members making decisions should be stressed in the
pre-group meetings where you brief individual potential members; it
should be stressed in the early sessions of the group, and again later,
whenever appropriate; and of course has to be demonstrated by the
leaders in practice.

However, group cohesion will only occur after the group has formed
and therefore in the early stages of the group the group leaders will have
an active role in achieving member-to-member communication. It is not
the sort of thing that just happens, unless you have a remarkably able
group. It is exceedingly unlikely to happen by itself among people who
have been or who are disabled or disadvantaged because their sense of
worth and of their ability to have any effect on their lives is so damaged.

How to achieve these tasks

In the actual group, we need to maximize member-to-member communication. We can do this in three ways.

1   We can select tasks where we know or can make an educated guess
    that the members *do* have something in common, do share common
    experiences. For example, if they were all brought up in the same
    part of the city or they all did National Service. We can gather
    biographical data from them before the start of the group to find out
    the common experiences.
2   Wherever possible, we can try to get the members to talk directly to
    each other, rather than through the group leader. We can put this
    visually. Imagine that at the beginning of a new group, the leaders
    are at the centre of a circle. As illustrated in Figure 3, you will find
    that almost all communications go into the centre from member to
    leader and then are sent out again, most usually back to the sender
    (1), but not always (2). What we want is for the members to talk to
    each other (3). We want the members to learn that talking to each
    other is fine and in fact we, the group leaders, prefer it to having
    remarks addressed to us. The only proviso we would make is that
    members stay with the group task. So if the group task is Our
    Working Lives', generally we would like the conversation to be on
    that topic, not on yesterday's television programme. The trick is to
    shape the behaviour we want gently, so that we don't undermine our
    main message of 'Address remarks to the group (one at a time)'.
3   We can increase the rate and intensity of interaction between
    members if they share a task. Such tasks can occur *inside* the group:
    making a collage of old photos, writing the texts accompanying

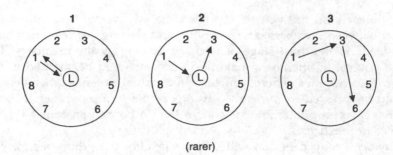

Figure 3   *Patterns of communication between leader (L) and members of a group*

photographs etc. Or they can occur *outside* the group: visiting the library or museum together, or just arranging among themselves to meet for a coffee on market day.

Since you want all the group members to be able to work with each other, vary which two or three work on a particular task together. If two or three members always work together, it is very likely that they will form a sub-group or clique, which can make the achievement of group cohesion very difficult.

In group psychotherapy there was and still often is a very strict rule that members do *not* meet outside the group. This is to get all their tensions expressed in the group, so that the members can work on them together. Although this model is not usually relevant outside of group therapy, it can inhibit us from encouraging members to meet outside the group. This is a great shame, since disadvantaged and disabled people are often isolated and have much to gain from stronger support systems. (However, this is something you should let happen naturally, rather than overtly encourage; and you may need to keep an eye open for members who are very unassertive being exploited.)

So, to repeat, Stage One, as with any group, is making it safe and welcoming. Stage Two is teaching members to talk and work with each other, and not depend on the group leaders for satisfaction and confirmation of self-worth. A key feature may be that the group leaders have transmitted their belief that the group members are, to borrow a phrase of clinical psychologist Anthea Sperlinger, 'people with histories that matter and experts in their own lives', and so can make sensible decisions and intelligent contributions (almost independent of their actual IQ).

Stage Three is for the group to move onto a task which the members decide they want to achieve. Obviously, they may want a bit of guidance and support, but the goal has to be theirs.

It may well be useful to end the group formally at the end of the Stage Two. The group can then review whether it wants to continue with activities aiming to increase its cohesion, such as a further number of reminiscence sessions, or wants to proceed to Stage Three. This formal closing also allows those who do not want to stay with the group to leave. Some members may not want more of the same; others may not wish to move onto a different task. The group members need to look at their options and decide on the future of the group. So make sure that there is an evaluation and a 'Where do we go from here?' session at the end of every block of sessions, allowing members to leave gracefully. Never force a group to stay in existence.

While it is important that the group members gradually take over the running and direction of their group, this does not mean that the leaders can disappear. They should be slowly giving up the roles of decision-maker and provider; but they may well be needed in the background to give impartial advice on the realistic achievability of the group's hoped for goals; to offer advice and reassurance; to suggest where resources are available; to suggest possible avenues through which the group can get help in solving problems etc.

The key word here is that leaders *gradually* phase out. We have seen groups collapse because the members accomplished the first two stages so effectively that the leaders felt they could leave them to get on with it. The group then completely collapsed in a few sessions. There are two obvious reasons for such collapses. First, the disappearance of the group leaders made the group a quite insecure place. Given that the members of the groups we have in mind are usually disadvantaged and often from not very happy upbringings, being in a group without leadership must be a frightening experience and one they will not readily submit to. The second reason is that 'power abhors a vacuum'. This means that, if the leadership of a group disappears, then new leaders must emerge if the group is to continue. Members may nominate themselves as leaders and not be acceptable; or two or more may nominate themselves and a vicious power struggle ensues, which destroys the group.

The opposite type of problem can arise: the group leaders don't leave at all! Some are very reluctant to trust the group to exist without them.

The gradual and sensitive phasing-out of leaders which is required to develop group autonomy allows the staff member who loves power or who needs to be needed or who believes his or her clients couldn't possibly do things by themselves, plenty of excuses to stay around and keep running the group, either openly or by influencing the weaker members to go along with their ideas. And they will be able to quote evidence of where the group has made mistakes. Because it will take time for the group to re-form and learn its own mechanisms of working, mistakes and lost opportunities are absolutely inevitable. As long as the members do not get disheartened by these mistakes, then no harm is done. The staff group leader must allow these mistakes to occur, and only intervene if the group requests their help. The trick is to be available and to have trained the group in the first two stages so that leader availability is used by the group appropriately, and is never used by the group leader to prove their indispensability.

It is a difficult balancing act to perform and is why all group leaders need regular supervision where leader behaviour that might keep the group dependent can be looked at. Less frequently, the group is abandoned too early by a 'they've got to learn to stand on their own two feet' disciplinarian. The transition stage is thus a particularly vital time when the need for supervision is crucial.

Examples of work for this purpose

1   A group home was created with residents who had been discharged from a mental handicap hospital which was closing. They had lived in a staffed flat for 12 months, prior to the start of the group. The clinical psychologist involved was Anthea Sperlinger, who kindly wrote the following synopsis:

> House staff were co-leaders and there was a compulsory pre-group briefing meeting of leaders and post-group de-briefing meeting, using a written format. The latter was intended to prompt the staff leader through a series of observations about process and content of the group and the contributions of each group member. There was one staff member who attended the group with one client as his 'interpreter' – as she could understand his speech as most others could not – and (after briefing) she acted purely as an interpreter, not as an extra group member. The group progressed from a house committee to a tenants group – where members of four flats met to discuss issues as tenants of the housing block.

2   An established day centre for older adults wanted to expand its numbers from 12 to 20. Since the existing group was very cohesive (over-cohesive?), there were concerns that it would reject the newcomers who might therefore drop out. To prevent this a two-stage process was put into practice. Firstly, to prevent the newcomers feeling unsupported, they came in an hour earlier than the existing members for eight weeks and had a reminiscence group. In this way, they got to know each other and gained some support and feeling of belonging. Secondly, each newcomer was paired with a group member, who had agreed to welcome them and make them feel at home. These two processes were both successful and after a couple of months, the new, larger centre was working well.

3   Ten younger adults (ages 18–40) with learning difficulties were moved from a number of day centres to form a new small one whose aim was to maximize client decision-making. To help achieve cohesion, a ten-session 'Our Lives' reminiscence group was run for all ten

members. At the end of this, the slot, as planned, became used for a house meeting with the day centre staff present. During this phase, one member learned to take minutes, so all meetings were minuted and later typed up; and all the members, even the shyest, learned to chair the group in rotation. In the third phase, the staff withdrew, although they were still on the premises if needed, and the members ran the group, deciding, for example, how to spend the outings and entertainment budget of the unit. Because all members attended there was, not surprisingly, a wide range of verbal ability. The group leaders had never managed to get the quieter, less verbal members to participate proportionally in the reminiscence sessions, but after the session was over, and the atmosphere was more informal, the good feeling built up in the sessions allowed members to engage in conversations quite independent of verbal ability.

4 Margaret Fielden, in a research paper published in 1990, compared the effect of running a Recall group for nine sessions in one sheltered housing unit, with the effect of nine sessions of a 'Look After Yourself' keep fit course in another sheltered housing unit. On two measures of psychological health, the attenders at the reminiscence group showed significantly greater benefit than the keep fit course attenders. What is of greater relevance here is the attendance at events held in the community lounges. While attending a keep fit group had no effect, attendance at activities in the lounge of the unit by those who had been to the reminiscence group increased between three- and seven fold.

> Over the period of the intervention the residents changed from a body of people seemingly unwilling to become involved with each other socially to a group of people requesting greater input from the warden and enjoying events organized. Finally, they began to be involved in organizing events themselves and in some cases have taken over the organizing role. The warden admitted to being quite disappointed at first when the residents no longer needed her to attend or organize all their social calendar, but was able to 'let go', aware that this was the situation she had been working toward. A further recent evolution is that people living close to the sheltered housing have been drawn in to join events. One gregarious gentleman has been known to invite people standing at the bus-stop to join them, with success! (Fielden, 1990 p. 30)

The excerpt shows the clear development of group cohesion. In addition, Fielden looked at friendship patterns before and after the intervention and was able to show the development of a number of new friendships. Note the dilemma of the warden as her success made her role much less central and her professional competence in responding to it. This shows in real life the difficulties of working on this kind of purpose that we discussed earlier.

6   We will mention two groups we were involved in where we would have liked to achieve group cohesion but failed. The first was a very odd group. It was composed of residents in an old people's home who were isolates and did not mix well. For reasons that were never apparent, they were all put onto one corridor, where after a while, perhaps not surprisingly, they got on rather badly. Two of us were asked to run a reminiscence group for the members of this corridor; of the six, four welcomed the idea but two spent all their time arguing with each other. We tried to sort out these two by behind the scenes interventions but this was a mistake. Had we but asked the other members of the group what to do about the situation, they would almost certainly have come up with a solution, most probably to give the two one last chance before excluding them, which we were too uneasy to do. Because we did not show our trust in the group in this way, the other members started absenting themselves and the group folded.

7   We shall describe in the next section a successful group for people who were hard of hearing. After the success of that group, we tried to create a similar group of people who were severely visually handicapped. We ran a successful reminiscence group and then handed over to staff who had been running the group with us. The group soon started suffering from absenteeism – old people are remarkably good at finding polite and plausible excuses! In retrospect, the group failed for a number of reasons:

1   We handed over without a 'fade-out' period.
2   The new leaders did not think it sufficiently important to work out ways of easing the problems of the visually handicapped, for example by spending time getting suitable tactile objects.
3   When we tried to rescue the situation, because we had not established a continuity between our work and their ideas, discussion degenerated into 'us' versus 'them'.
4   When gently confronting them about point 2, the new leaders' lack of belief in the ability and validity of the group became evident.

A detailed account of this purpose in action

In contrast with the experience just described, the hard-of-hearing group which we ran before that one was a great success.

When we were asked to start a group for the hard-of-hearing, we were clear that we wished to implement the strategy we set out above under the description of the goals of this purpose. We therefore ran the group with a member of the Sensory Impairment Team in order to decrease the likelihood of staff not understanding our goals, as well as one care assistant.

Of all the elderly people in a residential home, the hard-of-hearing are often the most overlooked, and as a result, become isolated and insular. (This situation can be exacerbated by residents who are too vain to admit to hearing loss as this might lead to having to use a stigmatizing hearing aid.) In the setting in which we worked, in the main, the cognitive functioning of those with poor hearing was good, which is why it was so wrong to overlook them, treating them with disregard, ignoring them and failing to notice their need. Their poor hearing made involvement in any large group activity organized in the home limited, almost impossible; bingo, quiz time, variety shows, a film, a sing-a-long, residents' committee meetings, visits to the theatre, all these they could watch, but as one woman put it, 'It's like window shopping, standing on the outside looking in, watching people laugh and wondering why?' With no sound, involvement has no texture or substance and little meaning. With poor hearing and because of their exclusion, these elderly residents become depressed and dispirited. The use of a hearing aid does improve communication in a one-to-one situation but in a large group activity, *all* sounds are amplified to such an extent that they become distorted and without clarity. This results in the hearing aid being turned off or the person retiring to their room.

Aware of the need and the neglect of these individuals, the officer-in-charge of the home (in the Borough of Newham), Muriel Johns, had installed a loop system in a small, infrequently used lounge. The essence of the loop is that for those wearing a hearing aid the sound is amplified, but *only* sound within a certain radius of a centrally placed microphone. With support from the Sensory Impairment Team, we looked at those residents with hearing impairment. Five whom it was felt would benefit from a group activity and who were intellectually compatible were approached. Bill, Frances, Cissy and Kit, once it had been fully explained to them, agreed to participate. Mary, however, was a little reluctant, but said she'd give it a try. A ten-week commitment was carefully planned, ensuring that ample visual material was available, giving maximum support to our topics.

The five residents came to the first session with some hesitancy. Prior communication had been limited to interaction mainly with staff, rarely with another resident and definitely not with a member with a similar hearing problem. This was not because interaction, albeit limited, was not possible, the main reason was because they had come into residential care over many months/years. Where they sat in the lounge or dining area had been pre-determined by where there had been a space (vacancy) in the home. The home was open plan with a large lounge/dining area. A new resident would probably have been seated around the periphery of the lounge alongside a confused or hearing older person, who was perhaps preoccupied with their own coming-to-terms with residential care and their own wellbeing. The need to talk slowly and deliberately to the newcomer, ensuring that they were facing them was not something they were aware of. In addition, for an old person seated facing forward, to turn through 90 degrees to face another is difficult and even painful.

A loop system means that people talk into a microphone and this is transmitted directly to other members' hearing aids, thus cutting out most of the extraneous noise. Because only one person can talk into the microphone at any one time, using a loop system means a group has a slower pace, but the group members were so pleased to have access to relatively clearly understood speech, compared to the confusing racket or total silence that were their choice normally, and so hungry to communicate with each other, that there wasn't really much work for the group leaders to do except notice who was wanting to speak and pass the microphone around.

Jill Lancaster, who was the support worker from the Sensory Impairment Team led the group supported by Peggy Kelly, a member of the care staff. The *Recall* slides were used and the topic was childhood. It had been decided not to use the audio tapes as the clarity of sound was poor. As with most first sessions, verbal spontaneity was slow and interaction between client and client was almost non-existent. However, it was obvious from the staff–client interaction and the non-verbal communication, that the members were enjoying this small group involvement. During the course of the week Peggy observed the five members outside the group. She informed us that Bill, Frances and Mary were now aware of each other as individuals, acknowledging each other when meeting.

As the weekly meetings continued, it was obvious that the members had become accustomed to and welcomed the individual and distinct conversations within the group setting. Conversation around the chosen subjects now went from client to client as well as to staff. The weeks progressed and so did the group, as the members recognized that they had life experiences in common and, in sharing them, formed friendships. Outings were arranged that supported the topics. Though not always able to hear fully what was going on because of overall background noise, they nevertheless enjoyed these excursions. Once this problem with noise was recognized (it could not be resolved), the group would return to the home after an outing in time to meet in the loop lounge, where questions were raised and discussion around the outing took place. Although some of the group had been involved in outings previously, it had been solely a visual experience, unless seated next to a member of staff.

As the group bonded, they became more confident and assured, participating in other activities within the home, i.e. the gardening club, music and movement (following the direction given by staff). However, it was evident that on such occasions they sought each other's company. All the women joined the handicraft group which left Bill at a loss. The visiting handicraft instructor initially introduced Bill to painting by numbers. This proved a costly exercise for the officer-in-charge, since as Bill became more proficient, the more paintings he completed! Eventually he tried his hand at original art work, which proved extremely positive. Some of his paintings were framed and hung on the walls of the home. The weekly reminiscence meetings continued to be enjoyed and looked forward to. At the end of the ten weeks, the reminiscence group sadly and reluctantly came to a close. Jill went on to support another home. From this group, however, another grew. The Hard of Hearing Group was the name chosen by the members, who met weekly in the loop lounge supported by Peggy, the care worker who had helped with the original group. Over tea they chatted about newspaper articles they had read and put the world to rights.

The talking book club had been used regularly by Frances, who had become a dominant member of the group. She praised this facility to such an extent that others tried it. Not all felt the same enthusiasm: some members had more profound hearing difficulties and others found the simple mechanics of the recording machine difficult to comprehend or manage with fingers swollen and twisted with arthritis. This did not deter Frances. During the afternoon, you could pass her room where Bill, Cissy and Kit would be crammed in listening to one of her story tapes going at full blast. (Crammed they would be, as both Bill and Frances were confined to wheelchairs.)

The group was such a success that residents with similar hearing problems from a nearby home were invited to join the weekly group. The officer-in-charge of that home agreed to finance the involvement, and three of her residents and a member of staff were taxied across weekly. The more homes there are that are involved in increasing the amount of social care, the more likely are the ideas of social care (and the implications for how many staff a home needs and how they should be organized) to be recognized and accepted by managers. Returning to the hard-of-hearing group: quite quickly, they had formed themselves into a club that met weekly and voted on whether new residents who were hard of hearing should join; they organized outings etc.

Factors that contributed to the success of this group were:

1 The room used had had the loop system installed, so that the message from the central microphone was heard without any other extraneous noises. This improvement in reception was greatly appreciated by the members.
2 There was enthusiastic support from the officer-in-charge.
3 A staff member was attending all sessions and co-leading the group so that staff knew what we were doing and could provide continuity between sessions.
4 We had trained the staff in this home in reminiscence work.
5 When the group became a self-help and support group, the staff member stayed on as a quiet, unobtrusive back-up to the group.

Our examples show that group cohesion is quite possible to achieve, but it does require some positive shared activity to bond it, a fixing agent, such as reminiscence. People living in isolation in a large group setting is not uncommon; people often get lost in a crowd. Other activities were going on in the home but to participate alone takes courage and self assurance. These are characteristics which, with age, are often lost and replaced with self-doubt. Staff could have encouraged those with poor hearing into another activity, but because of their hearing difficulties, they would have remained insular. To converse during some of the other activities is quite possible, but it is not the main element of the involvement, for example to sew and chat, to garden and chat. The bonding process eventually may occur, but may take a long time. Accelerating the process may be particularly important in units where people will soon move on, such as children in care settings.

A reminiscence group facilitates the process, allowing people to share common bonds. In the small group setting we become individuals, gaining in strength and self-worth, although personalities do not change. In our hard-of-hearing group Mary remained timid, but because of Frances, whose assurance grew, she became a little more adventurous. Bill, a modest man, became quite enterprising in a quiet way. Cissy, a cheerful person, remained so. Kit, who initially thought she was the only one with problems, left them behind when part of a group. These older people were not confused, they were physically frail and required the support of the residential home where initially they sat 'window shopping'. Through the process of group cohesion they eventually came in from the outside.

Conclusions

Group cohesion is an interesting purpose of reminiscence, demanding professional and emotional skill on the part of the group leaders, and so is not to be taken on by staff who are inexperienced in groupwork. It demands the ability to change roles as the group moves through the various stages towards greater decision-making by members. It demands good judgement as to where the group is in its development and how much to withdraw and expect the group to make decisions. It is demanding, but also very exhilarating work. This type of work, therefore, should always be supervised, so that the leaders have time and space to examine the group and themselves. It requires continual encouragement and prompting of the members to interact with each other and *not* with the leader, and in the end it requires the leader to ease themself from a position of leadership. This may be a very unusual process in the unit, both for group leaders and for other staff, and we will look at how to handle this challenge to the normal way of doing things in Part Four.

Finally, sometimes the achievement of group cohesion will sneak up on you, although you ran a reminiscence group for a different purpose. Perhaps you started with a fun group, but over the weeks, because it is enjoyable and well run, the same people have been coming, even when it was inconvenient for them, and they're starting to suggest ideas, some of which – oh so sweet and sour – don't involve you. You may well have a group that is ready for Stage Three. Seeing disadvantaged and disheartened people reach the autonomy stage is a fantastic experience, but it will only happen with the support of your colleagues in the unit. When it does, as you make your bow, have a good wake session with the group, so that you have an opportunity to laugh and cry at the group you are now leaving and being excluded from!

Useful reading and resources

Readers interested in how community work can help devalued people achieve a political identity and some political clout may find Saul Alinsky's work of use. Try *Reveille for Radicals* (Random House, 1969) and *Rules for Radicals* (Random House, 1971).

Richard De Board's *The Psychology of Organisations* (Tavistock/Routledge, 1978) is a good introduction to the major theories of groups.

The emphasis on security as a basic need comes from Abraham Maslow, whose basic text is *Toward a Psychology of Being* (2nd edition, Van Nostrand, 1968).

The two classic contemporary guides to group therapy are Dorothy Whitaker's *Using Groups to Help People* (Tavistock/Routledge, 1985) and Irvin Yalom's *The Theory and Practice of Group Psychotherapy* (4th edition, Basic Books, 1995).

Margaret Fielden's work was reported in the *British Journal of Social Work*, 1990, 20, pp. 21–44.

Purpose Eight

REMINISCENCE TO TEACH PEOPLE HOW TO USE GROUPS EFFECTIVELY

Rationale

This purpose is not one that immediately comes to mind when people think of reminiscence work, but people are scared of being a group – of losing their identity, of feeling forced to talk about things they don't want to talk about, of making a fool of themselves, of being rejected. In short, groups can be scary.

A *well-planned* and *well-run* reminiscence group can help people come to see that groups need not be like that – that they can stay in enough control to feel comfortable, that they do have some choice as to what happens to them in the group, and this will give them confidence to proceed to other types of groups (this is illustrated in the flow diagram in Figure 4).

We emphasized 'well-planned' and 'well-run' for the obvious reason that in order to show people that groups in general can be enjoyable/beneficial we first have to get them to experience an effectively run group. This chapter will therefore look at how the induction into a reminiscence group can be conducted, so that the member feels safe and confident enough to give other types of group a go.

To give people a good experience with/within reminiscence can be an end in itself, as much of the rest of this book suggests; however, it can also be used as an entry for other groups and other activities that will be of equal or even greater benefit to the person. If you like, going through one door into one room can give the person the confidence to enter other, different rooms. In short, we are offering reminiscence as a sample or starter for a range of groups.

Goals implied in the purpose

- To maximize information as to the purpose and method of a group.
- To maximize security within the group.

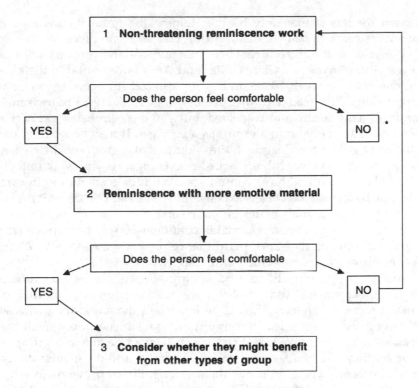

* Ascertain reason and offer appropriate individual/group treatment

Figure 4   *Helping people benefit from groupwork*

- To minimize anxiety.
- To maximize felt agency within the group.
- To maximize commonality/communality of experience within the group.
- To ensure enjoyment/satisfaction/benefit of members.

The tasks

- To be aware of how much anxiety being in a group arouses.
- To control that anxiety.
- To demonstrate to members that the group leaders are in control of the process.
- To suggest that groups can be enjoyable and also a learning experience.

The group leaders must have tight control of the planning of the group, selection of the group members and of the running of the group. The reason for this is that only by maintaining the group boundaries can members come to believe that a group can be a safe place.

We said in the introduction to this purpose that groups are scary places – for anyone. As Clare Gillies and Anne James put it in their book on reminiscence work, 'Being in a group can feel strange, dangerous and frightening.' The reader of this present book is likely to be reasonably professionally secure and respected, but you most probably get nervous the first time you go into a group as a stranger. It may be nothing more challenging than a colleague invites you to join a group of their friends who meet at a pub or club on Saturday evenings. As you walk in there's a fair chance you will have chosen your outfit or cosmetics with care – too casual/formal, too cheap/expensive? – and you will be a bit nervous – will your colleague's mates be your sort?

If we assume you are a reasonably confident person, how much worse must such an entrance and 'performance' be for someone with a much leaner history of being valued and respected?

Also, many of our clients find talking about their feelings difficult, especially as some of those feelings are painful. Moreover, as we'll discuss at more length later, their experience tells them that the expression of strong feelings can lead to very unpleasant scenes. So, for all these reasons our clients take a real risk when they agree to join a group. No wonder they often refuse such an 'opportunity': and the greater the gain if reminiscence work can prove them wrong. But to prove them wrong, the reminiscence group leaders must create a very secure and stable environment.

They do this by being in charge of their group and preventing disruption. This is done by creating and maintaining *boundary conditions*. A group is a place and time when people work together, and where they have different experiences than they do when they're by themselves or with only one or two others. To achieve this special time and space, the group's boundaries must be maintained. In Table 8 we specify some of these boundary conditions.

The group leader has to understand the importance of these conditions and find ways of achieving them in their unit. Without their achievement, no group can be successful. With their achievement, reminiscence work may be the group activity of choice when we want to introduce people to groupwork for the following reasons.

- The ease with which reminiscences can be elicited. Physical objects, pictures and so on, if relevant to the group, can aid people in recalling their past. So, if asking them about their past without any prompts is to create too daunting and anxiety-making a task, then we can move up and down the scale of 'strength of prompts' (see Purpose Six on work with the individual).
- We can vary what is asked about to reach an appropriate level of self-disclosure and comfort.

Table 8 *Necessary conditions for a successful group*

Leader interaction
1 Trust between leaders
2 An understood and shared purpose

Leader achievements/attributes
1 Informed consent from members
2 Shared purpose among members and leaders
3 Attention to members' contributions
4 Respect for members' contributions
5 Enjoyment/satisfaction for members from the group
6 Security for members in the group

Group conditions
Secure boundaries, which are provided by:
1 Closed membership
2 Continuity of leadership
3 Regularity of space
4 A private space
5 A space large enough to form a circle
6 A quiet place
7 Free from internal interruptions
8 Free from external interruptions
9 Regularity of time
10 Fixed start and finishing times
11 Fixed number of sessions
12 Known finishing date

- Reminiscence groupwork quickly demonstrates similarities among the group members *if they exist*. (It *cannot* create them.) So, if you have selected people with similar experiences for at least some of their lives, then the sharing of these experiences will create fellowship and a good feeling in a group.

For example, when two of us worked with Val Levens, a speech and language therapist, to run reminiscence groups for people with a learning difficulty, we were immediately struck by how bewildered they were as to what a group was about – What was it for? Why were they sitting there, just talking? Why were we sitting there, just listening to them? What were they supposed to offer us? Fairly quickly, because we had reasonable control of the group boundaries and because we didn't go away and the group *did* meet every week, they relaxed into enjoying it and sharing their sometimes painful memories together.

How to achieve these tasks

1 As we have already emphasized, you *need an understanding of the importance of group boundaries*. Group cohesion – the glue of the group

process – cannot develop without a quiet time and place for the group to meet.

It is quite surprising and a little sad how often it is not possible – or very difficult – to achieve these conditions. You find day centres with no side rooms for groups to meet. Sometimes the group leaders put up a screen to divide off a space, but of course this does not meet the boundary condition of undisturbed quiet. Many units for disabled or disadvantaged people are surprisingly noisy. In many units for older adults the television blares away unwatched in the corner, but the staff are surprisingly resistant to turning it off, claiming 'They all enjoy it', despite the empty chairs or the couple of people trying to doze.

Consistency of leadership is one of the most important conditions. It is very disruptive if various members of staff take the same group, and yet because groupwork is of low status and so misunderstood, such unprofessional behaviour is all too common. A group needs the same two leaders for each and every session – it needs more than two, again consistently present, if members are very cognitively or physically damaged. So this means the involvement and cooperation of management in rostering the group leaders on at the same time each week, and covering with other staff the tasks they might otherwise be doing.

2   You *need to select members carefully*. Remember, you are trying to maximize feelings of safety in the group. So common experience is important but not enough. Members need to be able to get on. It therefore makes sense to look at the patterns of interaction between people you have in mind for the group. Outright hostility between two potential members is obviously a contraindication for including both. Great differences in attitudes also need to be weighed up. Group leaders, first, must therefore do some careful homework before short-listing for a group. You need to know each potential member quite well and to know their biography and their views.

There is another reason for the need for a positive relationship between you and the potential member before the group starts. This is that the potential group member will surf into the group on their trust of you and your ability to deliver security. Without that they will probably refuse.

So, drawing up a list for the group has to be the group leader's responsibility. Obviously other people can suggest and advise, but group membership cannot be decided by a senior manager looking at names in their office, putting together all those with a gap against Tuesday afternoon or all the difficult ones that no one wants. Such 'methods' of selection provide little guarantee of security.

3   *The informed consent interview*. One way of reassuring people that they are letting themselves in for something safe is for them to take part in an informed consent interview. This interview is also important for another reason. People who have low self-esteem are concerned that, in a group, they will lose their fragile individuality; that it will

be submerged into the group, causing a frightening loss of self. The informed consent interview puts great emphasis on them choosing, or not, to join the group.

This interview is held between individual members and the group leaders (or only one if two would be intimidating). It

- explains fully the purpose of the group;
- answers any questions;
- and asks if the person wants to take part. (It further adds to the potential member's sense of having freely chosen if they are asked to go away and think whether they want to join and to let you know later. Additionally, to maximize this sense of choosing freely, you can ask them to let a member of staff who is not a group leader know their decision, to decrease the possibility that they are saying 'yes' only to avoid giving offence.)

So, at the end of this unhurried interview, the potential member should feel informed, consulted and, hopefully, motivated.

Note that the interview is held with the individual, so that they feel free to ask questions that might seem a bit foolish or embarrassing if heard by others. For all these reasons, *informed consent should always be sought in a private interview with the individual.*

4   *The group makes the rules.* We have talked about how the informed consent interview helps the individual potential member feel in control. Similarly, having the group spend time deciding on the rules which the group members will abide by helps the group feel in control.

We find it useful in the first session to start with all people – members and leaders – saying a little about themselves; to reiterate the purpose and hoped for gains/benefits of the group; and then, with the aid of a large sheet of paper, to get the group to work out the rules it wants to operate on. Members may need a little help to get started but the process allows fears and worries to be aired and shared in the group, and tackled.

The group leaders are not silent witnesses in this. There will be issues, such as confidentiality, that they will want the group to consider. As an example, the following are the rules worked out in the first session by older adults attending a life stages assessment therapy group at a psychiatric day unit.

1   Personal things to be kept in the group and not go outside it. Leaders may talk – only in outline, not detail – only to named staff and consultants.
2   Be honest with self and others in group.
3   Starts promptly at 1.30 pm.
4   Members to come unprompted.
5   Finish at 2.45 pm.

6   Tell the group if you will be absent for the next session.
7   If you can't make it, ring in.
8   Share what's comfortable.
9   Give it a fair trial.
10 If you decide to quit, come and explain *why*.
11 One person talks at a time.
12 Talk to the group, not to your neighbour.
13 Equal time share (opportunity).
14 No visitors, such as nursing students, without prior agreement of
    the group.

The rules, displayed each session, are surprisingly useful for sorting out disagreements or for pointing to when violated.

5   *Controlling the emotional temperature.* We have talked about the poor self-image and low self-confidence of many of our clients. Usually, low self-confidence makes people a bit reserved and shy but people can, of course, be noisy or aggressive to hide their low self-confidence. That's why we emphasize the need for security.

Less obvious is the fear of loss of temper. Our clients often fear they'll be left without any control of a situation, but they also often have had experience that when disagreements start and voices are raised, nasty things, like violent beatings, follow, with great unhappiness. Again, in these situations of familial violence they were helpless to intervene – they were powerless spectators.

With this in mind, the group leaders must have the skills to defuse disagreements, especially in the early sessions. Later, as the group members feel more relaxed and more self-confident, they can probably sort out their differences amicably. In the early stages, where anxiety is higher, confrontations may be sharper, more unpleasant and more difficult to resolve – the other members again being passive spectators. To prevent this, the group leaders may need to move in earlier to take the heat out of the situation. A good group rule to get agreement on is 'You are free to disagree with an opinion but not to criticize or mock the person with that opinion.' So, in the early stages of a reminiscence group with this purpose, you may need a tighter hold on the emotional tiller.

6   *Varying complexity of material.* You need to be familiar with a range of groups that have used a wide variety of materials – physical objects, music, photos etc. – so that you can vary the prompts you use to aid a discussion. Sometimes, you'll find the prompts essential; sometimes the prompts you spent weeks finding, quickly prove unnecessary.

Variation isn't just a matter of material either. It also requires the ability to alter the presentation and level of discussion depending on the capabilities and background of the members. Try to make your group failure-free.

7   *Varying depth of leader intervention* Group leaders must have the ability to move across the spectrum of intervention from light to heavy

involvement. A competent group leader runs an enjoyable bingo group as well as being able to handle the suffering of members of a bereavement group; and there is also a skill in moving across the light–heavy spectrum during a session. Thus, a session might start with pleasantries, move to painful issues, and then come back to pleasanter topics towards the end, without in any way denying the reality of the pain described in the middle of the session.

Looking over the last seven points, you can see that quite a range of skills is being called on. This is because you need flexibility of style – a range of possible behaviours and responses on your part – to achieve the twin goals of both security and growth; and to be aware of the great differences between one group and the next group you take, so that you vary your presentation with every new group to achieve the goals of instilling security, curiosity and self-confidence. You do need to know who you are – the boundaries of what you can do and still feel genuine – but there should be a lot of flexibility within those boundaries.

Examples of work for this purpose

Reminiscence with people with a learning difficulty appears greatly underused. Certainly, the work referred to earlier – with Val Levens – led us to believe that many people were hungry to be allowed to discuss their experiences; and once they had got used to a group format, could look at more personal areas. So we started with a group with a chronological approach – childhood, school, etc. – but in the next group, we looked at family dynamics and how relationships changed with time. This series of groups was for people with very severe learning difficulties and restricted cognitive ability. (In terms of speech development, these people were at the level of usually using less than three word sentences.) One incident that stayed in the memory was one young adult's realization that other people's fathers died. Up to that time he had clearly thought he was the only person, perhaps in the world, who had lost a parent.

One way of making groups less threatening is for members to share. In an inspired move, towards the end of this group, Val suggested an outing with a picnic. We all listed our favourite food for a picnic and then each member bought the favourite foods *of another member*. (Obviously, for some clients, this required a bit of help from their friends and family.) We found a picnic table in Epping Forest and the sense of anticipation and excitement as everyone produced their paper and plastic bags with goodies for someone else was palpable. Clearly, being in a group could be fun and could make you feel good.

We were never able to fully develop this group because we could not achieve acceptable boundary conditions – the tannoy could not be switched off in the room and the noise from the corridor frequently penetrated into the room, disturbing the session.

As indicated in Purpose Seven, Anthea Sperlinger used a reminiscence group for people who had left a large mental handicap hospital. A few knew each other but not in the context of community living. We have also used reminiscence to develop group cohesion among people with a learning difficulty coming to a new centre from a variety of different units. In each case, the group moved on from a reminiscence group to form a service users' committee.

So, in these examples, we can see *vertical development* – increase in depth in subsequent groups – or *horizontal development* – the group moves on to a different type of activity/purpose the second time around.

A detailed account of this purpose in action

I will describe an example of this purpose from slow-stream rehabilitation. I was called into a day unit to see if it could provide psychotherapeutic groups for 'chronic patients'. By this was meant patients who had been in the psychiatric system for a long time, including, for almost all of them, a number of inpatient admissions. These were people in their fifties and sixties, about two-thirds women and not employed.

My first attempt to work with this group was a near farcical disaster. It was coming up to Christmas; someone in the county was running an evening class for women to sort out how *they* wanted their Christmas to be, I thought it was an obvious idea to transpose it to this group. But the group rapidly became a nightmare. The members had little to look forward to over Christmas – for a minority, Christmas lunch would be courtesy of the Salvation Army. They had lost touch with most of their relatives; those who still knew where they were had quarrelled with them.

Besides completely misunderstanding the meaning of Christmas for this group, there was another problem. Most members, despite their long involvement in psychiatry, said they had never previously been in a group. Whether this was strictly true or not, they certainly acted as if it were – in terms of their insecurity and un-ease. One day – and this was a backhanded achievement in itself – three or four said they would not come to the session. When finally persuaded to come and state their concerns, they said they felt the group was far too personal.

When the group, thankfully, finished, my colleagues and I did a thorough debriefing. It was apparent that the members felt that they hadn't known what they 'had let themselves in for' and that the content was too threatening.

So, for the next group, we first strengthened the informed consent interview – a booked time, written notification of that time, a pamphlet explaining the purpose of the group given to them beforehand, and no agreement sought at the interview. They each had a key worker, so, to decrease the risk of compliance based on the fear of upsetting the group leaders, they were to relay their decision to their key worker. Secondly, we decided that the topics for the eight sessions would be holidays and leisure. The group members – very largely the same membership as the Christmas planning group – felt comfortable with this topic, and the group sessions were very relaxed and friendly. At the end of this set of sessions, the group decided that the next eight sessions would be about 'my brothers and sisters'.

Incidentally, we made these all-women groups. There were considerably more women than men in the unit and we thought that the amount of common/shared experience would be increased by doing this, leading to increased group cohesion and trust, making the group feel safer. Getting the members to feel safe is a key achievement in any group, but was particularly necessary with this set of people.

The final set of sessions was 'My life till age 11'. We chose to stop at 11 to avoid embarrassment regarding adolescent sexuality. By now, the group was far more able to handle sensitive topics, and the group was cohesive and confident. It went on meeting as a self-help, problem-solving group with the unit staff members there to facilitate, and I bowed out.

Conclusions

The purpose of using reminiscence groupwork to help people feel comfortable and not in danger of feeling overwhelmed in groups is an important aim, as it opens new horizons for the members, be they with regard to horizontal or vertical development. Implicit in such achievements are increased self-confidence; and with that increased confidence and, most likely, increased social skills to handle potentially difficult group situations. This increased self-confidence in handling potentially difficult situations may have important spin-offs outside their group in helping members to be more confident when tackling interpersonal or familial difficulties.

So, for clients with little group experience, low-key reminiscence groupwork may well be the group of choice early in their time in the unit. It is particularly relevant to psychiatric rehabilitation, learning difficulties and, generally, for people with a history of low-esteem, all of whom are likely to find groups bewildering and rather frightening.

Useful reading and resources

Mike Bender, Val Levens and Charles Goodson (1995) *Welcoming Your Clients*, Winslow Press. Provides a practical introduction to transmitting staff respect and welcoming.

Faith Gibson (1989) *Using Reminiscence*, Help the Aged.
Faith Gibson (1994) *Reminiscence and Recall*, Age Concern.
   The above are two manuals by a leader in the field.
Claire Gillies and Ann James (1994) *Reminiscence Work With Old People*,
   Chapman & Hall. An introduction to the theory and practice of
   reminiscence work for social workers.

Purpose Nine

REMINISCENCE TO RE-USE OLD SKILLS OR LEARN NEW ONES

Rationale

One of the strongest stereotypes about older people is that they cannot change (which is why Freud argued there was no point in giving them therapy); and that they cannot learn ('You can't teach an old dog new tricks'). This stereotype is very damaging as it fosters the view that old age is little more than time spent waiting to die, a period during which the person is unable to do anything useful or fulfilling. And, once again, remember that stereotypes are not just in the minds of younger people; they are internalized by many older people who then too believe this pernicious nonsense. This process, incidentally, starts long before retirement age: people start to become self-conscious about their ages even in their mid-twenties, and it worsens in the 'thirty-something' years.

In Purpose Nine, the worker's task is to prove the incorrectness of this stereotypic belief to the older person; to create an environment in which, perhaps to their surprise, the older person does engage in new learning, or pick up and polish and re-use previously acquired skills.

The motivational factors that we need to harness for this purpose are two-fold. First, we need to make the person feel positive about themselves, that they are able to do things. The key psychological term is self-esteem. The second aspect is that the task must be interesting to them or lead to a goal they would like to achieve. So, either the means or the ends must be motivating. Sometimes, with people who are down/depressed, we need to make an educated guess as to what they will be interested in if we are to get them started. Once they've got moving, the energy release will be considerable.

In the pages that follow (and in the next chapter, on using oral history), we will give examples of the activities we have in mind, such as older people writing up the history of the main street of their town; finding out the history of the hospital in which their day centre is located; putting on their own variety show; writing down accounts of their childhood and then giving lessons to local school classes; writing poetry and learning computer skills. In some of these projects, such as researching local history, word processing or poetry or teaching, new skills are being learned; in others, such as singing or reciting verse, old ones are being brought out and dusted off.

Goals implied in the purpose

- Creating a sufficiently high level of self-esteem in the participants to give them energy.
- Encourage the taking on and achieving of new skills, or the re-use of old ones.
- Creating valued activities or objects.

The tasks

- To give, where necessary, hope to the members so that they feel the effort and the risk are worthwhile.
- To share in the risk-taking.
- To minimize the risk of failure.
- To create good team morale, which generates its own enthusiasm and energy.
- To have the necessary teaching and training skills.
- To acquire the resources needed for the successful completion of the activity *before* beginning that activity.
- Where appropriate, to gain publicity for what has been produced, thus further raising the members' self-esteem, allowing the cycle of exploration and achievement to start again.

How to achieve these tasks

As with almost all these purposes, the key to achieving successful relearning of skills is knowing your group members – knowing their capabilities, knowing their lived lives and their interests. It is by having this information available to you in your head that it can be mulled over and ideas about what could and will work can be considered and rejected, till one 'fits' and looks like a runner.

It is useful if the projects are undertaken on a group basis, rather than each member of your group doing something separate and non-overlapping. This does not mean they all are doing the same thing. In 'A walk up Fore Street' each member of a group in a Liskeard day unit took on the task of investigating the history of a few shops in the town's high street. Together, they covered the whole street. In another day centre in Plymouth, each of three groups discussed and produced the material for one lesson about their lives, to give to local schoolchildren. In this way we harness the energy of the group process – the sociability, the rivalry, the encouraging etc. We also are encouraging member–member communication, cooperation and competition, which is far more effective in getting things done than staff–member interactions.

It will be seen that this purpose is perhaps most relevant for people, of any age, who are cognitively capable but have lost faith or belief in themselves. (Having said this, there is a tremendous amount of undeveloped potential in people with learning difficulties, so this purpose is most definitely applicable and useful for them.)

The creation or return of self-belief is in three phases:

1 Encouragement and assertion of members' competence by the group leader (and their trust in the group leader).
2 Seeing the task get under way.
3 Seeing the completed activity and product and knowing that they made a significant contribution.

When we talk of 'loss of self-belief' this does not mean that the person is clinically depressed, although fellow professionals may so mis-label them. They may feel useless because they've been bringing up children for a number of years and feel all their abilities relate to the past; because they are discriminated against in one way or another; because they are old; because their children no longer need them; or because they have chronic pain, such as arthritis.

Whatever the reason, you have to ensure *before* the beginning of the group that each member knows:

• that you value them;
• that you can see they have the ability to undertake the task which together you have agreed upon;
• that with your support they will not fail;
• that you have the required resources, be they for groupwork/the time needed/access to the word processor/volunteers to take someone to the library/or whatever.

It is unprofessional to start a project with this purpose without having guaranteed access to the resources needed, or to let people start work whilst you are still begging, borrowing or praying. In short, therefore, you require good interpersonal skills and the ability to forward plan to gain the resources that will be needed.

We can put society's prejudice against the elderly to good use in furthering this purpose. According to Attribution Theory, many decisions are made on the basis of what attributes are assumed concerning a person or group of persons. In our society, *general* expectations of elderly people are *low* – poor, frail, slow. So if one elderly person or a small group of them do something well, it is *against expectation* and therefore *particularly praiseworthy*. So if you and your group can do something reasonably well, members of the public will be surprised that they could do it at all and heap praise on them and you. If you are lucky you will get extra resources, and can smile at the cost of society maintaining its irrationality.

Examples of work for this purpose

We will talk about using oral history to develop new skills in the next chapter. We can develop the skills of selecting material and presentation skills in encouraging older adults to pass on their lived history to schoolchildren, and this will be discussed in the chapter on inter-generational communication.

When considering available but rusty skills, remember many older people were taught music when they were children – they were taught the piano, or to sing. They may well not have used these skills for a long time. At Lamellion Hospital Day Unit in Liskeard, one autumn, we wondered whether the clients could put on their own Christmas show, rather than the more usual practice of having an entertainer. Looking at the skills of the clients, the answer was almost certainly yes.

Two or three staff members each took patients who were interested and helped them decide on their numbers and write them up. By the staff communicating with each other and with a couple of dress rehearsals the whole show came together. But a note of caution is needed. A huge amount of work goes into putting on a show, over and above rehearsing the actors. In this instance the main organizer, Mo McGowan, a nursing assistant, put in many extra unpaid hours.

We called the show 'A Flight of Fancy' and the selling line on the advert was 'No one, but no one, not even the Chief Executive, gets on the stage unless they are over 70!', and that was true, because even the pianists were both over 70. On the actual afternoon, with a full house and a darkened room and a spotlight, there was inevitably stage fright, but with some prompting, and the audience – composed of all the day hospital's clients and anyone in the hospital who wished to attend – urging them on, the nerves were soon overcome.

There was great recognition and fondness for the material, which was very familiar to the client members of the audience. 'Rowing down the river on a Sunday afternoon', sung by four ladies in their long-flowing finery, brought tears to the eyes of many as it took them back 50 years. The day room, where the show was held, was packed with the other day clients, hospital patients and relatives, and this of itself created an atmosphere.

The thought arose that the show might 'tour' local and residential units, but it obviously wasn't of that quality, and this would have been a mistake. It was a show by the clients essentially for themselves; to take it out of the day hospital would have been to make it for other people, a more distancing process. Moreover, using external standards of excellence can damage the usefulness of the project to the participants: first, these standards are intrusive and not organic to the process, and secondly, they greatly increase the possibility of an experience of 'failure'.

Poetry and writing are two other skills that may be harnessed to reminiscence to help develop new skills. John Killick listens to people with dementia, and works with them to produce a joint piece of poetry. Some of his examples are striking and beautiful. This is a poem he 'assembled from conversations with a lady called Alice':

> MONKEY PUZZLE
> 'I would tell you the tale of my life, sir
> but I don't want my tea to get cold'
> . . .
> It's a different country here
> I don't like it,
> and they don't speak the language properly either
>
>   (Killick in Schweitzer, 1997: 98)

Writing skills can be damaged quite early in the dementing process, however, so do be careful that the person has retained their expressive and writing skills. Stay with skills that you are pretty certain are available to the person.

Returning to the wider population, an 'obvious' use of reminiscence is as an aid to adult literacy. If people enjoy talking about their experiences, it is only a small step to them wanting to write them down. So reminiscing could be the first stage in helping people develop their literacy skills. (See the book by Jane Laurence and Jane Mace on this.)

Poetry is, of course, 'available' to the cognitively able, if they can and want to think 'poetically'; prose writing may seem more 'natural'. A scheme called 'Write Away' was run by Julie Ward, Age Concern Newcastle's 'Creative writer in residence' in the early 1990s encouraging older people to write. An anthology resulted from it two years later. Its title, 'I Can Fly', is also a line from a poem in the anthology by Irene Dennison:

> ACHIEVEMENT
> Shoulders itching
> Nails are scratching
> Ooh! That's helping
> Wings are sprouting!
> I CAN FLY!

Play-writing would also come within work for this purpose. The Lamellion Day Unit got a group together to write a play about their lives to be acted by local schoolchildren. This project will be discussed in the chapter on intergenerational legacy.

A detailed example of this purpose in action

In *Reminiscence and Recall: a Guide to Good Practice* Faith Gibson describes a project named 'Teaching Older Dogs New Tricks'. The University of Ulster has pioneered teaching older people to use information technology. The materials used are available from the National Extension College. The older learners were highly motivated because they were working on a task that was important to them, such as writing their family history. 'The project showed that they can master word processing, even though it may take them longer to learn than younger people' (Gibson, 1994, p. 74). Taking part in the project also improved self-esteem, wellbeing and mental health and increased sociability.

The interested reader should obviously obtain copies of the teaching materials for themselves from the National Extension College. Professor Gibson advises twice-weekly sessions in a relaxed setting, with lots of encouragement and the minimum of technical language. The students, because they are working through their manuals individually, are working at their own pace.

An interesting lesson learned was to keep the class to people of the same age. Being with younger people would probably have highlighted the fact that it was taking the older people longer to pick up the ideas and therefore they would have been discouraged. 'Frequent evidence of achievement in the form of hard copy increased motivation and informal assistance from older mentors is most acceptable' (p. 75). Some wanted to write. Some wanted to publish their experience. What is written can then be shared, allowing for powerful group experiences as they share important aspects of their lives that the members all have in common. 'It validates or values in a public way the life that has been lived and the effort that has been expended in making the record' (p. 76). (Note again the framing of individual work within a group experience.)

You can see here how the ideas we outlined above in discussing how you might carry out the tasks of this purpose have been successfully applied in this project. The project leaders have started from something the older people wanted to do – to write about their lives; and then linked that goal to a whole new set of skills. Not only did that have benefits in its own right, but it led to other gains in terms of sharing experiences and having one's life validated.

Finally, since out-of-date computers are nearly valueless, they can be acquired very cheaply and still have lots of use left in them. Also, certainly among those at the younger end of the older age group range, many are now acquiring computer skills and so will be well able to utilize such equipment from the outset if it is available.

To give a final example, a centre is moving to new premises. The centre head wants an exhibition put up in the foyer of the new centre. One of the staff could do it. But why not a group of clients? They're also leaving the old place and feeling sad and a bit unsure. Some at least may wish to get hold of the pictures and photos of the old place and make a display with text. Even if because they are severely confused they can't do it all, they can create much of it; and if we want 20 minute videos of the key figures – councillors, the chair of the committee etc. who created the old place, then there is no reason why one of the members can't, with a bit of tuition, undertake these interviews.

Conclusions

The learning of new skills, and/or the re-using of old ones, requires the linking of a desired goal to the use of skills to reach that goal. Once the group has agreed its goals, group processes also aid the reaching of the goals as well as providing enjoyment and satisfaction in their own right.

We have given reasonably ambitious examples, but you can also use a group to 'warm people up' and remind them of old skills. For example, a group could meet for a few weeks to discuss gardening (the members having been chosen for their interest in gardening, ascertained from their biographical profiles). After a few sessions, they may well be prepared to ask for a patch of garden in the unit's grounds and to look after a few plants. Looking further ahead, they could possibly be made responsible for a small budget to keep the unit decorated with seasonal plants.

So projects with this purpose don't have to look dramatic, but for the person achieving new skills – seeing their life story in type on paper – or realizing that they can get tremendous pleasure from their existing skills, which they thought they'd lost – coming off stage after singing a love song their Mother taught them – the changes can be dramatic. Their self-view is stronger and more optimistic.

Remember, yet again, reminiscence can be used for people of almost any age to help counter the effects of almost any disability or misfortune. In that context, what this purpose does is both *specific* – it gives the person an increased range of usable skills – and *wide-ranging* – it allows them to look at the future with an increased self-confidence. The goal of using skills can be harnessed to a wide variety of activities, once you get the right 'mind set'. Travel light, think loose, and you will find this is a very valuable purpose around which to concentrate a group.

Useful reading and resources

Explanations of Attribution Theory are to be found in most textbooks of social psychology, such as *An Introduction to Social Psychology*, edited by Miles Hewstone and others (Blackwell, 1988).

John Killick has written about his work in several publications: 'Please give me back my personality!' in *Writing and Dementia* (1994), available from the Dementia Services Development Centre, University of Stirling; and *You are Words: Dementia Poems* (Hawker, 1997) and a chapter in *Reminiscence in Dementia Care*, edited by Pam Schweitzer (Age Exchange, 1997).

Julie Ward's edited anthology of new writing about age and change entitled *I Can Fly* was published by Age Concern, Newcastle in 1993.

Joan Barry records work with groups for elderly people to share their autobiographical writing in group settings in *Social Work*, Sept.–Oct., 1988, pp. 449–451.

Jane Lawrence and Jane Mace's *Remembering in Groups: Ideas from Reminiscence and Literacy Work*, published by the Oral History Society (1992), is full of ideas of using reminiscence to gain a written record of people's experiences.

The project 'Teaching Older Dogs New Tricks' is described in Faith Gibson's excellent *Reminiscence and Recall: a Guide to Good Practice*, published by Age Concern (1994).

Purpose Ten

REMINISCENCE AS ORAL HISTORY TO MAINTAIN OR IMPROVE SKILLS

Rationale

In this chapter, we will describe what oral history is and spend some time describing the benefits to older people of undertaking oral history. The main section will be its indirect uses – to provide social and cognitive stimulation.

What is oral history?

Oral history has been developed as a subject area in its own right over recent years. A key figure is Paul Thompson of Essex University whose *The Voice of the Past* has been tremendously influential. Basically, Thompson pointed out that we are taught history in school as if it were unbiased, and 'this is the only possible version of events'. In reality, he says, 'history' is the account of events that people in power when those events happened considered worth recording; and that people in power now – those who decide what should be taught – think worth teaching/transmitting today. The events so described and transmitted are those of importance to the ruling classes. They *may* be important to other members of society, but not necessarily – wars, conquests, treaties, trade, the coronation and death of monarchs etc., these events may be of little interest or concern to 'the man on the street'.

There are other aspects of 'official' history. It is not primarily gathered by seeking eye-witness accounts of participants. Rather, it concerns *written, official*, documents.

What Thompson and like-minded social scientists argued was that this mode of specifying what constitutes history left out the unwritten: it left out life as experienced by the vast majority of the population; it placed little value on these experiences and therefore did not record them. Particularly poorly recorded were the histories of low-status individuals, such as the working classes – both rural and industrial –

Table 9 *Differences between formal 'taught' history and oral history*

Formal history	Oral history
Written	Spoken
Major political and national events	More mundane, everyday events
Uses the entire country as its stage	Relates to a smaller, geographical area
Relates to the interests of the ruling classes and their property	Concerns the less well off
Propagated by books (nowadays also teaching videos) and through education	Handed down informally by word of mouth

ethnic minorities, women and disabled people. (The major differences between formal and oral history are summarized in Table 9.)

Oral history, then, tries to bring this wider meaning into the definition of history; and, for example, uses tape-recorded interviews of local people to try to get an account of what life was like. Such work is often a celebration of a community and its history. It also helps *create* community. Kay Isbell, a community work student working in the Barbican, the historical waterside area of Plymouth, in the late 1980s, found most of the pre-war residents were now living on estates further out of the city centre. In an unpublished essay about her work, she wrote:

> The oral history aspect took on the role of a communication tool. Interviewees suggested the 'next port of call' – often to someone whom they themselves longed to see. I likened my role during this period to that of a 'village postman' who read everyone's mail and passed on messages. So apparent was this aspect of the work that it culminated in a wonderful 'tea-party' where many old people who had not seen each other since childhood got together and pored over old photographs of their schooldays.
>
> Hopefully this party was the first of many.

It might seem that oral history sounds very like the things people in reminiscence groups talk about. There is certainly a similarity but there is a vital difference. In oral history, there have to be facts and factual accuracy. To this accuracy is welded the local people's experience of these events. In contrast, there is no need in a reminiscence group to be too fussy about accuracy. For example, a member may be expressing horror at the 'wrong' World War. Their horror may be appropriate and personal, so the group leader might well not attempt to 'correct' them. With a reminiscence group you're not trying to write a book, you're trying to run a group for the purpose you decided on. With oral history, a factual centre does matter.

Recording oral history

Obviously it will not be usual for you to work with people in an oral history project. Should you aim to do so, you need to think carefully about several aspects, especially who is going to transcribe the interviews. To give you an example, in one project I tape-recorded clients talking about important people in their lives. I aimed for 12 minutes of spontaneous speech. The interview takes half-an-hour and the 12 minutes speech takes 2 hours to transcribe. It has to be checked against the tape by a colleague – half an hour again – and then typed – 2 hours typing time after the transcript has been corrected a couple of times. So, to record 12 minutes of speech accurately takes, on average, 5 hours of concentrated work by three people!

So if you want to embark on an oral history project, you really must ensure that you are properly resourced – in terms of financial resources, person power and material resources needed – tape recorders, word processors etc. Most crucial is to properly quantify how much time you'll need, and to have some provisional target dates. So, even with a relatively small oral history project, you will need a rather large team of *like-minded* people.

This use of the word 'like-minded' requires emphasis. Oral history projects have floundered in the past because a large group of people have come together to research the oral history of their neighbourhood, but in their enthusiasm to get going nobody has noticed that half the group were hard-nosed historians wanting detailed accounts and the other half were welfare-types who wanted to listen to tales of the old days suitably elaborated and embellished by the slightly puzzled but pleased old folk of the neighbourhood.

A final point is that you will of course have to edit your transcript material. You really must know who you think will be interested in your oral history project even before you start the first interview. This potential audience will determine the content of the book/video/cassette and its length.

Using oral history to maintain or improve skills

We want to look at the use of history to help the older adult engage cognitively and socially. The key difference from the oral history we've talked about so far is that most oral history uses old people to *provide* information. In the use to which we wish to put oral history, the old people themselves *gather* the information.

We get this purpose rolling by getting together a group and agreeing with them a task that requires researching – the history of the local church/market/high street etc. The topic, of course, must interest them; and the oral history dimension means they will be working to a criterion of competence – to achieve accuracy.

Such a purpose is particularly useful for frail but cognitively capable older people. With the help of staff or a volunteer, a person in a wheelchair can go from the day centre to the library or local museum, perhaps meeting old acquaintances along the way, or stopping for a coffee on the way back to discuss with their helper what they have discovered.

Another suitable target group is people, again cognitively competent, who are socially isolated. The challenge of the task gives them a common purpose, making it easier to talk to fellow members and share information they've found; but also to relate to other people – people who have information about local events or buildings etc. So it can be a great boost for social involvement.

Anybody can benefit from using this purpose. People who have been in the psychiatric system for a long time and who mainly only talk to other people in that system might find getting oral history information very beneficial, as it helps them relate to a wider community. With sufficient support, and placing more emphasis on aural or visual material, the project might be very suitable for raising the self-esteem of people with a learning difficulty.

The results of the endeavours of the various members of the group will be discussed and pooled at meetings of the group, and will be put into some permanent record – or a wall display. Beware seeking to produce something like a book as an initial goal. At the very end of the project this may occasionally be possible, but you don't want to set such a difficult goal for your group from the outset or you'll minimize their work and their achievements. It may take a lot of effort and discomfort for a person with limited mobility to visit the local library and get one relevant book. This is a major achievement for them and should be applauded as such; but in the context of writing a book, it is a minor act, one very small link. So don't kill your project with over-ambition.

Goals implied in the purpose

1 To stimulate and stretch the group members' intellectual and cognitive abilities.
2 To help members share in the task and its challenge, and its achievement, thus increasing social engagement.
3 To produce a record concerning a given event/place/area etc. which highlights the local people's experience, as well as being factually accurate.
4 To put this record on display, be it an album, on a wall, in the local museum, on an audio or video tape etc.

The tasks

1 To select people who have the ability to undertake the research, and
2 To select those who have the motivation (or will have once in the group).

3   To resource the group properly, especially in terms of manpower, to
    help members move around in the community to get the information
    required.
4   To have access to the likely means of displaying the record – which
    may only be hard-backed board, but may require more resources and
    more negotiation.
5   To provide the facilities needed for the group to meet (see the
    discussion of 'boundary conditions' in Purpose Eight).

How to achieve these tasks

The first aspect you need to consider is client selection. We have spoken
of the need for cognitive competence and interest and motivation. Every
member in the group must be an active member, or severe tensions will
arise between those who are active and the excuse-making freeloaders,
who like the buzz of the group but each week parade an excuse for why
they have not actually done any work. You plan for this possibility.
Careful selection, discussed below, is the main key, but when discussing
the purpose and rules of the group with its members in the early
sessions and drawing up the rules of the group (again see Purpose
Eight), you need to discuss what will be done if this problem arises. It
might be agreed as an item on the agenda of each meeting; or agreed
that freeloaders will get one warning, and if that doesn't produce results
they will be excluded.

Of course, this is embarrassing and messy, so try to select carefully.
Also, look at their physical health. This kind of project goes on for
several months, so you want people who will last the course. To have
people dropping out of the group through ill-health, or even worse,
death, lowers the spirits of a group, besides, of course, decreasing its
size and its work capacity.

An informed consent interview with each potential member is thus
important, so that members know exactly what they're committing
themselves to. An oral history project is probably completely different
from anything else they do in your unit; and this difference may not be
readily obvious to them. So spell it out. It means:

- them using their initiative
- to gather relevant information or material
- from a variety of sources
- in their locality
- interacting with a range of people, some of whom will be strangers
  to them
- partly at least in their own time and when they're not in the unit.

Since the project will take some time, do clarify that this does not clash
with the discharge policy of your unit. Members must be guaranteed

that if they start the project they'll be allowed to complete it. (While it would be possible for them to leave half-finished work for someone else, such a policy is hardly likely to motivate them or the person who is supposed to pick up where they left off.) Of course, it is difficult to be sure how long a group will last, because it is hard at the beginning of this kind of project to know what it will throw up. The group should obviously go on till it has finished its task. If you are forced to give a finishing date, buy yourself as much time as possible.

In planning your project, if it involves frail people going out into the locality, do it during the months with the better weather.

One important aspect of this kind of work – or any work where the group fragments into sub-groups to do some work on their own – is to *re-form the whole group at the beginning and end of each session*. In flow diagram terms, the cycle looks like this:

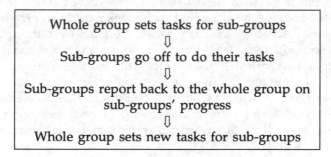

Make sure you have a regular whole group meeting at a fixed time each week to review the progress, pat each other on the back, see where things are going wrong etc. Don't let the fact that the tasks are being done by individuals blind you to the importance of people feeling they belong to a group which they value, as a motivator to keep on with the project. They can only do that if they take part regularly in the group. Also, if the group fragments into individuals and pairs, there will be no common bond and loyalty to the group. This makes it quite likely that differences in goals and agendas cannot get resolved, resulting in the group falling apart. You must maintain the reality and primacy of the group over the individual.

Obviously, you need to choose a topic that will interest the group members, but it should also interest you, so that you are excited by the project's development. Your enthusiasm is the starter fuel of the project. Do watch out for one pitfall in this. If you are an incomer to an area you may well enjoy finding out about it, visiting its nooks and crannies. People who've lived there all their lives will see it differently. They take it for granted – it's just their home town. So do check out the actual level of enthusiasm for the project *with the members* and don't just project your own enthusiasm on to them.

One final piece of advice: the intellectual challenge and the inter-personal challenge of meeting new people create a framework within which your members will experience success and, of course, the occasional failure. So don't get too task-orientated. In the same vein, allow opportunities of time and space for the members to share their reminiscences of the period you're researching; and also of their experiences in the field. Make sure your project has time for competence and also time for relaxation and camaraderie.

Examples of work for this purpose

A good description of the effect of an oral history project is given in an article by Liz Bartlett published in the magazine *Reminiscence*:

A colleague, Diana Senior, describes the work she has done with residents from a group care setting in Thame near Oxford:
'Eight residents from the home were brought over to the adult education centre where I ran a weekly reminiscence session. Topics we worked on were connected with the area as people remembered it. People had a sense of urgency about recording "how it was". We made a small exhibition from old photographs of rural Oxfordshire accompanied by comments and memories of the group. The exhibition toured local libraries and was the focus of much interest.'
Diana Senior adds: 'When they were in the residential setting members of the reminiscence group appeared disengaged from their surroundings, apparently taking little interest in life. At the education centre they were hardly recognisable as the same people, talking, questioning the accuracy of one another's memories, searching their own for telling details or stories connected with the places we were talking about. Members of staff who saw the exhibition were amazed at what people remembered and had told about.'

Because oral history is a discipline in its own right, we have not found many examples of projects using oral history for what is, effectively, therapeutic ends. For example, Maggie Potts and Rebecca Fido wrote down the experiences of ten men and nine women who had lived for many years in a mental handicap hospital – the average number of years they'd spent in the hospital was 47. As each chapter was written, so it was read aloud to the group members, stimulating yet more memories. This is a very useful contribution to our understanding of such institutions, but what we have been discussing in this chapter is disadvantaged people *doing the research* that creates the oral history.

We have used a town's high street as a focal point in groups of frail elderly we have run in different parts of the West Country. The first time the group failed because of the ethos of the unit. The group leader offered to help the members portray or learn about the town's high street in any way they wished, but was defeated by an ethos of much socializing among the clients but little effortful activity. There were some good individual efforts but the group members did not become cohesive enough to work on a common goal. This was made more difficult as some members 'freeloaded', causing resentment among the others, but the ethos of the unit was not sufficiently task-orientated to have them leave the group.

It became clear, once again, that it required a group leader with determination to see such a project through and energize the members. The next time we tried the group members were frail older adults attending a day unit in Liskeard. The group leaders were Mo McGowan and Jo Warrick. This time a narrower focus was used – the history of the shops in the high street since the 1920s. (The 1920s was chosen as a starting point as we wanted a time period that the members had lived through.)

The second improvement was to be more directive. We allocated two shops to each of the members and they had to find out their history in whatever way they wanted – ask the present shopkeeper, check old photos of the town, check records, check against the memory of their contemporaries. The group met weekly to pool information and share their experiences.

A large map of the high street showing each shop was drawn. As the information came in, so it was put next to the shop in question – a nice way of acknowledging the contribution the individual had made to the group's knowledge.

This was a very successful and enjoyable project with members working hard to get the relevant information. What was interesting was that it wasn't the Second World War that had changed Liskeard's high street, it was the advent of chain stores, like Woolworth, and the (small) supermarkets that removed the small shops.

The map of the high street with all the information on it was published in an article in the centre page of the local paper, with a picture of the group and naming the members, bringing praise to the members on the quality of their achievement and publicity to the unit.

After a break we started a new group with a more ambitious purpose. Lamellion Day Unit is on the site of the old workhouse, much of which is still standing, with its original architecture. A workhouse brings out very strong feelings in people who were alive before the advent of the Welfare State. Those who found themselves without funds were at risk of ending up there, where men were separated from their wives and children. It was a pretty hopeless existence.

The group task was to find out all about the hospital – and a fascinating history it proved to be, of the institution feeding its inmates from its farm, the local authority building a house for a leper in the grounds, the accounts, the governors' meetings etc. The group put on a display of old photographs with text at the hospital's summer fete, and wrote it up in book form. The management were so impressed by the achievement that they underwrote a print run of 200.

A reservation with this project was that the group leaders may have done rather too much of the rooting around to get hold of the records etc. This is not to say that the members did not contribute some information but it was a smaller percentage of the total compared to the project about the high street shops; and setting up the book and negotiating with a printer was all done by the staff. This echoes our initial warning on oral history projects: we need to keep the beast under control and develop projects that are achievable *by the members* within a reasonable time span.

After another break, we ran another group dedicated to producing 'a musical heritage' to remember what songs and chants were sung in this part of Cornwall 70 years ago – the lullabies, the schoolyard chants, the hymns. If possible, we hoped to get them recorded, sung either by the group members or by younger people. These tapes could then be used by reminiscence groups. This was a group that never got off the ground, as the members found it difficult to remember many of this type of song.

Some you win, some you lose, and this is especially true with groups where, despite your best efforts, the chemistry of the group may be wrong; or the work may not go forward because members perhaps become ill one after another, or the weather is so atrocious that people can't go out. As we said at the end of our book *Groupwork with the Elderly*, 'Inevitably there will be frustrations but don't give up. After all, the worst thing that could happen to you is that you grow a little older in trying again.'

Conclusions

The canny reminiscence worker can make good use of the demanding standards required by oral history to create a stimulating, challenging and enjoyable group. In no way is this purpose restricted to older, frail people. Because the end goal is a publicly visible record it is very suitable for showing disadvantaged people who have low self-esteem, such as those with learning difficulties or long psychiatric histories, that they can achieve and that their achievement is there for all to see.

But do make sure that what is being asked is within their capacity. A project requiring access to many buildings is probably not suitable for people with restricted mobility. Reading of old records requires a high level of literacy and a good vocabulary. You have a responsibility not to let your enthusiasm run away with you and to be realistic in what you expect from members in terms of their abilities, motivation and time.

This type of purpose needs good unit support, painstaking planning, teamwork and supervision to help keep your feet on the ground.

Useful reading and resources

For handling the excuses people give to avoid work, you need Eric Berne's *Games People Play*, first published in 1964 (Penguin and other publishers).

Paul Thompson's *The Voice of the Past* (Oxford University Press, 1984) is the pioneering introduction to oral history. Now a classic of the field.

Robert Perks has written a couple of useful books on doing oral history: *Oral History: Talking About the Past* (The Historical Society, 1992) and *Oral History: an Annotated Bibliography* (The Oral History Society, 1990).

The Department of Sociology, Essex University, Colchester CO4 3SQ publishes a journal called *Oral History*.

The article by Liz Bartlett, called 'Between life and death: a space for memory', was published in the magazine *Reminiscence* in May 1993, issue 6, pp. 6–8. Generally, the magazine is strong on adapting oral history. It is now published by Age Exchange, 111 Blackheath Village, London SE3 9LA (tel. 0181 318 9105).

Maggie Potts and Rebecca Fido's book of personal accounts of life in a mental deficiency institution is called *A Fit Person to be Removed* and is published by Northcote House (1991), Estover Road, Plymouth.

Reminiscence Reviewed, edited by Joanna Bornat (Open University, 1994) is a useful source of ideas for this purpose (and for others in this book).

The History of Lamellion is available from the Day Unit, Lamellion Hospital, Station Road, Liskeard, Cornwall.

If you want the history of the 1930s and the Second World War as seen by ordinary people and not as 'official histories' would have it, you could look at the Mass Observation Archive at the University of Sussex, Brighton BN1 9QL.

Purpose Eleven

REMINISCENCE TO AID INTERGENERATIONAL COMMUNICATION

Rationale

In this purpose, we aim to establish an initial relationship between young and older people, and then to embark upon a reminiscence project. In all probability the young will learn from the old, about custom, culture, and a way of life that was. These long-stored memories can then be documented. So, one key aspect is to create and further the process by which older people *impart their experience and knowledge to the young*. In so doing they will leave a record, a legacy of experiences of a passing generation, something to show they have been there, that they have lived. For the young, you may be assisting in their quest for knowledge of how people lived, how things worked, how people managed without a refrigerator/washing machine/inside toilet. The answers can be found in books but there is so much more richness and colour in stories which unfold in the telling of the tale. How much more rewarding to be told by someone who has lived it, binding it together with anecdotal episodes interspersed throughout. Which leads us to the second key aspect: in facilitating this process we make a bridge between generations, *opening up communication* between young and old.

This purpose can lead into learning new skills (see Purpose Nine). The young have the confidence of youth and therefore will readily try new techniques which the older person may approach with uncertainty and self-doubt. However, once respect and trust is established between older and younger members, new avenues may open up. The older person aided by their new-found companion may try the computer, the slide projector, the video camera, writing and painting, venturing into, for them, untried territory.

The point we want to stress is that intergenerational communication is and should be both ways – the obvious giving of knowledge and experience of the old to the young, but *also* the giving of vitality and

exploratory risk-taking from the young to the old – and in these interactions, opportunities arise for both to free themselves from prejudices
and stereotypes.

For example, Maria Faer described a '38-week Intergenerational Life
History Project designed to create a collaboration in a lower socio-
economic neighbourhood between 50 elderly people in the community
ages 80 and older [whose life reminiscences make them historians] and
50 high school seniors [who became scribes by writing down the elderly
people's oral histories]'. Her goals were: 'to impact positively the
physical and mental health of an adolescent and an elderly population'.

We have stressed communication with the young as the second key
aspect in this purpose. In this we do not mean the young person chatting
to Granny or old Uncle Fred, who are included in that young person's
family life and where the bonds for communication have already been
established. Rather, we are concerned with those older people who have
been assessed as being in need of the support and care of a residential
home, hospital, day centre or sheltered housing. For many of these
people communication with another person, let alone the young, has
become limited and, in some cases, non-existent. To the young person,
they are also strangers. The divide between a young person of 6/16
years and an older person of 80/90 is vast, not only in years but in what
the media portray as beautiful, young and productive versus ugly, old
and useless. In order that the young do not blindly accept these images
of the older person, we can assist in breaking down this picture of
worthless old age. By using the medium of reminiscence, interaction can
be facilitated and the young can come to acknowledge the older person
as having wisdom, experience, humour and a vast store of knowledge.
In so doing a mutual understanding may develop, with the older person
learning from the young about fashion, music, custom, culture and their
way of life. Older people have seen enormous changes since their youth,
with some still holding bigoted beliefs about people from other countries and cultures and narrow-minded views regarding a person's
sexuality. In an open and trusting environment these can be discussed
and, perhaps, dispelled.

Background

It is not clear when education and welfare workers began to attach
importance to linking young and old. Certainly one strand was a growing awareness, during the 1980s, of the need for input with regard to the
social and emotional needs of those older people in residential care.
Wanting to forge a link between the young and older people and to
utilize another source of input into a residential home, contact with local
schools was encouraged.

These ideas and schemes were being discussed and implemented in
many parts of the country. In our case, working in the East End, we

experimented by approaching the head teacher of a local secondary school to discuss a project on the lines of 'Adopt a Granny'. The title is patronizing, but the thinking behind it was valid, in that those young persons involved would befriend a resident. They would converse with them and assist in letter writing/reading, sewing labels or missing buttons onto clothes, or purchase small items from the local shops such as cards, sweets or stockings for them. We put the idea to a group of 15-year-old girls and it was favourably received. In retrospect, these young schoolgirls may have had a somewhat misguided picture of the elderly in care, conjuring up images of a sweet old lady sitting quietly knitting in a rocking chair. Of course, the reality was that the elderly people who were entering care were both physically and mentally frail. It was arranged that the girls would come along after school or during their lunch period. However, we failed to ensure that there was a real structure to the input and no one staff member was given responsibility for liaising with the school and for the schoolchildren when they were in the home. The new visitors were introduced personally to some of the residents in the hope that a befriending process would develop, but to the observer it was evident that the six schoolgirls were ill at ease with what they had encountered. The inability to communicate at a rational level with some of the older people left them tongue-tied and rendered embarrassed and afraid by the mutterings and incoherent responses of the more confused residents. This reduced them to fits of giggling, which did little to boost the self-esteem of those elderly residents who had some insight into their problems.

In this case the effect of the institution in causing visitor anxiety, and in causing loss of client individuality, meant that, without the initial meetings being carefully structured to heighten client individuality and ease communication, the very opposite effect to that desired was occuring – namely, the visitors' negative stereotypical beliefs were at risk of *actually increasing in strength*. However, this early attempt at an intergenerational communication project was not a complete disaster, as from this venture another idea grew and blossomed.

Goals implied in the purpose

- To facilitate communication between young and older people.
- To preserve a legacy of life passed from the old to the young.
- To assist the young in acknowledging older people for their store of knowledge and experience.
- To create a sense of community through encouraging shared creative activity and interaction between young and older people.
- To assist in narrowing the gap between young and older people.
- To assist in the building of confidence in the older person.

- To provide a setting where the older person feels valued and respected, and in turn respects the younger person.
- To provide a stimulating and enjoyable involvement for both the young and the older person.
- To assist in breaking down the stereotypical assumptions ascribed to older people by younger people, and vice versa.

The tasks

Having recognized and accepted the goals in this purpose, it is the group leader's task to facilitate the opportunity for them to happen. First, the project must be discussed with the relevant manager(s) and their clearance obtained. Then, clients need to be identified who would like to do this kind of project. It may be easier to work with a group that is already established, such as an existing reminiscence group (see Purpose Nine: developing new skills).

With these two building blocks in place, the leader moves into the role of facilitator, organizer and go-between – liaising between schools, youth centres and different religious organizations where young people come together. Having located a potential group of young people, you then go through much the same process as with the older age group – gaining the cooperation and interest this time of the teachers/youth workers and of the young people themselves. You will want to be satisfied that they are fully committed to the task with regard to the day, actual time of the input and over a specified number of weeks.

In facilitating communication between generations you need to create and support an environment in which respect and trust can be established. Through the medium of reminiscence, the group leader can provide a mechanism by which this can be achieved.

How to achieve these tasks

Initially it can appear that the divide between the young and the older person is so wide that to bridge it seems almost impossible. However, with the right materials, attitude and objectives, affiliation between young and older people is certainly achievable.

Because of their own self-awareness, the majority of young people aged 13+ often see older people solely in terms of how they present physically to them. At this adolescent stage in their life, taken up with their own self-image, they are not always looking at or thinking beyond the reality behind the presentation. With such a narcissistic focus, they will express beliefs like 'Old people are smelly, talk silly and dribble their food.' With a distaste for what they see (what age can do to the body and to the mind), some young people distance themselves from the older person. Not just in space but in how they interact, the physical contact involved in a giving relationship. This is an age effect, since the 6–10-year-olds, in contrast, in the main have an innocence, an honesty about them. Unafraid to touch, unconcerned with the physical damage that life has bestowed on the older person, they can interact fully at a far greater physical level. Therefore, when trying to bring about an intergenerational exchange, group leaders must bear in mind the average age of the younger group and the attitudes and likely behaviours for each age. However, interaction with groups of young people of whatever age *can* prove beneficial, since the fundamental principles remain the same, with the young learning from the old, and also the old from the young.

Maria Faer, in the article mentioned earlier in this chapter, writes:

> Research on the effect of intergenerational mentorships between elders and youth suggests that the optimal choice of a role model is an adult of like ethnic and cultural background who has survived similar life challenges.

This is probably sound general advice, but whether it should be followed depends on the purposes of the project (of course) and the degree of cultural integration/acceptance of a given neighbourhood.

Younger children will evoke more maternal and paternal feelings but the work will, of course, have to be simpler. Secondary schoolchildren, suitably prepared, should be able to work on a one-to-one basis. We hope to show that good quality and exciting work can come from contact with either primary or secondary schoolchildren.

Obviously, your assessment of the needs and interests of your clients will be the key to your decision about the nature of the project. However, also consider the distances involved: it is clearly simpler and less time-consuming to use a school or youth organization nearby. An added dimension can be that both the older and the young people will know the locality, so allowing for some shared experiences and knowledge. Transport – with its twin problems of availability and cost – will also need careful attention from the beginning of the project, and may even determine which group of children you select to work with.

Primary school involvement in a reminiscence-based activity

In order to prepare young schoolchildren for working with older people and in the environment of a residential setting, it is important that a certain amount of groundwork is carried out by the class teacher with the pupils. Through discussion, games and role play (What will I be like when I grow old?) the children begin to consider the needs of older people. They can practise techniques for communicating with people who are confused, shy or have sensory impairment, not just in the context of talking to older people but as part of learning communication skills.

An extremely successful method of initiating such a project is to have those pupils who are going to be involved take Polaroid photographs of each other in places they each choose within the school, for example at the computer, pointing to their place of birth on a world map, in the classroom. The photographs should then be labelled with their names and facts about their interests, hobbies and families. This information is taken, in advance of the children's first visit, to the unit, so that the clients are briefed and orientated. This pre-attendance session has a useful safety function, as it allows for discussion about racial and cultural differences. Occasionally, it will warn staff of prejudices that require the exclusion of a client from the project. Obviously, the schoolchildren cannot be subjected to prejudice or abuse, and it is a sad fact that xenophobia and race prejudice is quite common among this older age cohort.

This discussion may lead to a request by the older person to reciprocate the receipt of photographs by having their photograph taken. To send your photograph to someone is a stimulating act: it says 'This is me' and 'Let's share'.

The next step is to arrange a series of meetings between the older and young people. This requires some thought: one older person to two children? a group of older people talking on a theme to the class? Different activities will require different groupings, so what you intend to do will influence your thinking.

The younger child may soon become distracted and bored if required simply to talk to an old person. Younger children need something more tangible to stimulate and sustain their involvement. To produce something by the end of their interaction is more attractive and sustains their interest in completing the project. However, the work produced should not be so sophisticated that it discourages the older person's participation and willingness to try new ventures. We give ideas for such activities below.

DRAMA-BASED INTERACTION   By talking to older people on a chosen theme the children, together with support from staff and school, can formulate play-scripts. The end result will be the presentation of the creative work, either as a play or series of short sketches, with the children as the actors. These plays can be staged at the school, home, day centre or hospital. Themes for such productions have included: Preparing for Christmas, Rationing, The Pawn Shop, A Candle for Bed, Childhood Games, Bath Night, Four in a Bed. Parallels with the children's own life and other social issues which such themes can raise can then be looked at, highlighting changes across the years. By asking questions and making notes, the children will not only gain insight into the lives of older people but will be reinforcing that they are listening and are interested, restoring a sense of value to the life experiences of the older person.

CREATIVE WRITING From such interactions, short stories and poems can be written and read at the school, to the older people, and/or published in the school magazine or newsletter. Copies of these should be circulated in the home or day centre. Even the local newspaper could be approached with a view to publication. Creative writing also fulfils the goal of documenting a way of life that was.

A TIME LINE OF THE TWENTIETH CENTURY This activity can assist in helping people meet one another for the first time and get over their initial shyness. Working in child/adult pairs, each writes down four years that have been important or significant in their lives, for example for the old person this might be 1926 The General Strike, 1930 Bill got married, 1939 The Second World War, 1945 Peace is declared. For the child, 1989 sister Tracy was born, 1992 started school etc. The papers are then pegged onto a washing line across a room, stretching from 1900 to 2000.

ART-BASED INTERACTION Working in child/adult pairs the children interview their partner, discussing where they lived, families, childhood games, interests and experiences and illustrate the resulting biographies with drawings by the children of their partner in a setting where they wished to be shown, outside their home, work or with their family. Some of the older people may welcome the opportunity to draw the child in their chosen setting.

A HAND TREE With staff help, pupils draw and paint a large tree which is ultimately to be placed on the wall (of the home and in turn the school). Again working in pairs, the child draws round the elder's hand. The silhouette is cut out and painted and on it is written the name of the person together with what those hands did. For example: Kitty Brown – Seamstress, George Green – Builder; Mary Black – Mother of five. The hands represent leaves, which the children stick to the tree.

In all of the above projects children and older people have to interact, communicating in order to share their life experiences. In some of the projects both children and elders reminisce in recapturing the past, so that 'reminiscing' is seen as communication, not something only done by the old.

Reminiscence-based involvement for young people from secondary school

Reminiscence-based interviews or meetings can greatly assist younger people in supplementing their studies, e.g. Social Science, History, by providing first hand observations on local history, the first World War etc. From the teaching aspect, it becomes another strategy of learning, alongside reading, research, videos and so on. Many of the ideas suggested previously can be adapted to a broader and more searching level and used by secondary school pupils. However, it has been found that to have a small group of elderly people, say about four, going into the school with staff, where questions are raised by pupils on the past, has resulted in extremely positive exchanges; and of course, such exchanges do empower the older people and increase their sense of worth. Social issues with regard to the ageing process, health and social care and the changing supply and delivery of those services can be addressed. The arrival at some point in the proceedings of tea and biscuits made by the pupils assists in the creation of a more social setting.

There are no hard and fast rules to any of the suggestions put forward. Each can be adapted to suit your clients and the young people involved. Alternatively, the young people can visit the elderly people at the day centre or residential home. Where the home is organized in small groups, there will be few problems, and the young people can talk or work without distraction in adult/young person pairs or a group. Should the home be open plan, however, then a separate room should be provided.

General advice on intergenerational projects

We must stress again the importance of structure prior to involving children and younger people, preparing them in order that they are fully aware of the frailties, the physical, mental and sensory impairments, that age can bring. Timetables should be negotiated and commitment assured. We have found that with primary schoolchildren, one half-day a week over a 12-week period has been a sufficient undertaking. This allows for travel, preparation and organization of the session and tidying up at the end. Allow no more than an hour for the discussion or interview, so that the questions and the participants are still fresh. An hour on a regular basis is long enough to initiate and complete reminiscence-based work and for friendships to blossom. This can always be extended or restarted, should all concerned be agreeable.

Three final bits of advice. Make sure that the children know what questions to ask and that they understand their purpose. The children themselves may well have areas they would like to explore, questions they'd like to ask. So you or the teacher can start with brainstorming with the individual child or children and then the ideas can be brought together into topics for a semi-structured interview that should fill a session. The point is that anxious, uncertain interviewers lead to uncertain, unsatisfactory sessions, and must be avoided. So plan ahead to allow time for these planning sessions at the school.

The second point is that, if you are inviting children to a unit, you must take on board that serried ranks of older people, some with obvious disabilities, will be frightening to children, so you need quickly to establish the individuality of the elderly people working on the project. Move out of the day room, get some introductions started, and achieve some understanding of their past and present lives. You have to humanize and individualize the older informants for the children. If you don't, you'll get giggling and whispering from the frightened and anxious children.

Thirdly, if an older person is going to give a prepared talk, like anyone else they will be nervous. They may well write down what they want to say, and, if you don't stop them, read every word of their prepared text, which will be boring. Get them to rehearse it a couple of times using cue cards with the main points on – this gives a much more stimulating and 'alive' presentation.

Examples of work for this purpose

We ourselves have undertaken such work in a variety of settings. Our usual procedure is to get the whole group of elderly people to decide what they thought the children would like to hear – a list of topics (occasionally, the school would ask for certain topics to be covered). Small sub-groups then work on a topic each and build up the material. In the course of this, it usually becomes clear how many wish to talk, and the material is 'cut-up' so each person who wants to can say a bit. Alternatively, one member makes the formal presentation, and the rest chip in at question time. There should, of course, be a rehearsal or two of the whole presentation, preferably in the room where it will take place. This increases familiarity with the venue, ensures projector leads are long enough and reduces stage-fright. Remember, people who have been fine up to now will get anxious on the actual day, so be at hand to help and prompt, make recalcitrant projectors work etc. Group leaders must keep good control of the time, as sessions that start well with an interested and involved audience can be ruined by somebody who is anxious to give every last detail or just can't stop.

We usually allow about three months to prepare and present topics in this way.

A more ambitious project we ran was to have the elderly people write a play for the schoolchildren to put on. A group of older people wrote a very good script about life up to the age of 21, starting in the 1920s. Unfortunately, in this case *we* had not done our homework and eventually found that because of the National Curriculum, no local school had the time to take it on.

A detailed account of this purpose in action

The year 1993 was designated the 'The European Year of Older People and Solidarity Between Generations' and saw the promotion of involvements between young and older people. The area in which one of the authors was working had already forged bonds with local schools with some measure of success. However, in 1993 we were approached by a charity called 'Magic Me', which in 1992 had received the national Age Resource Award, being judged the best intergenerational project in the UK. Funding for a 10-week project was agreed.

The project ran from January until April 1994. Fifteen Year 6 pupils, aged 10–11 years, from Elmhurst Primary School, together with their class teacher, made weekly visits to William Kuhn Lodge, a residential home for elderly people. The programme, which involved a range of reminiscence-based art activities, was led by two project workers and supported by residential staff.

Contact with the school, within walking distance of William Kuhn Lodge, was made and liaison between the home, head teacher and senior staff led to agreed aims and objectives for the project. The head of the upper school was keen for his class to be involved and the project was planned with him. A timetable of visits was negotiated and a publicity leaflet was designed and distributed to residents and staff of the home. Two preparatory sessions with the children were arranged. In the first, Polaroid photographs were taken of the children to be involved. These were labelled with their names, interests and hobbies. The majority of the pupils involved were from ethnic minorities, whilst the majority of William Kuhn residents were white, and the Polaroid photos proved a useful introduction. The aim of the second session was to prepare the children for working with older people and in the environment of a residential home. The children began to consider the needs of the older people and practised techniques of communicating with people with sensory impairment. They then started individual project diaries which they kept throughout the programme.

At William Kuhn Lodge the project had been explained to the residents. With the exception of a few, most were delighted at the prospect of regular visits by the children. Not all fully understood, commenting 'Will they be singing like they do at Christmas?' The residents discussed the children's photographs and then, with some hesitation at using a camera, but with encouragement from staff, took pictures of one another to give to the pupils in return. There were shouts of delight as the photos emerged almost instantly from the camera. This proved an excellent and light-hearted way of engaging people in discussion with one another. The session took place at one end of the main lounge/dining room with two televisions being watched by other residents at the other end. No separate room was available for group activities. This initially made building a group atmosphere difficult, but it did mean that some residents, who at the outset were unsure about joining in, could watch what was happening and participate once they understood what to expect.

The first week's activity, a Time Line of the twentieth century, was designed to enable people to meet one another, get over their initial shyness and exchange experiences. Working in child/adult pairs, the group wrote on postcard-size paper four years that had been noteworthy in their lives. The papers were pegged on a 'washing line' across the room. This was an extremely simple yet positive activity which the residents enjoyed. Participants then took Polaroid photos of their partners as a souvenir of the afternoon and a link to the second session.

Prior to going to the home, each activity was introduced by a member of staff to the pupils in order that they could subsequently explain it to the residents. The children also began to suggest other activities they could share with residents. Each week pupils took part in follow-up discussions at the school, where they could raise issues or ask questions about what had happened and could recognize for themselves the progress they were making. At the home, in the morning, staff reminded residents of the forthcoming session. After 2 pm staff gathered together those residents who were involved in the sessions. This became easier as people got to know the children and looked forward to their visits.

Art activities built on personal details in the subsequent weeks. They included pupils drawing portraits of the residents in a setting where they wished to be shown. Florrie wished to be portrayed sitting in her favourite armchair on the beach with the sea in the background. Nancy wanted to be drawn with the background hills of her native Wales. This worked well, encouraging people to open up about their interests and lives and help shape the pictures. Many of the young and older people had been born in or had visited countries around the world: Egypt, India and Germany were featured. The children were keen to interview the residents about their lives and designed questionnaires about their likes, dislikes, experiences and families and illustrated the resulting life stories.

Over the weeks, collage pictures were made by adults and children working together, choosing magazine and newspaper images that interested them or reflected their lives. These were put together with photocopied head and shoulders photographs of the residents. The results were surreal, sometimes funny and very revealing! However, in feedback, the pupils said that this was their least preferred activity as they felt it was the most difficult for the adults to take part in.

The last week's activity was a Hand Tree, a group-produced picture of a tree, made up of cut-out hands as 'leaves'. Each hand was decorated with paint and stuck to the tree. This generated much energy and enthusiasm. The children said that they really enjoyed this activity because it involved most residents, including some people who had not joined in before. From an observer's standpoint it was a joy to watch. The children, without reservations, took hold of a resident's age-lined hand, gently spread the fingers out onto a piece of paper and carefully drew around them. The residents also enjoyed the physical contact with the children.

The end of the project coincided with the annual exhibition of arts and crafts made by the residents of homes for the elderly in the borough. This was to be staged in the Town Hall. Following on from the 1993 European Year of Older People, the theme was 'Solidarity between generations'. The Elmhurst pupils were invited to join their older friends on the day (along with other local schools). The work produced by the project was mounted on large screens. The exhibits looked good and were greeted enthusiastically by exhibition visitors. Merit certificates were awarded for some of the work produced, which drew cheers from the children.

The project was evaluated by those who took part. The class teacher at Elmhurst School was very pleased with the pupils' response to the project and benefited from gaining new insight into their capabilities. Most pupils, including usually quite shy children, were able to initiate and lead conversations with strangers in an unfamiliar environment. The teacher felt the activities worked well as a focus for interaction during the visits and was impressed by the high standard of the images produced. The children said they greatly enjoyed the project and would have liked more and longer visits. On being asked what they had found difficult the children said 'getting people to join in, especially at first and explaining things to people who couldn't hear properly'. Two children had found joining in very hard and had withdrawn from the project. However, other classmates not involved in the project had wanted to be. At the next parents' evening, some parents reported that pupils had spoken enthusiastically about the project. The manager and staff of the home felt it had been easier to encourage residents to participate in this project than in any other activities in the home. (Recognition must go to Magic Me here, who were innovative in providing new ideas for interaction.) Residents looked forward to each visit and their confidence grew as the project progressed and they got to know the children: 'When the children were there, the home was alive with noise, laughter and activity.' The residents, without exception, said how much they had enjoyed the visits by their young friends and were sad now the project had ended. Florrie said, 'I've never done so many things.' Both the school and home were keen to take part in further projects and to maintain the links that had been established. In May, a month after the project ended, the pupils invited the residents to a party and entertainment at the school.

There has perhaps been an emphasis so far on the benefits to the children. Lest there be any danger of an ageist bias, we finish with a quote from an older person garnered from an article by Bill Chandler, a head teacher on Humberside:

My first experience with this type of work was in 1974 with a seventy year old, Fred Watson, reminiscing about his experiences in the First World War at the Somme, Passchendaele and Cambrai. Mr Watson spoke sympathetically to eight year olds, avoiding the carnage but bringing to the children an illuminating picture of trench life and survival. He once said to me after telling stories of rats tunnelling to get at his cheese ration, trying to keep himself clean, trying to wash, avoiding dangers and trying to get food, that 'talking to these children was the only way I can come to terms with the colossal waste, carnage and devastation of mind and spirit'. As Christian Schiller, that great educationalist, said, 'The light in the late afternoon, with its shadows and colours of infinite gradation, is like the light of sunrise.'

Conclusions

In facilitating reminiscence-based intergenerational communication we help underpin social integration, supporting shared activity between two generations. It can provide the foundation for positive communication and remove the obstructions which impede a sense of community. It creates the opportunity for the young to acknowledge and appreciate the older person for their vast store of knowledge and place a sense of value on their life experiences. With work for this purpose we enrich the lives of young and older people and provide an environment that encourages awareness about issues of ageing, tolerance by the young of the old, and equally importantly, tolerance by the old of the young.

Useful reading and resources

As you have seen, there are a great number of ways that schoolchildren and older people can interact and share. The National Curriculum in History can give an impetus, for example, schoolchildren interviewing old people as part of an Oral History project.

You may find it useful to start with some material that is already available, to orientate the children to their informants. Many if not most libraries can help by providing relevant material. We have given the address of the National Sound Archive/National Life Story Collection, c/o The Curator of Oral History, The British Library, 96 Euston Road, London NW1 2DB (tel. 0171 412 7000), but there are also local organizations. For example, the Kirklees Sound Archive has 600 interviews with local people. (The KSA is at the Red House, Oxford Road, Gomersal, Cleckheaton BD19 4JP.)

Maria Faer's 'The Intergenerational Life History Project: promoting health and reducing disease in adolescents and elders' is in *Public Health Reports*, March/April 1995, 110, pp. 194–198.

Another example is the Mantle Oral History Project creating a sound archive of the people of North West Leicestershire. It has produced a number of cassettes of interviews and books (Mantle Oral History Project, Springboard Centre, Mantle Lane, Coalville, Leicester LE6 4DR).

Accounts of this type of work appear in the magazine *Reminiscence*, which is also a useful way of keeping up-to-date with developments. It is published by the Age Exchange Reminiscence Centre, 11 Blackheath Village, London SE3 9LA, which also publishes a wide range of reminiscence material including 'Reminiscence projects for children and older people', written by Pam Schweitzer (Age Exchange, 1993).

'Magic Me' describes itself as 'an arts education charity, founded in 1989 and based in Tower Hamlets, East London'. Besides its intergenerational purpose, it is highly sensitive to the differing cultural histories to be found in the East End. It works out of 33 Stroudley Walk, London E3 3EW (tel. 0181 983 3544).

The article by Bill Chandler appears in the Humberside National Demonstration Centre's *Newsletter*, No. 39, August 1992, pp. 20–21.

Purpose Twelve

REMINISCENCE TO ACHIEVE CULTURAL LEGACY

Rationale

In recognizing the wealth of experience and knowledge that older people have to offer, we can be of use to those whose past has been destroyed or lost, or left behind them when they departed their place of birth to start a new life elsewhere. We can assist by offering new ways of looking at the present, the past and the future, a coming to terms with where they are in life. We show that we value them and their history, by helping them to create and preserve a permanent record of historical interest that could be exhibited, or read or listened to, thereby establishing a cultural heritage.

Establishing a permanent record of particular peoples' history and experiences is an ambitious project. It is not necessarily a matter of documenting all the recent history of another country, but of one *way of life* within that country – the 'culture'. Examples might be the fishermen of a West Indian Island, the traders of an Indian state, the miners of Wales, the farmers of the West of Ireland, the dock workers of London. Of course, people whose families have lived in Great Britain for many generations equally have a culture to relate to, an account of a way of life that was, but, central to reminiscence for this purpose is to achieve a documented account in a permanent form from people who have left their homeland, their history and their culture behind them.

Background

Two lines of development have led to this use of reminiscence: the first is a revaluing of the migrants' experience, and the second, related development is legislative.

Peter Coleman's writings give illustrations of the first development – the re-evaluation. He points out that the famous psychoanalyst Carl Jung was particularly interested in the second half of life, and that 'the developmental psychologist Charlotte Bühler in Vienna had written, already in the 1930s, of reminiscence as an inevitable part of the ageing process resulting from the individual's need to substantiate his or her life in the face of loss of ability'. Such positive attitudes were not in favour up to the 1960s – we have already described the disengagement theory of Cumming and Henry, first published in 1961. Through the 1960s, however, a sea-change occurred. Coleman cites the example of Robert Havighurst, a leading American social scientist, who at the end of the 1950s was advising elderly people to *avoid* reminiscence (Havighurst, 1959), but a little over ten years later was researching the *benefits* of reminiscence (Havighurst and Glasser, 1972). This positive attitude, in a country with immigration waves as in America, would inevitably spread to the 'back-home' memories of those migrants. Thus, Rose Dobrof writes in 1984:

> I was then a very junior social worker on the staff of a home for the aged (in New York). I remember well being taught by our consulting psychiatrists and the senior social work staff about the tendency of our residents to talk about childhood in the shtetls of East Europe or arrival at Ellis Island or early years on the lower East Side of New York. At best, this tendency was seen as an understandable, although not entirely healthy, preoccupation with happier times, understandable because these old and infirm people walked daily in the shadow of death. At worst 'living in the past' was viewed as pathology – regression to the dependency of the child, denial of the passage of time and the reality of the present, or evidence of organic impairment of the intellect. It was even said that 'remembrance of things past' could cause or deepen depression among our residents, and God forgive us, we were to divert the old from their reminiscing through activities like bingo and arts and craft.

So, one aspect of the development of the ideas of cultural legacy was a re-valuing of reminiscence, including those of migrants. A second theme is political legislation.

There were campaigns in the 1950s by the British government to encourage West Indians to come and work in Britain in London Transport and within the National Health Service. These new citizens were, in the main, young men and women, some with young children; the older family members remained in their home countries. They were welcomed by poor housing, menial poorly paid work, discrimination and racism.

The 1976 Race Relations Act placed a responsibility on employers to take direct and positive action so that the imbalance in opportunities that existed could be put right. This saw an upsurge in the number of employers enforcing an equal opportunities policy which ensured equality of opportunity in the employment of staff and also in the *provision of services*. With the advent of equal opportunities legislation and racial awareness, the 1984 Registered Homes Act placed an obligation on local authorities to provide a model of service delivery which suited the cultural needs of the residents in their care. The essence of this model was that care was to be needs-led. It recognized that the needs of black elders were not different from those of the indigenous population but were *culturally specific*. There was also a recognition that those black people entering the elderly age group in the 1980s and 1990s were those who had come to Britain as men and women in their thirties and that they had brought with them their own cultural identity, which in many cases was lost or disregarded in British society.

Demographic trends indicate that there is an increasing ageing black population and the cultural needs of these older people have to be addressed if and when they enter the care system. Whilst information and literature is available with reference to the white indigenous population, only recently have the cultural needs of older black people started to be addressed.

The early 1980s saw the initial growth in popularity of reminiscence work with older people. At that time there were few elderly black people in residential and day care. Some staff using reminiscence were unaware that there was a problem in the material being offered to support this activity, in that it catered in the main to the needs of white people. However, as workers in various parts of the country set about meeting the needs of older black people and discussed with them their early lives, they became aware of the wealth of knowledge being imparted to them. Much printed or visual material has now been created (see the reading and resources list at the end of the chapter) and it is now recognized that reminiscence work allows both black and white to share their life experiences, thus gaining more understanding of each others' cultures.

Problems have been encountered, however. For example, when monitoring various groups taking place in residential homes, we started noticing unsuspected difficulties during supervision. For example, where we were working, in the East End, group leaders were often white or *young* black staff, and the language used was often inappropriate to the age or culture of the elderly black residents. Within the group, parallels could be drawn and with patience and endeavour excellent groups were run, but it was recognized that changes needed to be made. Also group members should ideally be of the same culture, involving people of a similar origin, in sharing and identifying with the recalled memories. This proved to be very difficult to achieve at the time, as older black people in residential care were very thinly spread over a number of homes.

During the group leaders' debriefing what was also being highlighted was that not only were the white staff unfamiliar with the stories of early life related by the black residents, but quite often so were the young black staff, born in this country, when the memories recalled early life in the older person's homeland or place of origin. While white staff and residents were learning about another culture and its customs, some of the young black staff on the other hand were relating these stories to their own families, having them reinforced, which evoked further questions that could be put to the elderly residents in the next reminiscence group. (Similarly young white staff were having the same experiences with the older white indigenous population within their groups.) The result of these processes was that the young were learning from the old concerning customs, culture, a way of life of a time gone by. Having an overview of numerous groups and bearing this information in mind, we began to think how we could hold on to these memories related first hand, these histories in miniature, thus passing on a cultural legacy. In so doing we would also reinforce that the older person's past and their history matters.

Goals implied in the purpose

In establishing a cultural legacy group we can help:

1 Preserve a cultural legacy related first hand by those who have lived it for those coming after.
2 Assist in breaking down ageism and racism.
3 Increase feelings of self-worth of the elderly history-tellers.
4 Recognize and value each individual for their experience and store of knowledge.
5 Actively involve older people in the process of documenting these related parts of their life.
6 Alter people's perception of older people, and of older people who had emigrated to this country.
7 Reinforce the staff/carers–client relationship.
8 Give staff an understanding of the way racism and discrimination can affect an individual's behaviour.

The tasks

The group leaders' tasks can be simply stated: to aid the achievement of a cultural legacy by a specific cultural group of people; to provide a setting in which stories can unfold and be documented. There will, at times, be a meld of different information and a telescoping of similar events but each story will be unique in its telling.

The group leader's role is that of a reporter, a scribe assisting in preserving those details that the older person feels should be selected and preserved.

You may well feel that you are embarking upon a more formidable task when taking on a group for the purpose of cultural legacy, compared to the other purposes. This is so: you are! More work will be required, in that careful notes will have to be taken of the group or individual reminiscing in order to render it into *permanent* form. The skills required are those of a *good listener*, an *active listener* and a *good recorder*, one who can recognize the value of what is being recalled in order that it can be recorded and is not lost forever. To participate actively in reminiscence is usually to interact verbally and listen, encouraging and supporting people in discussing their past. But to participate actively in reminiscence for the purpose of cultural legacy is to listen, encourage, support and question (the how, where, why and when) and then *record*.

STAFF SELECTION   When taking into account the qualities that have been mentioned previously, selection of staff to run such a group needs to be given careful consideration. You are embarking upon what will almost certainly be a lengthy project, therefore staff *commitment* is essential. This is not just 'another' group. Therefore, staff should be *enthusiastic* about such an undertaking. In recognizing that you are in the process of establishing a cultural heritage, a *resourceful* member of staff who is *intent* on achieving this end would be the ideal. They need to be able to *organize material* and also be *persuasive* in their dealings with people.

Check on how long possible group leaders intend to stay with the unit, or they may leave in the middle of the project, taking their enthusiasm with them.

How to achieve these tasks

Before setting up your group you must decide upon the aim of the project. What do you wish the group (or individual) to focus on? There are two main approaches:

1 **Oral tradition** – retained information that is passed on. This would take the form of detailing through discussion how things happened/ the process.
2 **Life stories** – personal experiences. The individual or group member relates incidents or happenings in their life and how it affected them.

For example, when looking at the subject of marriage for Oral Tradition you might pose questions such as: Did permission have to be sought? Were photographs taken? What arrangements were made regarding food? Where was the marriage ceremony held? Were specific clothes worn? An exhibition could be mounted about marriages of yesteryear relating to that particular culture, using photographs and memorabilia from the group which could be displayed in the unit or shared with others or loaned to a local school (this also supports Purpose Eleven: Reminiscence to encourage intergenerational communication). However,

Table 10   *Subjects that could be discussed in a cultural legacy project*

Childhood
Schooling
Adolescence (taboos)
Courtship
Marriage – weddings
Childbirth
Sex roles
Marital relations (expectations)
Ambitions
Cooking – keeping food fresh – recipes
Health care – medication – doctors – hospitals
Sickness – death – burials
Local industries – the work force
Religious festivals – religion
Major calendar events
Migration
Treatment on arrival and early days
Class differences
Major figures – famous and infamous (feelings regarding these)
Care of the elderly
Poverty
Superstitions
Work and working conditions
Budgeting – managing a home
Entertainment
Transport
Housing
The family unit
Shopping – food – clothing – household items
Holidays – days out

---

should the aim be Life Stories, then the individual would relate their *individual* experience. They may have had a church wedding, their photographs may have been lost or left behind in their homeland. Maybe there was little money so all of the family contributed by cooking something for the wedding feast. They will tell of the types of food that were eaten and how they had been prepared . . . and so on.

A non-exhaustive list of topics is included in Table 10.

In addition to the indignities of age suffered by white people, for elderly black people there may be yet another burden – feelings of almost complete isolation, the number of white residents by far out-weighing the number of black residents. They may also experience racist behaviour from some of the white residents. Staff must therefore be prepared for and competent in handling strong emotions, and being faced with the discomfort of hearing incidents of blatant and inhuman racism. This leads on to the need for supervision.

SUPERVISION   Supervision is an essential tool for any well-run group but none more so than that of a cultural legacy group. Pain and trauma have touched most people at some time during their lives and this may well be disclosed during the running of the group. You do not know *when* a painful episode will surface. While some white people will of course have had distressing periods woven throughout their lives, for elderly black people pain and distress are often a feature of everyday life in the form of racism. In all probability this will come to the fore in a cultural legacy group, and staff need somewhere to take this painful package. There is a danger a white group leader may leave a group carrying a burden of guilt; while the feelings of pain and anger, even resentment, may stay on for a black group leader. Planned supervision sessions will enable areas of anger, pain and guilt to be talked through in a supportive, trusting and open environment, which respects confidentiality.

PLANNING Planning, coordinating and setting achievable goals for the group, and evaluating and monitoring the group's progress, also assist the group leader in handling the stresses, enabling them to function effectively.

Before starting upon a group for the purpose of cultural legacy, you must ensure that all of the members involved are of the same culture. Do not assume, for example that all Asians or all West Indians will come from the same culture. Do not expect homogeneity of experience, even if all the members are from the same culture or sub-culture. You will get heterogeneity of experience because of the effect of class. Since class means that wealth is shared out unevenly in a culture, people's experience of what it was like living in a particular place in a particular period will vary greatly. Also, members may belong to different age cohorts. So expect a diversity of experience.

Discuss fully with the group what you are planning to do and obtain their advice and their agreement before you go ahead with the project (an informed consent interview). How often you plan to meet, for how long and over what period of time should be discussed with prospective group members. One hour each week for a period of eight weeks is normally sufficient for *one* particular topic. (That will allow the group to recount their experiences; but allow many hours for writing up your notes, preparing photographs, laying out the material etc.) A more wide-ranging discussion and recording of a culture will take many months. So the duration of the group depends on its task. You may find that the best way forward is to cut your milk teeth on a group that focuses on one particular topic, and then review what it wants to do next. In any event, predicting how long the group will need is a difficult business and management and leaders should allow for a few sessions over-run.

Staff must recognize that this is a time-consuming activity. Therefore management should be made fully aware of what you are embarking upon and time should be set aside not only for running the group but also for documenting it. It is vital that this agreement and understanding is obtained *prior* to discussing the project with prospective group members. Otherwise, everyone – management, group leaders and group members – will get disappointed and angry.

Finally, unlike most other uses of reminiscence, a cultural legacy group can become 'politically hot'. For example, a senior manager or a councillor may decide that an exhibition is giving an erroneous or unfavourable message, despite the fact that the words come from the members themselves. To guard against accusations that leaders may have biased the members, it is important to keep good records and to make accurate transcripts; and to have evidence that the members were involved in setting up the display.

MATERIAL REQUIRED   A note pad and an audio tape recorder – two is even better – are needed. A video recorder is useful if you are considering interviewing people. Should funds be available, outings that support your project should be arranged. Visit museums, exhibitions, areas that encourage the memories to be recalled. Outings to other establishments where people of the same culture reside or meet give differing views on the subject in question. This mutual support system can revitalize and enhance those 'blue, remembered hills', bringing them vividly back into focus. Your group could visit another establishment (residential home or day centre) or a group or individual could be invited to have tea with the elderly people involved in the project. Such meetings can widen the pool of memories to be recorded. In making such links, be sure to inform your clients what you are arranging and for what purpose as their agreement and cooperation are essential if you wish for a productive outcome.

Sometimes an individual group member needs to be interviewed in a one-to-one setting to gain more detailed material. Or someone who is ill cannot join the group sessions but the group is happy for them to make a contribution. When working on a one-to-one basis, the time commitment can be as little as 20 minutes, although longer is better (but finish before any exhaustion creeps in). Don't forget to feed back to the group the fruits of your discussion, keeping group and individual aware of the progress.

Should a situation arise where there is only one person in your care from a specific culture, then a cultural legacy project can still be embraced but it would take on a more personal stance, relating to personal experiences and an individual perspective. You will then have the problem of sharing the legacy. Members from different cultures might perhaps each make a display that is shown for a month.

Preserving a cultural legacy

Having established a cultural legacy project you have to decide what to do with the wealth of material that has been imparted to you. During the running of the cultural legacy group you will have either taken notes, or recorded the sessions on audio or video tape. You must then set about extracting from them those recalled memories that are relevant to your chosen topic and render them into written form. You need to edit ruthlessly until you get down to a paragraph or two that will explain the pictures and objects of the exhibition which may perhaps be loaned to you from members of your group or from their families. That is not to say that a video of a group is not a valid means of preserving your cultural legacy information. But remember, uncut video *cannot* be used; what fascinates you as a participant in a session will leave an audience fidgeting and bored. You will need access to editing facilities to highlight the points the group wants to make.

Secondly, remember that, with a video, there must be a *well-publicized* time and place for people to come to see the film. To invite group members to speak after the showing of their video which nobody has turned up to, is to give them a cruel and heartbreaking experience.

EXHIBITING OR DISPLAYING YOUR PROJECT You can be really enterprising and approach your local history museum, or contact your local paper offering an article for print. Should a room be available, you could create your own mini-museum, your own reminiscence centre where groups can be taken into a setting that re-affirms their culture and supports their memories. Should this be too ambitious and resources not be available, mount your exhibition on the walls of your unit's lounge or on the walls of corridors or entrance lobby. A good vehicle to display your pictures and written material are the room dividers that are often used in residential homes and day centres. An added bonus is that they can be moved to another room for others to see without disturbing the material. Take very good care of photographs or mementoes on loan; they are a very precious part of someone's life. A good photographer can reproduce photographs for you and take away the worry of them being lost or damaged. With items of value, insurance may need to be considered.

Examples of work for this purpose

We have difficulty in giving many examples of cultural legacy groups. This is because many units have only one or two members of similar cultures, for example Jamaicans or Sikhs, which makes a group unachievable. For this reason, we strongly suggest that the creation of such groups is shared by a number of units, despite all the problems of staff coordination and transport. The very act of travelling outside the unit to see other people can be stimulating. If this is coupled with a well-run group providing access to 'a community of memories', such a group will make a major contribution to the members' wellbeing.

As you will see in the first example given below, you *can* work with only one or two people, but do make sure that they really want to undertake the task and feel up to it. Make sure you don't impose your interests and hopes on them.

So we have to begin with an apology for an over-representation of British white sub-cultures that have disappeared.

One group we ran that developed into a legacy group did not start that way. We had been running a reminiscence group in a local authority residential home in order to produce social stimulation. Six residents with varying frailties met regularly each week. In the group were two men – Charlie and Henry – both involved in the group, but remaining on the periphery. However, when it came to discussing working life, there was a noticeable change in them. Both had worked in the London Docks. They painted a vivid picture of a way of life that was (sadly the Docks are now closed), informing members that the Docks had a life of its own, i.e. a culture. Inside the Docks had been shops, cafes, public houses and industries: there were shipbuilders, chandlers, a railway and a hospital. The life force of the Docks had been the people – customs men, lightermen (men who towed the barges), crane drivers, the dockers (who discharged the ships), the stevedores (who loaded the ships), the ship cleaners (scrubbers).

There was even a language: 'dockology' was how they referred to it. The words were English, but the meaning of those words could be quite different from what we understood them to mean. For example, the word *'under'* was shouted meaning 'take cover' as a warning of danger of falling cargo from above. Dock workers were not allowed to smoke in the docks and the Port of London Authority Police would keep a watchful eye out to curb this practice. At the sight of one of these figures, the men would call out *'cabbage'* to alert others that the police were in the area. Should the men say they were going to *'rover'* this meant they were going for a tea break. This name was adopted from a cocoa drink of years past called Rover. They spoke of the seamen sleeping on a *'Donkey's breakfast'*, which turned out to be a straw-filled mattress. There was even a name for the public toilet, *'The Iron Lung'*, which was built in the style of a French open toilet. (Although the Docks have closed and been razed to the ground the 'Iron Lung' remains and can be found situated at a junction between the Royal Albert Dock and the Royal Victoria Dock in Newham.)

Following the debriefing after the group, Charlie and Henry's memories of life in the London Docks were discussed. It was recognized that a way of life was passing and, in order to preserve this culture, it should be documented. Following a discussion with the officer-in-charge, meetings were set up with Charlie and Henry to record their memories of 'Life in the Docks'. Subsequent visits to the Local Studies Library resulted in pictures of the working life of the Docks corresponding with their recalled memories being exhibited in the home alongside their life stories. These in turn were exhibited and used many times as prompts and cues when discussing the topic 'Men at Work' with other reminiscence groups in the London area.

A second example concerns Lillian, who had come to England from St Kitts. She told of her first memories of England, of her first winter and the biting cold. She told of how the use of oil fires had been the cause of many accidents and even death. Developing a palate for English food had been another milestone to overcome. The biggest heartache was at having to leave her two children with her mother in the West Indies. She related her pain at her first experiences of racism, of having doors slammed in her face because of her colour.

Members of the community may wish to record their experiences of specific important events. This might be memories of the war, a 'Lest We Forget' record of what happened and who never came home; of a disaster – say a mining tragedy; or of the loss of a way of life – the end of a fishing community. The range of topics is vast, as is the range of people who might wish to contribute to leaving a legacy of their experiences.

A detailed account of this purpose in action

Having run a number of reminiscence sessions in a 'group living' residential home, what had come to the fore was how well the women had managed on very little money. Following the close of the group and subsequent discussions with the officer-in-charge, after an eight week break it was put to the women from the group that we would like to set up a cultural legacy group on managing a home called 'Making the Money Go Round'. It was explained that notes would be taken, the sessions would be recorded and the end result would be exhibited in the home and, with their permission, loaned to other homes or local schools. Should they wish to be involved then they might like to set their minds to thinking how they had managed. All eight women (there were no men in this unit at the time) were delighted with the idea and that we were re-assembling, as they had missed the weekly meetings. Following numerous questions regarding what we meant by recording and exhibiting what they had to say, they seemed extremely pleased with the prospect.

Our first meeting looked at the use of an audio tape for the purpose of recording the session. However, recognizing that some of the members spoke very softly, we felt notes should also be taken. Group leaders agreed to take notes in turn. We involved the members in the discussion from the beginning, deciding on what material was required, how long each session should take and how long the project would go on for. One of the group agreed to take control of the tape recorder. Actually, this involved little more than pressing a button to start and stop it, but the giving of control and of confidentiality was important. Another agreed to look after our book in which we were to paste our findings.

The second session opened with a discussion on pawn shops and how they were a source of additional funds. Towards the end of the week when the money had gone, items to pawn were sought: Dad's suit, china, clocks, watches, wedding rings, even the linen from the bed was '*hocked*'. The money obtained from the pledged item would provide for another meal. However, it was stressed that Dad's suit would have to be redeemed before the weekend as he would be wanting to wear it and would be unaware of the transactions that had taken place!

The third session told of the 'tally men', who sold various items of clothing, household linen etc., at the door. They would call each week selling their wares. Payment would be on a weekly basis. Should funds be low when the 'tally-man' called for payment 'you let him take it out on the knocker' or sent one of the kiddies to the door to inform him 'mum's out'. Another way of making the money go round was to purchase another item from this doorstep salesman, make the initial payment, and once he was out of sight take the new item to the pawn-shop to pledge.

In the next session the group members talked of the money lenders. There were not only men who did this for a profession, but also often seemingly ordinary housewives who had acquired a little nest egg. This windfall was often the result of a compensatory payment following an industrial accident to a family member. In general, the group felt this was the worst form of debt to get into, as the interest rate was very high and the debt just grew and grew.

The practice of purchasing goods 'on tick' from the corner shop required the shop owner to keep records of each purchase made by a customer who requested goods on credit. This resulted in a cumulative amount of money building up, which would be paid (or part payment made) each week. The members felt that they would have been unable to exist without this method of payment.

Another way of making the money go round concerned Provident cheques and the Co-operative Society cheques. These means of purchasing goods led to lengthy discussions. The members explained that a representative from one of these companies would call each week at your home. You entered a contract by which you agreed to pay weekly one shilling in the pound off of the money loaned, and a shilling in the pound interest was charged. You were not given cash, but a printed credit note which you could exchange for goods. The Provident cheques could only be exchanged in named shops. The Co-operative cheques, however, had far wider outlets and not only could they be used in any of their stores, but could be used to pay coal bills and funeral expenses. There was an additional bonus in using the Co-operative system as Co-op customers became a member of the Co-operative Society and were given a share number which they quoted after each purchase. A record would be kept and each year a dividend payment was awarded to each customer, the amount depending upon how much had been spent during that year. Group members laughingly pointed out that you may forget many things but you never forget your Co-op number! Amazingly all of them could recall them, with each member calling out a six figured number, one after another. Even one of the group leaders remembered their mother's number.

During their years as young mothers and housewives the women had been resourceful, taking in washing to earn extra cash, or ironing and cleaning for the 'more well-to-do'. Should you own a wringer or 'mangle', then you could charge a few pence to those who did not have the luxury of such an item. Staff were quite surprised at this revelation as it had been assumed that to own a mangle was commonplace.

During the course of the project, some weeks had been taken up with gluing written notes and pictures of a pawn shop into a book. Staff had even managed to get hold of a pawn ticket. Pictures of a doorstep salesman were found, in addition to pictures of a mangle, and a Co-op milkman and coal man. The son of one of the group members brought in some old coinage to support the project.

Having completed their project, and it was *their* project, they had imparted the information to staff and together they had achieved what they had planned, an exhibition on 'Making the Money Go Round'. This was displayed in the main lounge of the home for all to see, with the names of those members who had been involved, including staff. It had been a highly motivating involvement which had carried on over many weeks, with group members informing visiting family and friends of the most recent discussion in the group and of achievements. The exhibition was loaned to and exhibited in other homes.

Before leaving this project, it is worth pointing out how much of the culture it recorded had already disappeared. We decided to take the group on an outing to revisit their old haunts, only to find that the streets where they had lived had vanished under high-rise blocks, there were no shops left on the corners and the pubs were boarded up.

Conclusions

A cultural legacy project is a process by which we document a way of life that was, helping to preserve a lost heritage which can be passed on. It gives staff an insight into the lives of older people, establishing where and how their self-concepts were formed. By using the tool of reminiscence, the staff gather material on attitudes and customs from older people from various cultures. In developing this understanding we can also help combat racism.

Cultural legacy work is time-consuming, requires a long-term commitment and some awareness to avoid possible political pitfalls. But while these concerns need to be taken on board, it would be tragic if our note of caution in any way dampens enthusiasm for this purpose, as its achievement can do so much for people misled and mistreated by our society.

It may be useful to spend a few lines separating reminiscence for cultural legacy from using it for oral history or as intergenerational communication. Oral history has to be accurate and clearly factual, whereas, in cultural legacy, facts merely set the scene for members' history. So, let us say we are dealing with group members who were farmers in Bangladesh. We might have a map to show where Bangladesh is, and a one-paragraph introduction saying how many people live in that country; how many came to Britain, and why. After that, the members' memories, photos and mementoes take over, with a short explanation of each picture. Here we are giving enough information to let the pictures talk. In oral history, there would be much longer transcripts of interviews.

Cultural legacy differs from intergenerational communication because, whereas cultural legacy aims to create a permanent record, intergenerational communication consists of time-limited interactions between older people and younger people. They prepare a talk or talks; they are quizzed by the schoolchildren. The children may make notes but there is usually no permanent, public display.

This is not to say that the two purposes cannot be interwoven. Liz Bartlett, Coordinator of the Kensington and Chelsea Community History Group, has described such a project:

In the course of a project at a lunch club with elders from the Afro-Caribbean community, the topic of 'food' in one reminiscence session developed over time into a book with the title 'Nice Tastin': Life and Food in the Caribbean'. In it people described how, as children in the West Indies they helped to rear the animals; how crops were grown and marketed; how in the country areas food was communally prepared for events such as weddings and funerals and they shared favourite recipes and herbal remedies.

As the material for the book came together members of the club went in every week to two classes in a nearby primary school. There, as part of a carefully organized programme of activities which included art, craft, story-telling, cooking, songs, games and dances, they passed on some of their knowledge of the culture of the Caribbean. The children responded by producing wonderful drawings of Caribbean fruits and vegetables, they learnt how to cook potato pone (a Jamaican cake made from sweet potato) and other delicacies and they especially enjoyed story reading and story telling sessions with the pensioners. Over the course of the term the children noticeably gained in confidence, both in the work they produced and in their spoken English, something one of the class teachers had been particularly concerned about.

We will finish with one final example, a cultural legacy project in a poor area of New York, which has been powerfully written up by Max Kaminsky. He ran a Living History Workshop in the South Bronx in the late 1970s. This group was made up of elderly people from several different cultures. We pointed out above, when discussing the idea that intergenerational legacy should pair young and old from the same culture, that this may in fact limit growth and understanding. For example, in Max Kaminsky's group the members 'fell in love: less with each other than with the situation in which astonishing connections were made. The racial tension in the senior centre decreased, as an unlooked-for by-product of their work of remembering.' An obvious, if sad, commonality across the cultural backgrounds were race riots: one member's brother had saved his life in the race riots in Georgia in 1919 by 'shimmying on his belly' through the town, under two blocks of cars; another member recounted their experience of Kristallnacht, 9 November 1938, when the Nazis attacked Jewish shops in Germany.

The members worked up their life story into autobiographical narratives. Poems and images were intertwined with the text: 'At a ceremony held one Sunday at the centre, the old people handed these books down to their children and grandchildren.'

Kaminsky's article makes one aware of the worker's need to be able to handle not only individual tragedy and abuse, but to face up to and handle man's inhumanity to man. While we cannot take away these hurts and insults, we can reinforce and increase these people's present self-worth by recording their accounts of their previous lives and then rendering them tangible in a cultural legacy project.

Useful reading and resources

Re-framing reminiscence

Charlotte Bühler (1935) 'The curve of life as studied in biographies', *Journal of Applied Psychology*, 19, pp. 405–409. (Her 1933 book has not been translated from the German.)

Peter Coleman (1986) *Ageing and Reminiscence Processes*, Wiley.

Peter Coleman (1986) 'Issues in the therapeutic use of reminiscence with elderly people', in Ian Hanley and Mary Gilhooly (eds) *Psychological Therapies for the Elderly*, Croom Helm.

E. Cumming and W. Henry (1961) *Growing Old: a Process of Disengagement*, Basic Books.

Rose Dobrof (1984) 'Introduction: a time for reclaiming the past', in M. Kaminsky (ed.), *The Uses of Reminiscence: New Ways of Working with Older Adults*, Haworth Press.

R. Havighurst (1959) 'The social and psychological needs of the ageing', in L. Gorlow and W. Katkovsky (eds), *Readings in the Psychology of Adjustment*, McGraw-Hill.

R. Havighurst and L.E. Glaser (1972) 'An exploratory study of reminiscence', *Journal of Gerontology*, 27, pp. 235–253.

C.G. Jung (1933) *Modern Man in Search of a Soul*, Routledge and Kegan Paul.

Background reading on the migrant experience

Faith Gibson (1994) *Reminiscence and Recall: A Guide to Good Practice*, Age Concern (outlines various areas of concern that should be addressed prior to embarking upon reminiscence with people from different countries and cultures).
Dilip Hiroc (1973) *Black British, White British*, Pelican.
Paul Thompson (1988) *The Voice from the Past*, Oxford University Press.
A Place to Stay – Memories of Pensioners from Many Lands, Age Exchange, 11 Blackheath Village, London SE3 9LA.
Remedies and Recipes – Reflections on Health and Diet by Caribbean Elders, Age Exchange, 11 Blackheath Village, London SE3 9LA.
'Ethnicity and National Identity', *Oral History, Journal of the Oral History Society*, 1993, 21 (1) (whole issue devoted to this topic).

Other resources

Many organizations and libraries have started gathering material relevant to the cultural legacy of their residents. Some of these are:

Leicester Library Service, Bishop Street, Leicester LE1 6AA (tel. 0116 255 6699) have now established the 'Leicestershire Multi Cultural Oral and Pictorial Archive Project' and from this the following audio tapes have been produced:
Shari Songs – Wedding Songs as Remembered
Traditional Folk and Religious Tales – Jewel Language
Story Tape in Gujurat and English
'Memories of Highfield – memories of Black and White elders'

The Hammersmith and Fulham Community History Series (available through The Ethnic Communities Oral History Project, Shepherds Bush Library, 7 Uxbridge Road, London W12 8LJ):

The Irish in Exile – Stories of Emigration
Passport to Exile – The Polish Way to London
In Exile – Iranian Recollections
The Motherland Calls – African–Caribbean Experiences
The Forgotten Lives – Travellers on the Westway Site
Xeni – Greek Cypriots in London
Ship of Hope – The Basque Children
Aunt Esther's Story
Sorry, No Vacancies – Life Stories from Black Senior Citizens
Asian Voices – Life Stories from the Indian Sub-Continent
True Voices of Women Coming to Britain

The Somali Sailors, a VHS video

The Museum of London (tel. 0171 600 0807) held an exhibition in 1993/94 on 'The Peopling of London'. Numerous publications, photographs and posters relating to other cultures can be purchased from their shop.

Kensington and Chelsea Community History Group is at 240b Lancaster Road, London W10 (tel. 0171 792 2282).

In the UK, Carvie Supple and Rob Perks have compiled a resource pack of a book and four audiotapes entitled 'Voices of the Holocaust' published by the British Library. Be advised to listen to it first before using it with any group – parts of it are very harrowing.

Max Kaminsky's article 'All that our eyes have witnessed: memories of a living history workshop in the South Bronx' was published in the *Journal of Gerontological Social Work*, 1988, 12, pp. 101–109.

Purpose Thirteen

REMINISCENCE AND SPIRITUALITY

Rationale

Many of the values that are explicitly or implicitly espoused and advocated in reminiscence work – respect for the other, valuing them, listening to them, sharing – seem to have a clear spiritual or religious component. These values are common to most religions. It follows that spirituality informs or is integral to reminiscence; and that a familiarity with and competence in reminiscence work should be useful in religious or spiritual work.

One of the authors, Andrew Norris, trained as a clinical psychologist and worked for a number of years with older adults, then later left the NHS to become a priest in the Church of England. To help him put across his views on reminiscence and spirituality this chapter departs from the usual format and uses the more free-flowing method of a semi-structured interview. The interview with Mike Bender took place in October 1997.

MB: Reminiscence and spirituality – how do you see the two relating?

AN: I think where I would start is to define spirituality, and without coming up with a sophisticated definition, I think the spiritual dimension to life is something to do with that which gives meaning and purpose to people's lives, and I guess particularly with older people, but of course, I don't want to confine it to older people. I would say that as older people's role in society is undermined, as they become less valued, then their meaning and purpose is much more difficult to establish in relation to those around them.

Putting on my clergy hat (or collar), in an increasingly secular society, people feel unconsciously/subconsciously that they can only get their purpose and meaning through materialism, through social status, through achievement and success and so on. In other words, they get their value through those things which relate to that which is around them. So they don't look to the Church and they don't look to a faith or to a belief or an omnipotent being to actually give a purpose to their own existence, to life. But I would argue that particularly as people get older, those material/status things are not available to them so readily and so they must look elsewhere for them. This means that, as they get older, people are confronted with the spiritual dimension to their lives in a much more intensive way as they are faced with devaluation in social terms.

MB: Does awareness of death have anything to do with it?

AN: Absolutely and inevitably, because as you face death, you are becoming aware of the limitations of mortality and of what mortality can give you in terms of worth and value. So again, the individual has to look elsewhere for that and has to try to put it in a broader perspective; and I think that perspective comes through a spiritual dimension.

MB: I see where the spirituality comes in but where does the reminiscence join up with spirituality?

AN: Well, everybody knows that part of the declared rationale for reminiscence is in terms of how it can actually support people's sense of worth and identity. On top of that, a person when they reminisce can reflect on their patterns of living, of recurring themes in their life, in terms of networks of relationships across a period of time. What it means is that people are actually being taken away from the immediate and are reflecting on a broader plane. I think often people will talk about how the events they have been through in life – they didn't make sense at the time but when they look back at them they can see that they actually fit into a theme. So I think that reminiscing about life events and their experiences helps to put people in touch with that broader perspective. Again, we are talking about spirituality in its broadest definition. The importance of reminiscence is that it is not about historical recall but is actually about experiencing events; it is actually about relationships; it is about living through events; it is actually about distilling the essence of events and experiences – rather than the factual happenings of those events and experiences. So I think the person is inevitably put in touch with that spiritual dimension.

MB: What would you say are the goals for reminiscence work – individual or group – in the spiritual context?

AN: I would put it, broadly speaking, as helping people to recognize that they actually have a place and a value, not necessarily in the values of their society, but by dint of the person that they are; that people can be valuable for what they are and what one person is, is inevitably going to be different from what another person is. Again reminiscence is important in terms of actually helping remind not only the person themself, but others, about their uniqueness. In so doing it is actually affirming who that person is and the fact that what they are has a particular place and contribution to make, maybe mainly to other people, maybe to art or music, or whatever. So I think essentially reminiscence is about affirming the value that people have and actually affirming how, and what happened in the world during their lifetime.

MB: So what are the tasks of the worker – you are mainly talking about working with the individual, aren't you?

AN: Yes, although I think within the group situation that people can be encouraged to affirm each other. Because some of our affirmation does come from how others perceive us and so on, that can be something which a group leader could seek to encourage. So they might highlight one set of skills – 'isn't it wonderful that Mrs X has got one set of skills/gifts – but isn't it also wonderful that Mrs Y has got a different set of skills, gifts and talents?'

Turning to individual work, I think it is about helping the person become aware of their distinctiveness and how things which they may have felt have been a liability in their lives actually may well have made a positive contribution. This isn't to do with trying to gloss over all the parts of themselves that are less easy to come to terms with. But it is actually part of acknowledging that we are all different. Like we might say that someone who is abrupt/blunt and to the point is probably someone who gets things done, whereas somebody who is compassionate and warm may not be the most dynamic person in the world, but they are people who are good to be with. So you put people in different situations – I suppose if I was thinking of it biblically, St Paul used the analogy of the body and the fact that every organ in the body contributes something unique to the body; and that without each organ the body is not whole; and that each organ, although it is different from all other organs has a unique contribution to make; and the other organs rely on it. It is actually translating that into lives and lifestyles that people have led and to say that 'you may not be a politician', 'you may not be a scientist' or whatever, but actually what you have done and have is something which is unique and important.

MB: Which parallels Erikson's line that the task of old age is 'the acceptance of one's one and only life cycle as something that had to be and that, by necessity, permitted of no substitutions'.

Can we hear about this Purpose in action – some examples?

AN: Part of the problem is that most of the examples that come my way are from dealing with individuals and so it doesn't necessarily mean that they have an earth shattering and dramatic content. But take a personal example first of all: Alison, my wife, and I met up in Scotland and a person who was very important to Alison, and who then became very important to me, was her great aunt. She was actually very formative in me getting involved in work with older adults in the first place. Now she was a person who was very reflective in her life and she had a very strict religious upbringing – Scottish Presbyterian, a hell-fire and damnation type of religion. I think what she saw in the happenings in the society around her were that moral standards were declining and she found that kind of change quite difficult. But in both Alison's and my involvement with her it was apparent that the upbringing that she had had provided her with a shape – a shape to how life should be led and how she led her life and indeed, passing on advice to Alison and I about how our lives should be led. That exercised itself in a quite explicit way when she made her first trip down from Scotland after 84 years and came to our wedding. That was a symbolic gesture from her setting us on our way, in accord with the principles in which she believed. We could have said to her that the kind of religious values and the kind of moral standards that she was subject to, we considered to be quite oppressive; but in actual fact they were her way of making sense of life and provided an order to her life. Our involvement with and devotion to her was, in effect, an affirmation of the values that she held to and our way of taking them on board as something which provided a significant perspective and direction in life. She was actually physically quite weak, but she was psychologically and, I would say, spiritually a very strong person. So here was somebody who actually had a very strong purpose and meaning in her life and that carried her through with great strength.

MB: And the link between reminiscence and her spirituality?

AN: We spent a great deal of time talking with her about her life and life experiences and things which were important to her and those in turn were translated into what was going on in the present. Our interest and involvement was a way of expressing affirmation in the things which she held to be important in life, and helped her to make sense of the experiences she faced – especially as she was growing older.

MB: Are there any examples of using reminiscence in your pastoral work?

AN: One example that comes to mind – a chap whom I got involved with, taking the funeral of his wife, and he felt naturally lost without her and he had been very dependent upon her, so it was a double blow in the sense that in effect he not only lost his companion but also his support. One of the things he was desperately seeking for was reassurance that she was going to be alright now; which perhaps at the same time indicated that he was actually looking for reassurance that he was going to be alright now.

Now he wasn't particularly a religious person so he didn't have, as it were, a natural faith which he could fall back on to give him something to help make sense and give meaning to his wife's death. Yet in talking to him, I could identify various experiences that he had had. In theological terms we would say we were made aware of the numinous – the otherness of the situations – things, like what it meant to fight in the war; and the sense of being protected and supported that he felt throughout that period, and then, the sense of companionship with his wife even though they were at a distance from one another. The birth of their children was an experience which he said in some ways was beyond words and yet had a very special significance.

There were several experiences like that throughout his life, where there was a sense of otherness. Through that, we were able to agree that 'well, yes perhaps there is a spiritual dimension in life'; for this person there had been a sense of 'a force' or 'a purpose' and 'a direction' which had carried him through many of his life experiences. And (although I wouldn't say that we got down to agreeing on points of doctrine!) actually from that, there was a sense that he was able to acknowledge that there was still a 'force' at work in his life – that there is something which holds on to us even though we might not be able to put our finger on it. That was a matter of great reassurance to him, so yes, if you analyse that, then you would say that was using reminiscence to reinforce the spiritual dimension.

MB: What are the implications of this approach, this purpose to mental health workers, on their daily rounds?

AN: I think the first thing is that it is important that everyone acknowledges that there is a spiritual dimension to people's lives. It may be implicit or explicit but it is nevertheless there; and also that people's lives are influenced by that spiritual dimension – sometimes positively, sometimes negatively. If we fail to take that into account, then we are actually failing to take on board the whole person, and we are potentially missing out on a very important driving force in their life. Elderly or vulnerable people are going to be particularly susceptible, particularly open, to exploring that spiritual dimension. And actually what we have here is potentially very powerful in a person's life.

Now as with anything psychological, when we are dealing with things that are powerful, we are dealing with things that are subject to our abuse as well as subject to positive use. I mean there are things which people consider to be manipulative or exploitation. But what I am saying here is: look, when we are presented with a person and we are presented with a whole person's life, what we are endeavouring to do is actually to identify what are the significant forces and influences on that person's life and we may talk about it in terms of, if they are deaf we may need to give them a hearing aid; or we may think about it in terms of, if they have short-term memory problems, we need to present our stimulus in particular ways and so on. But we also need to think about it in terms of, this person has particular moral values. These may be political values which may come under a spiritual umbrella. Those are the sort of values which give a lot of people meaning and purpose in their lives. But if they have particular religious values as well, then we must listen to those and we must see how those are helping the person, for better or for worse, actually either to cope with particular stresses in their lives or indeed to maintain their optimum quality of life. It is important that we are looking at a person holistically and I believe that that is one of the important contributions that reminiscence has made – that it actually has opened the door to aspects of older people's lives particularly, but others' as well. It has opened doors – it has validated parts of people's lives which other therapies haven't reached! I think that that is important for mental health professionals to take on board.

MB: Can I pick up on a point you made, that spiritual values can be negative?

AN: Oh yes, very much so. There are those who have a negative image of God – a God that is judgmental – and punishing – as being oppressive. And those images can reduce the quality of life of people. To give an example, I don't know whether you happened to see last night they had one of those television debates – it was about 'Should fewer people be sent to prison?' I was frightened by the tone of the debate because there were so many angry people there. There were angry police officers who felt that they were being let down by the Courts; there were angry victims; there were angry criminals who felt they had been dealt an unjust blow. There was this real sense – well, I would describe it as an evil that was around in this debate and it was bringing out this side of people. It was a destructive thing – it was appealing to the selfish/self-centred side of people's lives.

MB: Can reminiscence touch that?

AN: [pause] I would like to think so. The trouble is . . . Yes I would like to think that, for instance, that by kind of putting those sort of values, those sort of ideas in the context of what people have experienced – that perhaps that might moderate those views. But with some of those people you felt they were psychologically damaged.

MB: So how should reminiscence influence the clergy – either in present work or future?

AN: Well, I think the Church, in the past, has deluded itself that it has actually had an influence in peoples lives, above and beyond that which it deserves. I would say that the Church has tried to exercise a sort of bullying influence on peoples lives in saying 'These are the sort of standards you should follow.' I think what the Church has got to do is to, as it were, get alongside people and the kind of lives that they are leading and the meaning and purpose in what they actually experience and in a sense almost help people to reflect on how that meaning and experience expresses itself in their lives. It's the difference between God working from within and God working from without. I'm a believer that God is there working from within everybody – but actually part of our job is to, as it were, hold up a mirror so that people can see something of that and see the source of it. I think that people sometimes see that it's there. Sometimes they see that it is there but they don't actually recognize the source of it. So I think that reminiscence is important. I think that the Church, the clergy, have a lot to learn from other people's reminiscences because it actually should help provide a reflection of how God is working within the lives of people. It is actually showing people's meaning and purpose. If you are going to speak to people – you have to speak to them in terms of things that they actually understand. Unless we acknowledge what the values of people are, wherever they are; unless we try to tie in and understand and reflect on that (and I think that reminiscence is a great vehicle for that) then the Church will continue to become increasingly irrelevant.

MB: So they would need to know how to help people to reminisce?

AN: Yes – because unless you know how to start where people are at – then you are going to lose them anyway. In the past, the Church has expected people to come to where the Church is at – that is the difference.

Take the recent outpouring of grief over the death of Princess Diana. There was the nation, I believe, being put in touch with the spiritual dimension to life. The Church did OK in reaching out to people in this particular time of need, but here was a rare opportunity to help people explore what Diana's life and death meant in terms of their own life experience.

The media gave so much coverage of Diana's life that this obviously had a part in enabling the public grieving to take place. And perhaps people started looking at – reviewing, if you will – their lives in the years that Diana had been living hers. And to reflect on what was important about life, what mattered. And the Church helped the formal grieving but think of the value of what might have been gained if the Church had used the opportunity to encourage people to examine and explore the spiritual issues in their own lives.

I know Diana's death provided this sad *opportunity* to help people get in touch with their spirituality: but there are *ways* of helping people do this that the clergy should be familiar with, and reminiscence – including life review – is certainly one of them.

Useful reading and resources

The Erik Erikson quote is from 'Eight Ages of Man', a chapter in his *Childhood and Society* published by Granada in 1977; and in many other editions.

We cannot offer any specific references linking reminiscence and spirituality. This is less of a problem than it might appear as many of the leading clinical psychologists working with older adults are very active religiously, way above the national average, and they could help you make links in your work. There is a network for Christians in Psychology, so if you cannot find someone to help in your area, Esme Moniz-Cook, Consultant Clinical Psychologist, Coltman Day Hospital, Coltman Street, Kingston-upon-Hull HU3 2SG (tel. 01482 328807) has kindly agreed to see if the network has someone in your locality.

In the field of dementia, Alison Froggatt and Eileen Shamy wrote Occasional Paper Number 5 on 'Dementia: a Christian Perspective' for the Christian Council on Ageing (3rd edition, 1995).

The recently set up South West Dementia Services Development Centre, besides its general brief to support workers in the field in the South West, has a special interest in 'Spirituality and dementia; the spiritual needs of people with dementia; links with local churches; the spiritual and cultural needs and differences of individuals'. The director of the centre is Jane Gilliard and she can be contacted at Dementia Voice, Blackberry Hill Hospital, Fishponds, Bristol BS16 2EW (tel. 0117 974 1117).

The journal to help you keep in touch with related work is the *Journal of Dementia Care* published by Hawker Publications, 13 Park House, 140 Battersea Park Road, London SW11 4NB (tel. 0171 720 2108).

REMINISCENCE IN ASSESSMENT AND TREATMENT

In this section of the book, we look at reminiscence in the context of the delivery of services, particularly mental health services, by statutory agencies. Such services would include the assessment of need by social workers; counselling; and psychological therapies. So, the next three chapters, covering Purposes Fourteen, Fifteen and Sixteen, look at assessment and individual and group treatment.

We first look at the use of reminiscence as an assessment technique; and then at its use with depression. Life review work is now very popular and we describe such work, before going on to look at what we consider its most beneficial use – to help disadvantaged and disabled people come to see themselves in a more positive light; and from this improved self-valuation, start to be more effective in gaining their goals and fulfilling their needs.

Purpose Fourteen

REMINISCENCE IN THE ASSESSMENT PROCESS

Rationale

In this chapter we discuss various ways in which reminiscence can be used to understand a client and their difficulties by placing those difficulties in the context of their lives. This is in contrast to seeing their problems in isolation. Reminiscence used as part of the assessment process in this way can also aid the formulation of treatment plans.

At first glance, using reminiscence, when undertaking assessments, may seem a little surprising. Surely assessment is something that is done by ticking off – either the client's or your own ticks – items on a schedule or well-established tests of anxiety, cognitive ability etc. The problem with the use of standardized tests is that the person who is answering the questions *will do their best to tell you what they want you to know*. So, what you are actually measuring is their stance with regard to the variable they think you're measuring. All too often we see a very depressed person given a Depression scale who answers it to score as 'non-depressed'. Why? Because they didn't like being in hospital *or* they fear they might be given electroshock therapy if they scored as 'depressed' *or* they saw themselves as having something physically wrong with them but there was nothing wrong with *their* nerves. So what is measured is how they want to be seen and interacted with, *not* some underlying quality of theirs.

Another problem with the 'standard' approach to assessment is that it isn't honest. We don't tell people what the tests are about in any detail. So, there is often an air of mis-information about the testing situation.

Even when the client knows what they're being assessed on, they don't know the criterion of success or how the information will be used. For example, they are asked to make the occupational therapist a cup of tea, which they do reasonably well. Was that good *enough*? Was she assessing whether I'm fit to go home or whether she'll recommend residential care? So, there is often ambiguity about what their performance means, what will be done with the information, and how it will influence decisions.

The reminiscence approach may provide an alternative, or at least a partial alternative, to this maze of confused and confusing communications. One reason for this is that the person who is reminiscing is in charge of what they choose to disclose, so, in power terms, the relationship is more equal. A second is that the person listening is trying to understand that person's experiences, so behaves in a more respecting manner than is usually the case on the part of an assessor.

One starts finding this use of reminiscence in the literature in the 1980s. Basically, besides being more honest with the client, the underlying premise is that to make sense of present problems, you have to understand the past; and secondly, you stand a much better chance of doing so if you spend time getting to know the person. Probably the best-known or best publicized exponent of this approach is Naomi Feil, who developed Validation. We will discuss Validation Therapy in a later chapter but her basic premise is that people who are living with severe dementia are responding to *past* events. So, if we want to communicate with them, we have to learn what those past events were. We will then be in a much better position to make sense of present behaviour and speech.

So, in this use of reminiscence, we aim to elicit the client's life history as they wish to tell us, talking for as long as that telling takes; and in this way, we hope to illuminate their present.

Goals implied in the purpose

1   To achieve rapport with the life-story teller.
2   To achieve trust between the life-story teller and listener.
3   To get them to describe detail, light and shade, emotional nuances, not just global evaluations ('wonderful days').
4   In these ways, to help the person give a rounded picture of their lives.

The tasks

The tasks of the worker, as listener/scribe, are:

1   To value and respect the person.
2   To make the time spent together worthwhile both for life-story teller and listener/scribe.
3   If, for any reason, the listener/scribe is not achieving the above, to have sufficient awareness to arrange for another person to take over the role.

4   To make sufficient time available since it will not be clear at the beginning of the 'assessment' how long it will take.

5   To make flexible time available. It will often be the case that the informant will not be in good health and may rapidly tire; have good or bad days; have periods of greater lucidity. So the scribe needs to have a flexible timetable so that they can be available at the 'good' times.

6   To have an understanding of interviewing and communication skills to be able to elicit the autobiography.

7   To have the time to write it out properly.

8   To develop an understanding of the life they have scribed.

9   To be able to transmit that understanding to other staff working with the client.

10   To create the opportunity to do so.

How to achieve these tasks

We do not see the elicitation of an autobiography as being necessary for all clients. If a client is living in a very cold house, at risk of hypothermia, they need the means to heat the house, not the taking of an autobiography! We don't see that this use of reminiscence should ever become routine. 'We elicit the autobiography of all our clients' is probably the death knell of its usefulness. This gets back to the unthinking use of reminiscence we advise against throughout this book. Reminiscence work must be targeted.

But targeted towards whom? In this case, the people for whom it will probably be of most use are those who are puzzling you; those whose behaviour or speech/conversation doesn't add up. Here, an autobiographical account may provide the missing links.

We would also say that we do not see this method of assessment as a 'stand-alone' procedure. We may still need to know the client's physical abilities, cognitive or intellectual level, their Activities of Daily Living skills etc. – whatever else may give an understanding of the problem(s).

Besides not being a stand-alone technique, it is also most useful if the autobiography is shared with other professionals who see the client in a wide variety of settings. This is because we all tell different people different things about ourselves. What each friend of ours knows about us is slightly, but importantly, different. It makes sense, then, for the people involved with the client to match their knowledge of the client with the autobiography.

This, of course, raises the issue of confidentiality. Once the client has begun to trust you, they may well be happy to reveal quite intimate details about their lives, but they may well not want other staff being party to them. You will therefore need to discuss who will see or who will be told their autobiography before the start of the taking down of that autobiography. You will also need agreement with your colleagues on how you each see confidentiality so that you can clearly tell clients what the boundaries of confidentiality are, and what will happen to their life story.

This seems to be a problem not sufficiently discussed in the literature, which is full of cosy descriptions of life stories. If the person believes that a large number of people will see their autobiography, they are likely to censor painful or confidential events, and to simplify their account. All of which defeats the purpose of taking down their auto-biography. Time and care therefore need to be taken in drawing up *the contract of confidentiality*. The importance of other professionals being able to understand this contract needs to be stressed; for example, the contract might be permission to give an outline of certain events that happened in the client's life but not the details.

Time should be spent building up a relationship of trust before the biographical work is undertaken. It is unlikely this time will be wasted, as it can be used to help the client with urgent, practical problems, which helps build up the credibility of the worker.

What we are saying is that the usual concept of 'assessment' of people is flawed – that people are complicated, and to understand takes time; and that the role of the life story and its importance will vary depending on what the purpose of the unit/service is; what the client believes they are getting from it or should be getting from it; and their relationship with the various staff. The elicitation of a life story requires a high level of empathy and good interviewing skills. An unhurried atmosphere needs to be created.

Generally, a fixed time each week is best, and let the person know the time or topic you will be going on to in the next session, so that they can think about it, and bring in relevant material – photos, records, mementoes etc.; or write something down about the topic(s) you wish to discuss.

Staff interest in the project will prevent or decrease the jealousy of other staff members who see involvement in the sessions as 'taking it easy'. It is not a good idea for only one staff member to be 'in charge' of life history gathering as this will create jealousy, can cause blockages if that staff member is off for any reason; and also a team approach allows growth and improvement of skills through the sharing of experience and ideas. Meeting an external supervisor may also be very beneficial.

Examples of work for this purpose

Romanick (1983) wrote up a case study of a widow who refused all formal assessments. Since she was verbally and physically abusive, the referring staff had quite a problem. Using her photographs to engage her did allow for 40 minutes of conversation, compared to her stopping all previous interviews after 5 minutes; it also allowed a care plan to be formulated. ('It became clear that attention-getting and manipulative tactics directed at reassurances of acceptance and love were her way of coping with the loneliness, rejection and abandonment of her husband and being institutionalized', p. 42).

Faith Gibson used the biography of a person to make sense of troubling behaviour. In 'The use of the past' she describes a systematic approach to biography and observation, and discusses its implementation. You will recall that we advised that life history-taking should not be a stand-alone technique. In this project, staff did gather a detailed biography but also undertook careful observation of the person's behaviour to pick out rhythms, patterns, interactions etc.

The Gloucester Project in the mid-1980s, headed by Malcolm Johnson of the Open University, put care coordinators into GP practices. One of the tools the team developed was a biographical approach. Johnson stresses that it is an *approach*, not a *technique*. By this he means it is a way of relating to people – in this case older adults with a variety of problems known to GPs.

The team felt that the advantages of this approach included:

1 Understanding family relationships.
2 Finding out which kinds of help/services would be acceptable or unacceptable.
3 Finding out what strategies the person had used to cope with difficulties in the past, so that the type and method of help accorded with their ways of coping.
4 Uncovering particular talents and aspirations, so that, again, the care package could take these into account and be individually tailored.

The client also benefited from getting traumatic events into perspective through talking about them. (It seems likely that the process had elements of a life review – see Purpose Fifteen.)

Not surprisingly, the length of time spent eliciting the life story was a problem. The care coordinators found it more realistic to deal with immediate needs first and gain the life story more gradually. The life story took between two sessions of about one hour to several visits where autobiographical data was gathered at the same time as more immediate problems were tackled. Clearly, there was the issue of 'fitting' the biographical approach into a system of care for older people that, like everywhere else in this country, was under pressure. An approach which values the individual and which requires the building of a relationship will inevitably be slower and more time-consuming than high volume, sticking plaster approaches.

An approach we have used in a psychiatric day hospital whose staff were familiar with Erikson's life stages was a ten-session 'Getting to Know You' group. With the first session being 'Introductions' and the last 'Evaluation', the middle eight were used for chronological periods, for example years 1–5; school years; adolescence and so on, with a session on the Second World War and its effects on the individual during the war and afterwards. The Evaluation session allowed the members to specify events in their lives or current difficulties they would like to examine further. These groups, for newcomers to the unit, took place twice a week and so were completed within the six weeks allotted to assessment. Staff certainly found they gave a more rounded picture of their clients. Since the same staff did not take all sessions, good record-keeping and handover were essential.

Finally, Bender and Stephenson have suggested that individual cognitive assessments done by psychologists have limitations. Only the psychologist sees the person tackling the tasks and if they are not full-time on the ward, the transmission of the information may not occur. It seemed sensible to see whether cognitive ability could be assessed in a social situation run by the ward staff. Working with Cathy Douglas and Chris Garcia, of the occupational therapy department of an assessment ward for people with organic difficulties, we structured a reminiscence group in such a way that responses could be noted by an observer. So 'Can we introduce ourselves?' can be scored as to whether the person *does* give their name when asked. Similarly 'please pass this to the left'. Verbal recognition of familiar objects etc. can be noted. This method was found to agree highly with individual assessments; but it allowed us much better understanding of how the person tackled difficulties with regard to memory and cognition; and, being run by full-time members of the ward team, such information was much more available at ward rounds and other times when decisions about the person were being made.

A detailed account of this purpose in action (carer-information sharing on a long-stay ward for people living with severe dementia)

The admission of a person with severe dementia is a very sad and conflictual time for their relatives, especially the one who has been caring for them up to that point. For them to have to admit defeat – that the task has gone beyond their capabilities – is a bitter pill to swallow. There is guilt – perhaps they should have tried even harder, digging even deeper into their physical reserves (despite the fact that, if they are a spouse, they are likely to be in their seventies; even a daughter, or less likely a son, may well be in their fifties).

The admitting staff also have a problem, although in units which are primitive in their concept of care they may be unaware of their problem – which is that they know nothing of the likes and dislikes of the person being admitted. They know nothing of their history. They are in the ridiculous position – again perhaps without realizing it or only realizing it partially – of pretending this person's experience and habits started the day they were admitted to the unit, at the age of 75!

The relative is asked a few perfunctory questions that mainly seem to concern their loved one's dying – such as what type of priest to call – and shrinks away full of guilt and anxiety. The nurse has missed the opportunity to learn about the individual they have just admitted.

We have piloted a semi-structured interview for such a situation – where the patient cannot give an autobiography. The caring relative who knows them best is asked to come back and hand over the information they have on their relative's history; but also their habits of living – how they like to get up, their rituals of rising, their rituals before and when retiring, food preferences and dislikes, their hobbies when they were active, how they structure their days, anniversaries and other dates of importance to them, in short – everything that goes to make us the person that we are. We use the Biographical Profile (see above pp. 78– 104) with 'you' replaced by 'he' or 'she'.

Carer-information sharing has two main goals:

1   It allows the unit to become well briefed about the person being admitted.
2   It allows the relative to let go – to share their parent or spouse with the unit; sharing that is not without sorrow, quite often not without tears, but hopefully tears of catharsis.

The interviews go at the pace of the carer. As Johnson found, two or three sessions are usually enough. In that time, hopefully, a bond will be made between the carer-informant and the nurse-scribe, a bond that will move forward during the relative's stay on the unit; and which will develop because, in the process of information sharing, the carer has hopefully shed some of the guilt and recognized the inevitability of the admission; and shed some of their anxiety about the handing over of their loved one because a unit that takes the trouble to want to know all about that person's life, is likely to provide high quality care.

A longer-term benefit is that because the carer's energies are not tied up (or are less tied up) in their anxiety or guilt, they are freer to re-build their own lives and also to contribute to improving the activity level and quality of life on the ward, not only for their relative but for all the other patients. (See Purpose 17 on the use of reminiscence for relatives.)

Although we have described work on a unit for people with dementia, it is equally valid across a whole range of difficulties, as the Gloucester Project illustrates.

So far in this chapter we have looked at the gaining of the life story as a major way of assessing. The life story can be used in a more one-off, trouble-shooting way. For example, an elderly man became very disturbed at night on a general ward. An hour's conversation about his life revealed that he had been a Japanese prisoner-of-war and the night lights on the ward brought back traumatic memories of the lights in the prison camp. The therapeutic solution to his problem was to ensure that his bit of the ward was practically dark. Another example was when a lady's disturbed behaviour was due to the fact that she recognized one of the nurses as a person her husband had had an affair with.

There really is no substitute for gaining an understanding of the person's life before deciding what a piece of behaviour (a 'symptom') means; or what is best done about it.

Conclusions

Assessment through the use of reminiscence challenges conventional ways of assessing, which place a premium on speed, throughput and scores. Such assessments will only tell you what the person is like at the moment of assessment, and so provide a very thin cross-section of that person.

In contrast, assessment using the ideas of reminiscence makes little sense until time has been spent building up a relationship of liking and trust. On the basis of this relationship, it is the past, not the present, which is explored in depth. To be exact, the past is explored so that it is linked up with the present, so that it provides clues as to the meaning of the present for that individual.

Useful reading and resources

Mike Bender and Sue Stephenson (1994) 'The use of reminiscence as an assessment tool', *Reminiscence*, Issue 9 (October), p. 5. Describes the Reminiscence Assessment group mentioned in the text.

Naomi Feil (1992) *Validation: The Feil Method – How to Help Disorientated Old-Old*, Edward Feil Productions (Cleveland, Ohio).

Faith Gibson (1993) 'The use of the past' in Alan Chapman and Mary Marshall (eds), *Dementia: New Skills for Social Workers*, Jessica Kingsley, pp. 40–62.

Tom Kitwood (1997) *Dementia Reconsidered*, Open University Press. Stresses the importance of understanding the behaviour of a person with dementia in a biographical context.

Michael Romanick (1983) 'The application of reminiscing to the clinical interview', *Clinical Gerontologist*, 1 (3), pp. 39–43.

The Gloucester Project was written up as a series of reports from the Open University Department of Health and Social Welfare. Their report, *Care for Elderly People at Home: a Research and Development Project in Collaboration with the Gloucester Health Authority: Final Report*, written by Tim Dant, Michael Carley, Brian Gearing and Malcolm Johnson, is dated June 1989.

REMINISCENCE AS PSYCHOTHERAPY

In this section we shall look briefly at using reminiscence as a type of psychotherapy: 'reminiscence therapy'. We shall describe a few studies and then give our reasons for thinking that this kind of work is misguided, because it does not specify how reminiscing relates to the solving of the problems. It fails to explain the link between the process (reminiscing) and the desired outcome (lessened distress or whatever the problem was). In short, there is a lack of clarity as to how the purpose is to be fulfilled.

So far in this book we have been examining purposes for which no formal training is required. In considering reminiscence as therapy or used for life review, training in counselling or psychotherapy or clinical psychology or equivalent forms of professional accreditation would usually be considered necessary, and the reader is warned that they need to ensure they are suitably qualified before undertaking such work. This is especially the case as the amount of litigation increases annually. Even if qualified, they should seek suitable insurance.

Given the wide-ranging claims made for reminiscence, it was perhaps inevitable that reminiscence should be proposed as a means of psychotherapy. The most frequent target group is people with depression. For example, Fry (1983) found that structured reminiscence was more effective with depressed older people than unstructured. In the unstructured format, the patient/client was in charge of how much they explored a stressful event in their life; in structured reminiscence training, the therapist encouraged them to examine stressful life events in some depth. Presumably, this procedure prevented them from using their usual modes of avoidance and denial, and allowed catharsis and working through.

Fry had used five 90 minute weekly sessions for five weeks. So five negative events were explored in the context of individual therapy. Bachar, Kindler, Schefler and Lerer (1991) used a group format and compared reminiscence therapy with a 'traditional reflective nondirective' approach with severely depressed hospitalized patients. The members of the reminiscence group benefited more.

However, not all studies are so positive. Eleanor O'Leary in *Counselling Older Adults* (1996) has done a thorough review of such studies. She found nine studies, of which she says five 'did not provide evidence for the effectiveness of a reminiscing intervention' (p. 133). Two of the positive studies are by Barbara Haight and concern life review, which we will consider in the next chapter. As we shall see, Haight considers reminiscing and life review as separate activities.

We have used reminiscing as a way of tackling blocked grief in a day hospital context. Here, reminiscence was used for a specific end. There were a number of clients who found it very difficult to talk about their deceased spouses, and therefore could not process their grief. Working with a psychiatric nurse, Barbara Crispin, who had done a lot of bereavement work, one author used a format of asking members to describe their lives from when they were young. Since this inevitably involved courtship, marriage and family life, the members could talk about their loved and lost ones in the context of happier and less traumatic events. By the time – a number of sessions later – they came to describe the illnesses and deaths of their spouses, they were able to do so freely, of course with emotion, but it was no longer a topic that needed to be avoided. The group ended with the members cheerfully discussing how they wished to be buried/cremated etc.

In this group, then, we had used reminiscence as an indirect way of accessing and processing painful memories, where more direct approaches would not have worked.

A similar rationale for groupwork was used by Julie Lloyd in the field of learning difficulties. She co-led a small group of five women who had experienced pregnancy. For some, the pregnancy was the result of rape and only two had contact with their children. It was clearly helpful for them to share the horrific experiences they had been through and gain strength from each other.

When the group finished, they identified reducing their loneliness and continuing the relationships they had built up with each other as very important. (Julie Lloyd, unpublished)

We have, for the sake of completeness and even-handedness, looked briefly in the last few pages at reminiscence as therapy. However, we would counsel against such a use. This is because, of itself, discussing the past is *not* therapy unless it relates directly to any particular problem or difficulty the client may have, as in the examples above.

To elaborate, a good psychotherapist should be able to select from many techniques the one most relevant to the client and their particular difficulties. Where there has been a very traumatic childhood, they might choose long-term psychodynamic therapy; where there are difficulties between the couple or in the family, they might choose one of the various types of marital or family therapy; if the person has a phobia, such as agoraphobia, behaviour therapy or cognitive behaviour therapy; if they keep repeating destructive relationship patterns, transactional analysis may be most appropriate.

The analytic schools – Freud, Jung, Adler etc. – have done psychotherapy a great disservice by making their training consist of several years of the *same* approach. What is needed is that the would-be therapist undergoes several years' training working at the use of *various* approaches. It is the same with reminiscence. It is not sensible or professional to give the same method to all your clients.

A good example is provided by Lesser and others (1981). They found reminiscence group therapy more effective than traditional group therapy. This sounds impressive until we read that the patients were diagnosed as 'psychotic'. One explanation is that *traditional group therapy was never an appropriate approach for this group*, not that 'reminiscence therapy' was a particularly effective treatment mode.

So we are concerned with the logic of offering reminiscence as a therapy. We are, however, of course aware that there are reports – such as we have described – of people getting better after individual or group reminiscence work. These two points are not in conflict. This is because of what we call *non-specific effects* in therapy. By this we mean the effect is not specific to any one school or approach. It is common to them all.

Non-specific effects are the results of being a patient/client in a therapy setting and are *independent of the orientation of the therapist*; they are almost *independent of what they do*. For example, it is to be hoped that, whatever type of therapy the person is being offered, they will be treated with respect and be valued. In a group setting they will meet other people with similar, or equally severe problems, and so realize that they are not the only one with that problem. Also, meeting people is anxiety-reducing. Anxiety-reduction is helped by being in the company of another person/other people you can relate to. Anxious people exaggerate how bad things are if they're alone with plenty of time to let their imagination run riot; the presence of another person/people seems to limit this gallop towards disaster. At the simplest level, the presence of other people 'takes their mind off their worries', but it is probably more complicated than that, and may have more to do with them feeling safe. A good example of reminiscence activity reducing anxiety is a report on its use to reduce preoperative stress by Rybarczyk and Auerbach (1990).

Of course, this effect only works as long as the people are around. Take the people away and the anxiety returns. However, if the person remembers the group fondly or is tested quickly after the session, the client will rate themself as feeling better.

These then are examples of non-specific psychotherapeutic effects. It seems that, as long as the therapist is respectful and valuing of the person, it doesn't matter much what type of therapy they receive. So why not reminiscence?

What is missing here is a rationale: how does it relate to the client's problems? For example, a good cry or perhaps, under encouragement, a good outpouring directed against unsatisfactory parents or spouses or ungrateful children, may make the person feel refreshed and even invigorated. But this outpouring, which is called *catharsis*, is insufficient. Certainly, it can help clients to experience how helpless or angry they feel and felt about a relationship/situation/event, but having experienced that force of emotion, they need to move back into the 'here-and-now' and decide how that hurt can be mended; and how they can change their present way of life. Catharsis, of itself, has a weak and ephemeral effect. In the same way, the reminiscence group worker may be very impressed by the raw emotions expressed by members about the war – the anxiety, the fear, the losses. But from a therapy point of view, the real work hasn't started, which is, what will they do with all that anxiety, fear and grief now that the war is over?

To sum up, psychotherapy is a very confusing and confused topic. There are lots of ways that people will benefit from almost *any* activity, but this does not mean those activities are therapy. Reminiscence needs no exuberant sales pitch. There are enough valid uses of reminiscence without the hype.

We turn to two more coherent uses in the therapy field: life review and aiding (positive) identity creation.

Useful reading and resources

E. Bachar, S. Kindler, G. Schefler and B. Lerer (1991) 'Reminiscing as a technique in the group psychotherapy of depression: a comparative study', *British Journal of Clinical Psychology*, 30, pp. 375–377.

P.A. Fry (1983) 'Structured and unstructured reminiscence training and depression among the elderly', *Clinical Gerontologist*, 1 (3), pp. 15–37.

J. Lesser, L.W. Lazarus, R. Frankel and S. Havasy (1981) 'Reminiscence group therapy with psychotic geriatric inpatients', *The Gerontologist*, 21, pp. 291–296. Suggests that reminiscence groupwork is more useful than traditional group therapy; but the evidence is clinical, not statistical.

Julie Lloyd and Margaret Todd have written a chapter on psycho-therapeutic interventions with people with learning disabilities in Margaret Todd and Tony Gilbert (1995) *Learning Disabilities: Practice Issues in Health Settings*, Routledge.

Eleanor O'Leary (1996) *Counselling Older Adults*, Chapman and Hall. A good introduction to the various types of therapy mentioned in this section.

Bruce D. Rybarczyk and Stephen Auerbach (1990) 'Reminiscence interviews as stress management interventions for older patients undergoing surgery', *The Gerontologist*, 30, pp. 522–527. The preoperative stress reduction experiment.

Irving Yalom (1995) *The Theory and Practice of Group Psychotherapy*, 4th edition, Basic Books. Has a good section on catharsis and on therapeutic factors.

Purpose Fifteen

REMINISCENCE FOR LIFE REVIEW

Rationale

With the purpose of life review, we are very clearly in the area of psychotherapy, so practitioners in this realm will need formal and extensive training. They do need a good grasp of the major theories of personal development and of mental illness/emotional disorders. They should also have considerable experience of working in therapy groups. So, we begin this chapter with a disclaimer: **you can't start from here in terms of running such groups**.

Expanding on what we wrote in Part One of this book, the classic underpinning for life review therapy is one chapter, a few pages long, called 'Eight Stages of Man' in a book entitled *Childhood and Society* by the Danish–German psychoanalyst Erik Homburger Erikson (1902–1994). The book came out in 1950. Basically, Erikson argued that there were eight major periods in human development, and that each period or stage posed a particular problem to be solved, a task to be tackled and achieved. Table 11 gives details of the eight stages.

There are obvious similarities with the original formulations of the founder of psychoanalysis, Sigmund Freud. Indeed, Erikson felt he was only smartening up the basic model, but he was being over-modest and over-loyal to Freud and the Freudians. (His personal analysis had been with Freud's daugher, Anna.)

Erikson made two important changes. He put less emphasis on instinctive drives, such as sexuality and aggression. Instead, he put greater emphasis on how the person's society and culture shape a person's personality and the difficulties and problems they will have to face. His is therefore a more social approach. Secondly, Freud believed that a person's personality was basically developed by early adulthood. As you can see from Table 11, Erikson extended the age during which personality changes. In fact, he extended the period of change and development to the whole life-span (so that change over the lifetime now has its own sub-discipline, called 'Life span psychology').

Table 11   *Erikson's Eight Stages of Man*

Stage	Age (years)	Erikson's dichotomy	Task
1	0–2	Trust vs. Mistrust	Developing trust in the world; believing your parents value you
2	2–6	Autonomy vs. Shame and doubt	Developing independence and own choice
3	6–10	Initiative vs. Guilt	Developing initiative, planning and doing things alone
4	10–14 (Latency)	Industry vs. Inferiority	Learning to apply yourself to work (at school)
5	14–20 (Puberty)	Identity vs. Role confusion	How you look to others, and maintaining an identity independent of peer regard
6	20–30 (Young adulthood)	Intimacy vs. Isolation	Being able to develop close relationships
7	30–60 (Adulthood)	Generativity vs. Stagnation	Bringing up children/creating works that outlive you
8	60+ (old age)	Ego integrity vs. Despair	Acceptance of past, of limited time left and tasks to be completed

The task Erikson believed the older adult had to work on and achieve was to sort out what their life had been about and to achieve some integrative meaning.

It is the acceptance of one's one and only life cycle as something that had to be and that, by necessity, permitted of no substitution . . . he knows that an individual life is the accidental coincidence of but one life cycle with but one segment of history. (*Childhood and Society*)

Erikson's major conceptual achievements are summarized below:

- Motivation related to life tasks, not predominantly to sex and aggression.
- Awareness of wider society – such as school and work and not just the family.
- Development goes on throughout life; it does not stop at adolescence.
- Achievement of a stage was not once-and-for-all. The issue, e.g. intimacy, could arise again later in life.

The creation of a therapeutic task for the worker was given an even sharper focus by the psychiatrist and psychotherapist Robert Butler. Although Erikson was an analyst, *Childhood and Society* was a book of ideas about culture and the development of personality. So, for example, there are chapters on the cultures of the Sioux Indians and Yurok fishermen in Alaska. Butler, in contrast, writes as a therapist working in New York City with patients to see. His is a more focused and pragmatic approach.

Basically, Butler argued that older people, toward the end of their lives, undertook a **life review**. This stocktaking was unique to the elderly as it related to the nearness of death. In his key paper in 1963, Butler wrote: 'This paper postulates the universal occurrence in older people of an inner experience or mental process of reviewing one's life.' If the person found reviewing painful and depressing, then they might or should seek help from a mental health professional.

Like Erikson's 'eighth stage', the concept of 'life review' was very influential among workers with the elderly. Their charges were no longer dozing in their chairs, they were undertaking their life review! And the idea fitted very neatly into Erikson's work. Erikson had shown us the *task* – to achieve ego-integrity. Butler had shown us the *method* of achieving that integrity – the life review.

It is perhaps difficult to understand now how important Erikson's and Butler's writings were to people who were working with older adults in the late 1960s and the 1970s. For the first time, two separate psychotherapists were taking older adults seriously; and, therefore by implication, taking workers with the elderly seriously. This helped the workers feel that their work was of importance and did have some prestige. Peter Coleman, Professor of Psychogerontology at the University of Southampton, was doing his PhD on reminiscence in the late 1960s. He describes the feeling of the time in the first few pages of his *Ageing and Reminiscence Processes* (1986):

> When I was beginning my post-graduate studies . . . I soon came across and was impressed by Robert Butler's article on reminiscence and 'life review'. . . . I also had the opportunity to speak to Robert Havighurst, while on a visit to London, about his own research on reminiscence, and I began to feel part of a developing crusade. . . .
> I remember very well the excitement I felt when reading Butler (1963) . . . Rose Dobrof (1984) testifies to the influence this single article had on attitudes to the elderly.

Innovation and the excitement of innovation is very bound by time and place. Looking objectively at Butler's article now we see it is full of literary quotes. Just as Erikson seemed to believe that Ingmar Bergman's film *Wild Strawberries* explained old age, so Butler (1963) analyses at length William James' *The Beast in the Jungle*, and the article is full of literary allusions, with not a statistic to sully its imagination.

Perhaps we can see Butler's article in this light now that the battle has been won and the reframing of reminiscence has occurred, because the importance of this giving of purpose should not be underestimated. Prior to this time, since the creation of an industrial society, old people were perceived as having no value and as not doing anything useful. So those who looked after them also did nothing useful or valuable. Like their charges, their activity did not have much point. Now there was a theoretical framework within which to place and structure their care. If older adults had a task – to achieve ego-integrity – so workers with them also had a purpose and a task: to help their clients achieve ego-integrity.

Historically, interest in using the life review as a therapeutic method took some time coming. When reminiscence groupwork came in in the 1980s, workers would use the names of Erikson and Butler to give their work respectability – a quick tug of the theoretical forelock as it were – and then get on describing or doing their reminiscence work. And the main point of such work was to liven up residential units, by giving the residents an activity which they were good at, because their long-term memories were intact, and which they enjoyed. (See Andrew Norris, *Reminiscence with Elderly People*, published in 1986, for more on this approach and purpose.) However, neither Butler, full of his literary quotes, nor Erikson, not a native English speaker, are easy reads, so the influence of their ideas remained somewhat restricted. But by the 1980s, people in the field started wondering whether contemporary models of therapy could be developed for older people.

Barbara Haight, an American Professor of Nursing, has been influential in separating life review from reminiscence. She argues that while reminiscence is a communal, a sharing experience, life review is an individual process of examining one's life in the presence of a therapist. So, the pay-offs are different. At the end of a reminiscence group, the person feels good and their communications with others are richer. At the end of a life review, in contrast, the person is (more) at peace with themself as they have put away 'old baggage'; or to use a phrase from Fritz Perls' Gestalt Therapy, sorted out 'unfinished business'.

Haight then went on to develop a package of '8 one-hour visits approximately a week apart' with a checklist of questions. This package is presumably for the American nursing home market and shows how economics shapes service. Eight sessions does not seem generous, and in many cases would barely allow the creation of trust necessary before the client starts taking risks. The risks are the pain that may result from a more open examination of one's life, and the risk of entrusting these doubts, shame, guilt and regrets to another. Secondly, it seems odd that each person gets the same number of sessions. In our experience, people vary greatly in how much they want to explore their lives. Some have worked out 'a story' that they do not wish to examine; others have only one area, say the war, that they wish to look at and work through.

Finally, a checklist of questions – presumably developed to allow less highly trained (and hence less well paid) staff to undertake the life review process – runs the risk of 'flattening' the life. As indicated, clients characteristically do not want to work with equal intensity on all periods of their lives (if only because not all stages of their life were equally problematic; and some may be *so* problematic that they do not wish to examine them closely – let sleeping dogs lie). Rather, for example, they may spend sessions looking at the effect of a violent parent on their primary family and their early life; or their own disastrous marriage. Of course, all periods of their lives should be examined, but a time-limited checklist runs the risk of losing light and shade, and of reducing the life review to a march past and the creation of an artificial role – 'lucky guy' 'poor but happy' – to agree with this galloping series of questions.

Naomi Feil's Validation Therapy fits into this chapter as a life review approach. Feil propounded a stage beyond Erikson's last stage (Ego-integrity vs. Despair). For those unable to achieve ego-integrity, they move to another stage, Resolution vs. Vegetation, where they continue, albeit with decreasing cognitive and physical abilities, to try to resolve their unfinished business. She says there are four stages or types: mal-oriention, time confusion, repetitive motion and vegetation. However, individual Validation Therapy is less a therapy but more a way of relating to confused people by accepting their time frame. Group validation therapy has even less to do with traditional psychotherapy: it's a very highly structured activity with everyone being given roles – hostess, song-leader etc. Its achievement seems to be to provide a safe place where very cognitively damaged people can feel some minimal sense of competence.

Validation Therapy has been very influential in nursing homes, especially in America. In terms of purposes, it fits best into the reminiscence used to produce emotional and social stimulation; and its achievement is, by putting emphasis on security and predictability, to effect this with very damaged people. But its theoretical approach is infused by a life review concept; hence its place in this chapter.

We should point out that the respected psychologists Graham Stokes and Fiona Goudie suggest that Validation Therapy 'is not appropriate for people suffering from Alzheimer's disease or multi-infarct dementia, with the possible exception of when the dementia is in the earliest and therefore mildest stages. Validation remains a relatively un-tried and unproved method of counselling in terms of both its underlying premises and principles of practice' (1990, p. 183).

In Britain, psychologists such as Jeff Garland and Peter Coleman have written papers on developing life review therapy. One of the present authors, working at the Nuffield Day Hospital in Plymouth, a psychiatric day hospital for older adults, has also developed therapy based on life review. We call it a Life Stages Assessment and Treatment group, because it operated on the following cycle:

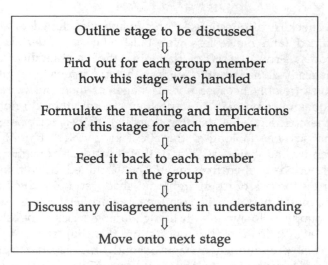

Outline stage to be discussed

⇩

Find out for each group member
how this stage was handled

⇩

Formulate the meaning and implications
of this stage for each member

⇩

Feed it back to each member
in the group

⇩

Discuss any disagreements in understanding

⇩

Move onto next stage

You can see the assessment component of this group. By the end of the group, the leaders should have a very extensive and intensive understanding of each member's life. Members will also hopefully benefit because stages are *not* like hurdles – over and away. They cast shadows into the future. Thus, a violently explosive father can damage a baby's sense of security (Trust). This internalized belief that the world is an unsafe and unpredictable place may well influence the person's behaviour in later stages – for example, choice of friends and behaviour in adolescence (Identity stage) and choice of partners (Intimacy stage). Group leaders therefore need to keep good records and to try to see how the threads of the stages intertwine; and to feed their perceptions back.

The treatment (the therapy) arises from the client's having plenty of time to look at their life and get some gentle feedback. Also, the last two sessions look forward: where does the client go from here? What do they want to do now with (hopefully) their new found understanding? What have they decided – to use Perls' phrase – is the unfinished business?

We operate on a 10-stage model – Erikson's eight plus an early career/early marriage stage, when major roles are consolidated. We also found we needed to break the very long period of old age into two stages – the last is Erikson's 'Integrity vs. Despair' but we need a stage to look at the effects of stopping work/becoming a pensioner. We call this Social Re-integration, as the person has to make new relationships and re-negotiate old ones.

We also spend time looking at the effects of the Second World War on the members; not just the efects at the time – a time that was very traumatic for many of them, for the servicemen and the civilians being bombed night after night – but also the subsequent effects, effects of marriages made because they were scared, or through pity for a man who might not come back; effects of bringing up children who might die any night of the raids; difficulties for the men, settling down again after years of service discipline and routine, with a quite different way of life and values.

We select members who are cognitively able so that they can understand the purpose of the group. They should not be in acute crisis. The group is most suitable for those dissatisfied with their life in a non-specific way – the existentially dissatisfied.

The group meets weekly for an hour and a half. It is scheduled for around 20 sessions but it lasts as long as it takes to achieve some security and trust at the beginning; work through the cycle of exploration and feedback for ten stages, and cover the war; look forward to what their experience in the group has taught them about what they want to do now; and finally to tell us how well or badly we ran the group. So it can take 16, 20, 24 sessions, depending on how many clients there are with how much to discuss.

A group of this duration should have three leaders, so that, allowing for leave and sickness, there will always be two group leaders. So much communication in a group is non-verbal that it is unreasonable to expect one group leader to pick up all these messages. A life stages session can, of course, be run single-handed, but you miss things and cannot be as finely tuned as two leaders working well together. Colleagues helping to run our groups have been occupational therapy staff – Pauline English, Marlene Hewitt – and nursing staff – Amanda Brown, Claire Booth and Claire Gemmell.

We are still developing techniques to help group members get back more strongly to the 'there and then', and the emotions they experienced at the time, not the conclusions they came to later. So more recently, we have, before discussing a stage, asked the group members to fill in forms: one asking who, alive or dead, was important to them during the years of that stage; the other asking about important events that happened in their lives during those years. We also have made the therapy 'more open' by giving the members beforehand a list of the questions or ideas we want to discuss that relate to a particular stage and how the way they handled that stage affected their life afterwards; and we ask *them* to make the formulation of how they handled that stage. So the life review process now looks as illustrated in the box on p. 244.

It can be seen that this form of 'open therapy' is quite demanding on the ability and openness of the members. It may be more useful as an additional therapeutic input alongside more practical or more focused work. By increasing the person's understanding of what has been and what has still to be undertaken, we may make them emotionally stronger and more psychologically competent to handle difficulties that being old in contemporary Britain brings at a personal and a social level.

Bennet and Maas (1988), Australian occupational therapists, compared music-based life review with verbal life review. The members of the two groups were in nursing homes but were not confused. The groups only ran for six sessions. In the verbal group, the topic was introduced and

---

Revised life stages group

Before each stage

1   Group member fills in
    • Important Others form
    • Important Events form
    for the relevant years.
2   Group member reads questions and ideas about that stage
    and is free to discuss them with others, e.g. siblings, partners,
    children.

In the next session(s)

1   Each group member describes their life during that period,
    drawing on the Important Others and Important Events forms.
2   Members explore how they tackled that stage
3   and what effect the way they resolved the task of that stage
    had on their life afterwards.
4   When satisfied, each member presents to the group their
    formulation of how they handled the task of that stage and the
    long-term effect of their resolution of the stage.

---

explored verbally; in the music group, the topic was introduced with a
piece of music and then the topic discussed. Members in the verbal life
review group stayed at much the same level of self-rated life satisfaction:
the music group's life satisfaction increased significantly.

The obvious explanation is that the members of the music group
enjoyed listening to the music more than the verbal group enjoyed
talking, and measures of enjoyment show this to be the case. In point of
fact, six sessions is far too short for a meaningful review of one's life, but
for the reader, the interesting point may be to widen your ideas on how
a life review group might be presented.

Finally, William Borden (1989) has applied life review as a way of
helping young adults come to terms with AIDS. He gives a case example
of a client, aged 39 years, referred after becoming depressed. A quote
from this client sums up life review work well:

Using an allegory from Ingmar Bergman's [film] (1957) *Seventh Seal*, he
compared himself with the Knight engaged in the struggle with Death in the
chess game. 'We all play chess with Death' he said. 'The question for me is
how *well* and how fully we live the life we have, given the givens of our fate.
This is the only way I believe we can hope to win. . . .'

Despite progressive impairment, the client began to re-experience a sense of
control and completion, and developed a greater sense of what he called 'the
history and the mystery of life'. (p. 257)

Summarizing then, taking Erikson seriously, we would try to see a life in terms of component stages that must be passed through and some adjustment made; and the increasingly complex interweaving of the experiences of the stages. It then makes sense to try to convert such a theoretical understanding into practice. There are many miles of development in life review therapy yet.

One final point. Butler distinguishes between a 'life review' undertaken by older people and 'stocktaking' undertaken by younger people. We do not know of any research evidence for this distinction. Nor do we think it particularly valid or useful. We suspect that people review their lives when there is a crisis. Indeed, Butler wrote:

> Reviewing one's life then may be a general response to crises of various types, of which imminent death seems but one instance. (1963, p. 67)

So, older people may engage in life review or stocktaking more than younger people because they suffer more life crises and losses. So, although we have focused on older people in this chapter, we are sure that this purpose has equal relevance to people of whatever age who could benefit from time and space to take stock of where they've come from and where they would like to go.

Useful reading and resources

Ideas and theories of life span development are discussed in Leonie Sugarman's *Life Span Development'* (Methuen, 1986).

Erik H. Erikson's 'Eight Stages of Man' in *Childhood and Society* (1950; various later editions by publishers such as Penguin and Granada), is not an easy read. A bit more digestible is Eric H. Erikson, Joan M. Erikson and Helen Q. Kivnick's *Vital Involvement in Old Age* (Norton, 1986).

For those wanting to become familiar with Freud's ideas, there are a large number of introductions to his work. You may enjoy Ernest Jones' biography *The Life and Work of Sigmund Freud* (Penguin, 1964).

There is no simple introduction to Butler's work. You will have to get hold of the original classic paper: 'The life review: an interpretation of reminiscence in the aged', *Psychiatry*, 1963, 26, pp. 65–76. See also his 'Successful ageing and the role of the life review', *Journal of the American Geriatrics Society*, 1974, 22, pp. 529–535.

Barbara Haight has a book coming out with Robert Woods. An introduction to her ideas is her chapter in *Caregiving in Dementia: Research and Applications*, edited by G. Jones and B. Miesen (Routledge, 1991). Irene Burnside and Barbara Haight's paper distinguishing between reminiscence and life review is entitled 'Reminiscence and life review: analysing each concept'. It was published in the *Journal of*

Advanced Nursing, 1992, 17, pp. 855–862. The 'how to' paper by Haight is 'Reminiscence and life review: conducting the processes', *Journal of Gerontological Nursing*, 1992, 18, pp. 39–41.

Eleanor O'Leary in *Counselling Older Adults* (Chapman and Hall, 1996) gives a brief but coherent account of Gestalt ideas.

Naomi Feil's book *Validation: the Feil Method* has gone through various revisions and you should be sure to get hold of the latest (Edward Feil Productions, Cleveland, Ohio, 1992).

Two articles of interest concerning Validation Therapy are 'Validation therapy with the demented elderly', by Christine Bleathman and Ian Morton in the *Journal of Advanced Nursing*, 1988, 13, pp. 511–514; and the same authors' 'Validation therapy: extracts from 20 groups with dementia sufferers', again in the *Journal of Advanced Nursing*, 1992, 17, pp. 658–666.

Graham Stokes and Fiona Goudie's comments on Validation are in *Working with Dementia* (Winslow Press, 1990).

The first few chapters of Peter Coleman's *Ageing and Reminiscence Processes* (Wiley, 1986) is a very thoughtful discussion of the role of reminiscing in the lives of elderly people. (The article by Rose Dobrof he mentions appears in our list of literature for Purpose 12.)

Jeff Garland has a chapter in R. Woods (ed.), *Handbook of Clinical Psychology for the Elderly* (Wiley, 1996).

The implications of the Second World War in Eriksonian ideas is treated in Mike Bender's article 'Bitter Harvest' published in the *Journal of Ageing and Society*, 1997, 17, pp. 337–348. For the reader interested in the war, Angus Calder's *The People's War* (Panther, 1971) is a long but very readable account. The traumatic effects of the war and possible treatments are well described in *Past Trauma in Late Life: European Perspectives on Therapeutic Work with Older People*, edited by Linda Hunt, Mary Marshall and Cherry Rowling (Jessica Kingsley, 1997). The chapter by Peter Coleman and Marie Mills, 'Listening to the story', is particularly relevant to life review work.

S.L. Bennett and F. Maas describe their research with music-based life review in the *British Journal of Occupational Therapy*, 1988, 51, pp. 433–436. The measure they used was the Life Satisfaction Index, most usually associated with B.L. Neugarten, which can be found in 'The measurement of life satisfaction', *Journal of Gerontology*, 1961, 16, pp. 134–143.

William Borden's paper 'Life Review as a therapeutic frame in the treatment of young adults with AIDS', is in *Health and Social Work*, November 1989, pp. 253–259.

Purpose Sixteen

REMINISCENCE TO AID THE CREATION OF A POSITIVE IDENTITY

Rationale

If we think about the way the words 'depression' or 'depressed' are used in contemporary Britain, the concept has four meanings:

1 Misused to mean *'unhappiness'*. Unhappiness is a rational response to a negative event; depression is an irrational or exaggerated negative response to an event. So 'he is depressed because his roof blew off last night' is a misuse of the term 'depressed'. He became unhappy after his roof fell off, which is hardly surprising.
2 Misused to mean *'grieving'*. Grieving is the response to a loss and does not imply loss of self-esteem, a key feature of depression. So 'he is depressed after his wife's death' is much more likely actually to mean 'he is grieving for his wife'.
3 *Clinical depression*. Clinical depression is one of the more severe mental illnesses. We can use the term 'mental illness' as the condition has very clear symptoms – loss of appetite; loss of sexual interest; catastrophic loss of self-esteem; and retardation. 'Retardation' means 'slowing down' and someone who is clinically depressed doesn't talk much, and says it very slowly with long pauses. All aspects of their behaviour are slowed down – the simplest thing like making a cup of tea takes an age – if it ever gets made, because another feature of clinical depression is poor memory and inattention. Once you have seen clinical depression, you won't mix it up with the next meaning or the previous ones.
4 *Depressed mood*. Depressed mood (or 'sub-clinical depression') is a bit further than unhappiness, but a long way short of clinical depression. You don't get anything like the same degree of retardation, nor the conviction of uselessness. But you do get chronically low mood, low self-esteem and loss of confidence; everything seems likely to be a long haul that will end in failure.

It is depressed mood that this chapter will mostly be about; and before getting started, we need to add that depression and anxiety go together. Anxiety is the feeling you don't know what's going to happen next, but it will probably be nasty. 'Ominous' is a good adjective in connection with anxiety. There is a bit of a puzzle here. Psychologists and psychiatrists have no trouble distinguishing between the meanings of anxiety and depression – anxiety as uncertainty, depression as loss of self-esteem – but nature seems to intertwine them, at least in contemporary Britain. So usually when you have someone with low mood and low self-confidence, you also have someone who is anxious and uncertain.

We are interested in sub-clinical depression because it is so common in people attending units for the mentally ill, elderly units and units for people with learning difficulties; in fact, common in disadvantaged people generally.

What causes this low mood or sub-clinical depression? As in any other mental health condition, the causes can be various and multiple – genetic inheritance, early upbringing, traumas during the person's life, early family difficulties, crises and so on, and a mixture of some or all of these factors. All these causes work at the *individual* level, as a function of the individual and what has happened in their life. But there is another way of looking at the causes of depressed mood; and that is to see it, at the *social* or *societal* level, as the internalization of social devaluation.

Our society does not like people not to work, and one way of encouraging people to work is to devalue those people who are not working. Whatever they *are* doing is not considered real work – and, almost by implication, they are not real people, just statistics. So who is discriminated against? Many groups:

- The chronically sick or ill.
- People with learning difficulties.
- Young blacks (more than young whites, as more are unemployed).
- Women running a home/bringing up a family (and men if they take on that role).
- Relatives caring for others.
- Retired people.

In short, a great many people of varying types. We are not saying *all* prejudice is based on people not working; you get prejudice against people of different races and cultures; and different sexual orientation. But discrimination against people who don't work is the largest single source of prejudice.

From here it is just one more step for the unemployed person to internalize the societal devaluation. They start saying things like, 'I'm no good because I can't get a job' (despite knowing that the local unemployment rate is 20 per cent – that there are no jobs). They say, 'If you're old, like me, you're on the scrap heap', instead of revelling in the

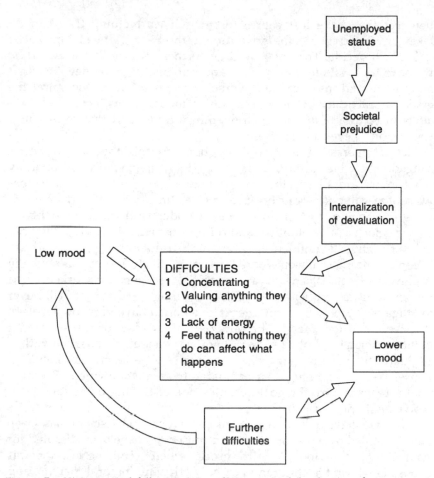

Figure 5   *Vicious spiral following internalizing societal devaluation of unemployed status*

freedom from the tyranny of work. Or the woman bringing up children can feel she is becoming a vegetable, because she 'hasn't read a book for years', ignoring all the skills that she has had to learn during the course of child-rearing. The ability to revel in freedom from work or just concentrate on and enjoy bringing up children is made easier if the person has money available to explore and develop these aspects of themselves. However, since many occupants of these 'unemployed' roles will not have money, it is much more difficult for them to appreciate potential benefits and possibilities in their life situation.

Once people start accepting (or to use the psychological term, internalizing) these negative valuations they will become depressed in mood and we will start seeing a vicious spiral (Figure 5). One further aspect of this spiral is worth highlighting, because it is something we should bear in mind when we undertake reminiscence work with this type of client.

They feel they have lost control of their lives. Nothing they can do makes any difference – the government/the benefit office/their social worker will decide. They may well go further and say that it would be unwise to try to talk to these people and put their point of view 'in case I annoy them and make matters worse'. At the bottom of the spiral the person is practically in free fall, as lower mood causes increasing difficulties in concentrating and getting things done, and this results in a progression to even lower mood.

What is interesting is that throughout all this the person hasn't changed. Their life-history, their personality, their relatives, hopefully their friends, are all still the same. But the way they frame their continuity, the value they put on it, decreases. In psychotherapy or counselling one would try to help the client understand the irrationality of accepting such a self-definition, and reframe the situation so that they can have sufficient self-confidence to look at their options.

People who have never worked are quite likely to have chronically low levels of self-esteem; as are people who have not worked for a number of years and believe – rightly or wrongly – that they will never work again. So, the long-term unemployed often have very low levels of self-esteem and low mood. The reminiscence worker, of course, cannot get the person a job, but where employment is a realistic possibility, they can help the person gain/regain enough self-esteem and belief in themself to start planning their campaign to gain employment. Where it is not a realistic aim, the goal becomes one of finding other sources of involvement and self-worth.

So far we have talked about people whose self-esteem has been severely dented over a short time; and those who have been disabled for a much longer period. A third group where reminiscence for this purpose is relevant is children in care. Not having 'natural' parents and not having a past that those parents can construct for you is likely to cause considerable uncertainty and anxiety about who you are. The making of a 'life book' with a fostered child can give them a platform of a known past – unhappy as it perhaps or probably was, but at least there is some solidity on which to build a future identity.

We will spend no time here arguing whether helping someone create a more positive identity is psychotherapeutic. Obviously, if successful, it is therapeutic. If done insensitively, it can damage. So once again, therapeutic skills and good supervision for the carrying out of this purpose are essential. It is an ambitious goal and potentially one of the most important uses of reminiscence.

Goals implied in the purpose

1   To raise the felt worth of the individual member.
2   To increase the sense of wellbeing of the individual member.

3   To locate (or re-locate) the basis of their identity on their worth as a person and not on the role of disabled or disadvantaged person.
4   As a longer-term aim, to increase the person's felt sense of agency – that they can change their environment; that what they do will have an effect.
5   To transfer the increased sense of self-worth to the world *outside* the session or unit. It is what they do *outside* the session that proves the value of what happened *inside* the session.
6   To achieve these goals without the person becoming dependent on the therapist, but realizing they can achieve desired goals by themselves and/or with the (non-professional) help of others, such as friends or family.

If the work is being undertaken in a group context, an additional goal is:

7   To help members support each other, thereby increasing the chances of achieving Goals 1 to 3.

The tasks

We will focus on the reminiscence worker's tasks in a group context, which is most likely to be with adults, and then move to individual work.

Essentially, the group leaders use a variety of known therapeutic factors to achieve these goals. (Therapeutic factors, which we discuss in more detail later, are processes that are known to cause positive therapeutic change in group therapy: see Irving Yalom (1995) and the chapter on Purpose Twenty: Reminiscence as the working philosophy of the unit). The tasks are thus:

1   To make the group feel a safe place.
2   To communicate their respect for the individual members.
3   Thereby encouraging individual members to respect and value each other.
4   Through reminiscence, to help them realize that they have led useful and valuable lives, and this fact is still true – they are still useful and valuable.
5   To give members strength through encouraging group cohesion.
6   To encourage members to help and support each other, thus decreasing their sense of isolation; and also enjoying shared activity.
7   To help them plan how they will utilize this greater sense of self-worth.
8   To help them transfer the fruits of feeling good inside the group to the world outside, which is where it matters.
9   To be aware of the environment in which the group operates, so that they maximize external support for the above goals.

10   But not to put at risk members' wellbeing by encouraging them to
     initiate and undertake behaviours or projects that important others,
     such as the unit's staff, will not support and/or may discourage or
     even punish.

How to achieve these tasks

Doubtless there will have been many times when a respectful reminiscence worker will have, knowingly or unknowingly, helped a client
gain or regain their self-respect. The purpose of this chapter is to make
the process *conscious*. We could not find many examples of this purpose
in the literature. This is probably because this aspect does have psychotherapeutic overtones but psychotherapists, sadly, tend not to work with
people who are disabled, be that disability physical, learning or associated with old age. It is therefore worth giving a bit more detail here
about what is entailed in such work.

The group setting is of particular use where we are (re-)constructing
an identity based on shared experience. It is therefore particularly useful
where the members do come from the same locality and are of roughly
the same age, so that they have lived through some of the same events.
So, for this purpose, it is easier if all your members come from Plymouth
and are in their seventies, compared to two people from the South East,
one from Birmingham etc., with an age range of 60 to 90.

This purpose has a very wide-ranging applicability across disabilities
– be they difficulties in mobility, learning difficulties, or those of people
who have spent many years in the psychiatric system.

The basic process is to allow the sharing of memories so that the
members feel they have led valued lives. To this end, we want the group
to define and produce the memories. So, physical prompts should be
kept to the minimum necessary, as their presence can take away from
the central task of the group defining its past.

The discussion of common experiences has a number of pay-offs.

1   The development of group cohesion (Purpose Seven).
2   Aiding the processing of grief. By discussing the past, when they felt
    more valued, they are in some way saying goodbye to it.
3   Experiencing positive respect. People with low self-esteem do not
    value themselves *nor* do they value people like themselves, thus the
    group member values neither themself nor the other group members.

The group leader starts breaking this negative system of valuation by
expressing clearly their positive valuation of the members and of their
experience. The group leader, perhaps for the first time, creates time and

space to listen to them. They also express their interest in what the members are saying by positive non-verbal or body language messages. So the key task, the key achievement of the group leaders is the transmission of respect and worth.

Probably the next stage is finding that the other members are interesting and likeable, despite their disability; and finally, trying out the hypothesis that you too might be likeable and of worth. It is on the basis of increased self-worth that the person may now be able to shed the need to hold onto the disabled role and have the confidence to take some control of their life. Where and how this further development can occur would be the focus of the last few sessions.

Again, we would remind you not to encourage any behaviour or activity that will not be supported by the people – be they parents or staff – in the environment in which the individual member will be operating. It is not ethical to put them at risk of disapproval and even punishment; and the fragile growth of the self that has occurred in the group will be rapidly undone. Consolidating small steps and maintaining a support system may often be a more useful strategy.

Figure 6 on p. 254 summarizes the process whereby the depressive spiral can be reversed.

Examples of work for this purpose

We have used this approach with people who had been discharged from mental handicap hospitals. This 'decanting' process was happening to large numbers of people in the late 1980s and early 1990s.

The factors – group experience, grieving and the transmission of respect – were all very relevant. We ran such groups in the East End of London (with Val Levens) and in Plymouth (with Fran Seeley). The material presented by the group members was similar in the two locations – the complete staff power, the segregation of the sexes, and also the mental hospital having been a nearly self-sustaining society, with its farm, its vegetable gardens, its laundry, shoe repairs, chapel, recreational hall etc. What we had not bargained for was the frequency of loss in the lives of people with learning difficulties. One could not predict what type of loss – of parent or grandparent, moving and losing friends, poor education – would be raised by a member, but such unresolved losses came up early in a group's life, earlier than we were used to while working with older adults. (The reader may be interested in other differences we found, and these are given in Table 12 on p. 255.)

As indicated by the last point in that table, the members' strongest felt hurt was not at their experience of being in these institutions, it was at their parents for having sent them there. This betrayal appeared far more hurtful than being a powerless inmate.

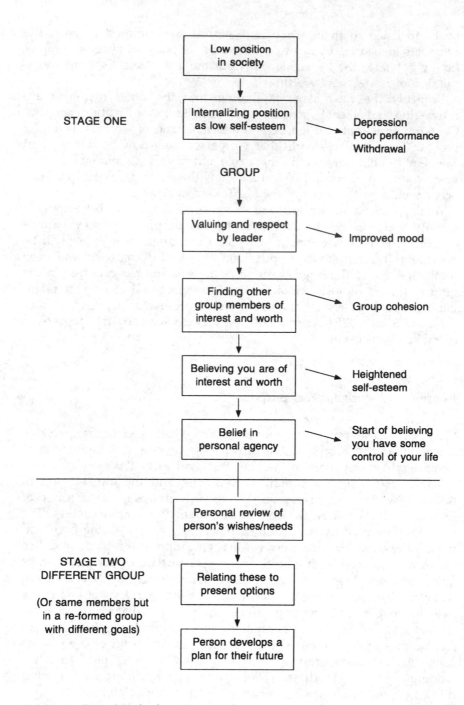

Figure 6   *Reversing the depressive spiral*

Table 12 *Features differentiating people with a learning difficulty attending day centres from older people living in residential units*

People with a learning difficulty	Older adults
Never experienced a period of being valued – except perhaps when very young	Usually valued from birth until retirement (and especially when working)
Limited range of social and interpersonal experiences	Much wider range
No history of decision-making; life-long powerlessness	Long history of decision-making until recently
Major events happen to them without explanation – passivity in the face of experienced chaos	Major events were more predictable as more under their control
Chronic loss of self-esteem, but lower frequency of depression	High frequency of depression
Physical infirmities not a major cause of depression	Depression linked to physical losses
Over and above linguistic deficits, linguistic skills have not been encouraged in educational/training settings	Received schooling with great emphasis on 3 Rs. Social interactions further reinforced linguistic skills
Have a hunger to talk about their lives	Attach greater importance to presentation of a socially acceptable self
More frequent 'disinhibited' statements of painful and powerful events	Greater censoring of accounts; willingness to play to 'cheerful' stereotype
If placed in institution, most devastating loss was rejection by or loss of parents	If placed in institution, key damage was to self-image and having to admit to loss of coping skills

We ran such groups for ten sessions and these included a trip to re-visit the site of the mental hospital, whether it was standing or not. Members with quite restricted verbal ability became remarkably fluent when showing the group leaders around the site.

We carefully researched one group and measured the amount of interest shown by the member, and the degree to which therapeutic factors were present. The term 'therapeutic factors' was coined by the leading group therapist Irving Yalom; these are the 'effective ingredients' of successful groupwork (see Table 13). We compared the level of these factors in a day centre group for people with learning difficulties with findings with the same measures taken from a psychotherapy group for older adults and could find no differences in therapeutic level.

This group moved on, becoming a clients' committee, with its own small budget and meeting by itself with staff only present when invited.

The focus does not have to be so specific. People with a learning difficulty who live in the community can look at various aspects of their lives – early days, relations with siblings, schooldays etc., and again can pool and share their experiences.

The benefits of a more positive identity should hopefully be seen in individual decisions and changes; or, as in this case, may also result in a

Table 13   *Therapeutic factors*

	Factor	Meaning	Examples
1	CATHARSIS	Emotional release	• Anger at treatment in hospital • Bitterness at rejection by parents • Grief at loss of loved ones
2	SELF-DISCLOSURE	Information of a personal nature	• Describing being hit by parent(s) • Being told of parents' death
3	LEARNING TO BE MORE OPEN	Experimenting with more open ways of relating	• Member feels able to discuss loss • Member starts talking to other members, not just to staff
4	UNIVERSALITY	Realizes problems are not unique	• Member finds out that other members' parents have also died • Members find out that others hated school • Members comment on similarity of *personal* experience (*not* 'we both live in Honicknowle')
5	ACCEPTANCE	Member feels they belong	• Member expresses solidarity, loyalty to group • Member expresses wish for group to continue to meet • No evidence of felt rejection by group *or* if evidence, rejection is nullified by end of session
6	ALTRUISM	Offers of help and encouragement. May be verbal or non-verbal	• Member encourages others to speak, in helpful (*not* bullying) manner • Member, with other's agreement, speaks on their behalf • Member stands up for another member, at some personal cost • Member helps another member come to group
7	GUIDANCE	Group leaders give information (Is *only* concerned with group leader behaviour)	• It's OK to cry • If we talk one at a time, we'll hear others speak • Things from a long time ago can still hurt
8	SELF-UNDERSTANDING	Member indicates evidence of new insight into self and/or their behaviour	• They can't hurt me any more • I could do hairdressing again
9	LEARNING FROM OTHERS	Learning through the observation of others' behaviour and acceptance of its value	• Member checks with other members if it's OK to cry (or whether it's better done at home) • Member sees others not impressed by bullying and starts to question its value

continued

Table 13   (*cont.*)

	Factor	Meaning	Examples
10	INSTALLATION OF HOPE	Optimism expressed as to progress in group and/or in life generally	• I feel more free now we've talked about things • Maybe things will get better now
11	AGENCY	Member expresses 'ownership' of their behaviour and does not place responsibility for their action on others or external events	• We could ask that the record player be turned off • It wasn't all my dad's fault. I was a handful • If I want to go there, I'm going to have to ask

Modified from Yalom, 1995

group or collective change. Here the person achieves desired ends by working with others – these end achievements may well have been unrealizable without the positive group experience. The chapter on Purpose Seven, Reminiscence for group cohesion, discusses the achievement of group goals.

A positive identity group may be more usefully run in an evening class, with its greater surround of adulthood, than in a day unit, with its implication that the person is a client or patient. Two quotes may give the flavour of such work. First, the group was discussing visiting their old hospital:

At this point, Avril was quietly sobbing . . . Shirley, who had rather restricted verbal ability, was very attentive and said 'What's the matter with her? She's missing her mother, that's what the matter is.'

And the second quote: at the end of the group, one member gave the following feedback:

Feel free . . . for 30 years, shut up! now feel open. . . . Under carpet, say nothing – No!

We have discussed increasing self-esteem in groupwork. Of course, this can also be done working with individuals. Maintaining self-esteem in the face of dementia is described in Marie Mills' account (1997) of counselling 'eight moderately to severely demented elderly people'. She uses the concept of 'a narrative identity'. Her exploration and support of narrative identity in an individual setting contrasts with and complements Rik Cheston's similar approach (1996) in a group setting.

A detailed account of this purpose in action

The work we intend to describe in more detail here concerns life story work.

For children who are in care or who have been fostered, there are often great gaps in their knowledge of their own history. It has become good practice in many child-care units to use life story books as a means whereby the child and a worker try to fill that vacuum concerning the child's history.

> When children lose track of their past, they may well find it difficult to develop emotionally and socially. If adults cannot or do not discuss this past with them, it is reasonable for children to suppose it is very bad.
>
> A life story book is an attempt to give back to the child in care his or her past life through the gathering of the facts and people in that life and to help him or her accept it, and go forward into the future with that knowledge. (Ryan and Walker, *Making Life Story Books*, 1985, p. 5)

Obviously, one would only undertake this in a professional context, having received proper training and receiving ongoing supervision. Here we only *outline* how a life story book is made and its possible uses, in the context of reminiscence, and cannot give guidelines as to professional practice. The reader should seek out the specialist literature if they actually wish to undertake such work.

The life story 'book' can be structured in many ways. For example, the National Foster Care Association have *A Book about Me*, but a photograph album with pages that can be written on will do nicely. It is useful and less fiddly if plastic envelopes are the means of keeping the photos/drawings/letters in place, as this makes re-arranging easier. The headings or topics are, of course, decided between worker and child. Finding out the relevant history and gaining visual material to illustrate that history will take some time, and plenty of time for discussion, the development of friendship and trust, and self-exploration should be allowed.

It is important that there is no hurry, so that there is sufficient time freely available to follow where the child wants to explore; that there is purposeful activity in terms of finding out what happened to them – but the gathering of information is not overly constrained by pre-determined headings; and that the resources needed – the camera, film, bus fares etc. – are available when needed, so that management requirements do not cause stuttering and misfiring in the work.

This type of usage of reminiscence work is not limited to children in care. It can have a use where people of whatever age are moving units. If, for example, a hospital ward is closing, each member can be helped to develop their own life book of *their* individual experience of their time there. It may also be good management if staff are given time to do the same, so that they too have a memento and they too are allowed to grieve for what will inevitably be lost. (For example, the large mental hospitals had recreation halls which were packed on Saturday nights for film shows. There was usually an Open Day, and so on.)

But we must not focus exclusively on big units. As the cost of accommodation and land space increases, so units will move site more frequently. In Plymouth a unit for people with dementia was moved just a hundred yards to larger premises. By running a 'Goodbye–Hello' group, some of the sorrow of leaving their familiar old unit and some of the anxiety about the new unit could be dealt with; and given that change is difficult for people with severe dementia, such gains are not to be sneezed at. The material they worked on became the basis for a display stand of 'Then and Now' in the foyer of the new building and was ready in time for the formal opening, the members thus gaining some prestige for their work. It was members of the group who asked the questions in video interviews with key figures in the organization who had created the new building, which again gave them prestige through the role of interviewer, and the prestige that goes with the creation of film and a permanent record.

The key rationale for life books is their use with people who do not have a past that is available for them and others to communicate about; thus a joint search is needed by the person with a helper to find out about and record their past. This 'loss of past self' is actually quite common in society – people discharged from psychiatric hospitals and people entering nursing and residential homes often come with very limited biographies. Charles Murphy has surveyed the use of life story work in various units in Scotland, and has a chapter on how to develop life story work in residential and day care settings for older adults. A life story book is an excellent channel whereby communication and cooperation in friendship can be built up. Really no client should be in a service unit without a detailed biography being available about them to allow intelligent, individualized care/treatment/ service.

There is another, and overlapping, group of people for whom life books may be useful. These are people whose lives have been considered too unimportant or valueless to be worth recording, either in writing or visually. A person with a learning difficulty may thus know very little about their past and have very few mementoes or pictures of that past. If there is willingness among those who do have that information, a life book may well help increase the person's self-esteem and firmness of identity.

Life story books thus have two important goals:

- to allow the person to know who they are;
- to allow people working with that person to provide a focused service for and to them.

Conclusions

There is, of course, much mental illness in our society. But there are far more people who are very unhappy and perhaps confused as to who they are and what they are worth. These people often only receive help if their unhappiness is re-framed as mental illness, but that creates its own complications and confusions. Far better if we have services that do not need to label or stigmatize but can help people pick themselves up, look at themselves and their world and re-discover hope, optimism and self-belief. They may need further support as they test out their re-created self-image and self-worth.

Reminiscence, then, can provide a vital first stage of gaining or re-gaining self-belief for a very large number of disabled and disadvantaged people today.

Useful reading and resources

For people's accounts of the effects of disability, see Steve Humphries and Pamela Gordon's *Out of Sight: the Experience of Disability 1900–1950* (Northcote House, Estover Road, Plymouth, 1992). It has many moving stories and the photographs do a lot of talking.

Therapeutic factors are discussed at length by Irving Yalom in *The Theory and Practice of Group Psychotherapy* (4th edition, Basic Books, 1995). Our research showing that the level of therapeutic factors was as high in the groups of people with learning difficulties as in a formal therapy group for older adults was written up by M.P. Bender, D. Tombs, S. Hodges, S. Finnis and R. Morris, entitled 'How should we measure the effect of groupwork with adults with a learning difficulty?', *Clinical Psychology Forum*, 1992, May, pp. 2–6; and June, pp. 3–5.

Readers who want to take their understanding of psychotherapy with people who have a learning difficulty further, will find Valerie Sinason's *Mental Handicap and the Human Condition* (Tavistock, 1992) fascinating, but a familiarity with psychoanalytic ideas is probably needed. *Psychotherapy and Mental Handicap* is a collection of papers edited by Alexis Waitman and Suzanne Conboy-Hill, (Sage, 1992) and covers a wider range of approaches.

Marie Mills' account of her individual counselling work with people who are suffering from dementia is in 'Narrative identity and dementia: a study of emotion and narrative in older people with dementia', *Ageing and Society*, 1997, 17, pp. 673–698. Rik Cheston's use of a similar theoretical approach in a group setting is written up in 'Stories and metaphors: talking about the past in a psychotherapy group for people with dementia', *Ageing and Society*, 1996, 16, pp. 579–602.

We are not attempting to provide a detailed guide to the specialized world of life books used with children in care. The National Foster Care

Association, Leonard House, 5–7 Marshalsea Road, London SW1 1EP (tel. 0171 828 6266) has a catalogue of relevant material. Tony Ryan and Rodger Walker's *Making Life Story Books* (1985) is published by the British Agencies for Adoption and Fostering, Skyline House, 200 Union Street, London SE1 0LX (tel. 0171 593 2000).

Charles Murphy's survey of the use of life books in services for older adults with dementia is in *It Started with a Sea-Shell: Life Story and People with Dementia*, published in 1994 by the Dementia Services Development Centre, University of Stirling, Stirling FK9 4LA (tel. 01786 467740). The Centre is an important resource for workers in the field of dementia.

PART THREE

USES OF REMINISCENCE TO BENEFIT CARERS

In this section, we look at carer uses of reminiscence. These are uses aimed at both professional and personal carers, the latter usually being relatives. These range from making the relationship between relatives and, say, a person who has had a severe stroke more rewarding, to providing a group experience within which the staff member can learn groupwork skills.

The main purpose in writing this book was to try to clarify what workers are or could be doing within the framework of reminiscence. So, it is very important that the uses for the benefit of staff are *not* subsumed under client purposes. When that happens, the clients are short-changed because some of the energy and thought is not aimed at them, but at staff needs; and because the staff needs are not stated clearly and met, so the training lacks quality.

Carer needs are a perfectly valid use of reminiscence. The next two chapters address their fulfilment.

Purpose Seventeen

REMINISCENCE TO AID COMMUNICATION BETWEEN A PERSON WITH A DISABILITY AND THEIR FAMILY

Rationale

Note: This chapter is addressed to the family member or person engaged nearly full-time with a disabled person. It is obviously, we hope, of use to advisory staff, but it is not addressed to them.

In this chapter we will consider the utility of reminiscence in the situation where one person is spending many hours a week looking after another. The latter may have become physically or mentally frail, for example, due to a stroke or dementia. We shall assume that any rehabilitation/reablement programmes have been undertaken so that the situation and the level of competence is fairly stable.

We start with two general points. The first is that we need to maintain the identity of the disabled person but also *the identity of the carer*. Hopefully, nowadays, we know that we need to consider the emotional needs of people and not just top and tail them. Less obvious, perhaps, is that caring requires that the carer *cares for themself*, as well as attends to their relative. We therefore need to get away from much of the huge 'carer' literature, which changes the relative from an individual person into a 'carer'; and changes the person with the disability into a 'sufferer' or 'victim', who is causing a larger or smaller 'burden'. In this death-like world where humanity is reduced to roles and tasks, it is very difficult for living, changing relationships to flourish. Such a framing of a relationship almost encourages its death as a living process.

So, the giving of time and caring by one person to another should be in the context of a boundary or limit. We believe that this limit should be where the relative creates time and space to maintain *themself* – their interests, their hobbies, their friendships. Failure to maintain their own identity reduces their ability to operate as a person, rather than as a drudge, and also greatly reduces the amount of stimulation available to them. So, they become over-focused on the caring role and have nothing other than the disabled person's health to talk about. Because they are so boring and the disabled person's health – or rather ill-health – is an embarrassing and difficult topic of conversation, they rapidly lose most of their friends, thus accelerating the loss of their personal identity.

Therefore, the relative – if they are the person who is most concerned with the wellbeing of another – must be assertive and insist on help and time from other members of the family/the person's previous support and friendship system and from professional sources, such as social services or voluntary agencies. As Errolyn Bruce (1998) points out, the story that you may have heard a hundred times and makes you homicidal, can be fascinating to a volunteer. So, before proceeding, we wish to emphasize the carer's *right* to have time for themselves, and not just for worthy reasons like hospital appointments, but also for having a lie-in, window-shopping etc. As Khalil Gibran wrote in *The Prophet*, 'let there be spaces in your togetherness'.

The second point is that spending much more time than you are used to in someone else's company is stressful and also requires re-negotiation of the contract between the two people. If you like, they need to create anew and re-negotiate their relationship. Colin Murray Parkes has a useful phrase in this context, 'the fine print of the marriage contract', and many – if not most – couples do not bother to read the fine print, until they are actually in the situation.

Examples of this disruptive change are honeymoons – how many men and women, especially those who married in earlier times – have come back from their honeymoon wondering how they will ever survive their future life? Or retirement, where suddenly the wife's routines are disrupted by the presence in the house of a man who has little idea of how to spend his time now that he's no longer working. And of course, long-term sickness. In cases such as these there is little point – quite independent of the effects of the disability – in pretending that what is happening is the same as before, but just more of it. In that hopeful delusion lies inevitable trouble and stress.

One obvious way in which the relationship must change and move is for both parties to successfully grieve for those abilities or capacities of the disabled person that are permanently lost. Failure in that task can result in stultifying denials and distortions. So, we stress the need to maintain identity, to be part of a supportive system and not be isolated.

Reminiscence can be used and be of use in various ways. It draws on the common experiences of the two people, allowing them to share again the good and bad times, thereby creating topics of conversation and reinforcing the bonds between them. It can give meaning to activities – like getting photographs in order; and outings to places they've been to before or said they would like to visit but never got round to it.

By the use of an illustrated diary, a memory bank can be created to be shared with others and allow communication.

Goals implied in the purpose

- To aid communication and the enjoyment of that communication.
- To frame activities within the home.
- To encourage activity outside the home and to give it shape.
- To allow communication with others.
- To form a legacy or record for future generations.
- To maintain a record of present life.

The tasks of the relative or carer

Note: these are tasks for the *relative* to try to achieve (*not* for the professional helping the relative)

- To become familiar with the rationale and ideas behind reminiscence.
- To be interested in the memories of the disabled person.
- To encourage them to get out and keep living, even if that requires some overcoming of pain, discomfort and inconvenience.
- To continue to see them as a person with a past and also a future, and being part of a wider network of people.
- To encourage them to maintain such a view of themself and of their network.
- To know where the physical, time and psychological boundaries to your caring are, and to keep within those boundaries.

How to achieve these tasks

An understanding of human needs is important in work for this purpose and Abraham Maslow's hierarchy of needs, shown on p. 135, is very useful. It moves from basic, physiological or physical needs to higher-order needs of creation and cognitive stimulation and also artistic and spiritual needs. To make this more practical, we create a framework for interaction (Figure 7).

Respect for the person and valuing them as a person is needed if there is to be energy and purpose in our interactions. Our respect for the other fulfils, at least to some extent, Belongingness and Love needs, and Esteem needs. In our attempts to communicate with and encourage stimulation/enjoyment for a person who is disabled, we need to provide security – Maslow's Safety needs. Creating or making something

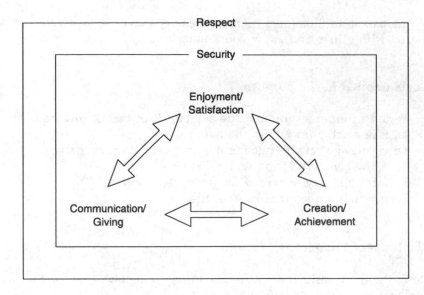

Figure 7   *A framework for therapeutic interaction*

obviously satisfies Creative needs. Concerning communicating and giving: when a person is ill, all the giving flows towards them – the time taken to visit them, the fruit, most of the conversation etc. Of course, we can't alter the basic process but carers can try to create opportunities for the disabled person to give also – to reverse the 'gift process'. Helping the disabled person to make a gift where and when appropriate will help maintain networks, as will keeping in touch and consciously striving to maintain communication.

Examples of work for this purpose

Clearly a carer would be ill-advised to use *only* reminiscence methods and material to achieve these goals, but certainly reminiscence has a place and an important one in their toolbag. This is for two reasons:

1 If there is any memory damage, then it will affect short-term and more recent memory more than memories of what happened some time ago. So reminiscence will draw on strengths.
2 It is likely to draw on experiences that both participants either did together or both know about, allowing for good verbal and emotional communication.

In the previous chapter we discussed creating life books or life story books, and this can be a good way of organizing material scattered in boxes or in the attic. Some of that material – not needed for the book –

may make nice mementoes for other members of the family. Sometimes photographs being used in life books or similar material will be of people whose names are forgotten, but you know someone who will know. Renewing acquaintances is much easier if there is a particular purpose on which to hang the suggestion of meeting. Kay Isbell, working in the Barbican area of Plymouth, found old school photographs an excellent way of linking people together.

All the time, you are looking for ways to get outside. Staying indoors can be stifling. The person has far too much time to think and reflect, feel aches and pains and generally feel sorry for themself. If the carer needs to be with them to ensure their safety/wellbeing, the home soon becomes like a prison. The stimulation is outside. Backman, a Scandinavian psychologist, has made the important point that with people with dementia there is not much point in training their memory, what matters is to *make their day memorable*.

Visits by others can be memorable events, but a major way to punctuate life is to get out. Obviously, there will often be major logistic difficulties. These may relate to moving the person, suitable transport, moving around once you've got there, finance and so on. You need to become an expert on what types of transport and car services are available locally and how to access them. You may well need extra help and there may be financial costs. All these are real disincentives but we cannot emphasize too much the importance of overcoming them in terms of the benefit to the mental health not only of the disabled person but also of the relative, and to their quality of life.

The framework that we outlined in terms of **enjoyment** – **creation** – **communication** can inform such outings. So the outings can be used to make more personal gifts. The shells collected on a trip to the beach can be made into a necklace for a young niece. Of course, not all material can go into gifts but can go into the visual record; or to make a picture or its frame.

Thinking of communication, the choice of destination for the outing will of course depend on many things, but previous experiences will be one of them. Once there, you can buy a postcard or some other visual memento (see below) and communicate with others who were there with you on earlier occasions.

Outings needn't just be to visit places: they can be aimed at seeing people. As we said earlier, an important task in caring for a disabled person is to prevent their (and your) network from diminishing, yet one of the problems for older people is that not only does their mobility decrease, but so does that of their cohort. So, it is quite likely that to visit an old friend, for example, it is the person who you are caring for who will have to do the tavelling. Again, human and financial difficulties may well have to be overcome.

An important point to bear in mind is that outings are even more important in winter than in summer. In winter, if not countered, there can be months of low level stimulation and little mobility with correspondingly low mood, too much time together and heightened irritability. With a little planning, there are plenty of places and people to see and the festive season provides an excellent opportunity to make contact with people.

Of course, not all outings need to be days away. If we are trying to maintain interests and hobbies, then that needs trips to town to purchase the relevant materials. With a disabled person, the temptation is to bring the services to the person rather than the person to the services: the nephew picks up the material needed for the person's hobbies and drops them off; the hairdresser comes to the home to do the person's hair; even the priest offers communion at home. Such temptations need to be resisted.

Another aspect – perhaps a less obvious one – is that we need to lay down material *now* if we are going to reminisce about the event *later*. This point may seem so obvious as to be hardly worth making, but we take our snaps of the holiday, the video of the wedding as these events happen so that they are available to us later to enjoy and to prod our memories. Without such records there can be no re-living. But for the disabled, quite often, their photographic records become much thinner. There is less to talk about, less to show to visitors to get communication flowing. So reminiscence requires replenishing – a visual diary if you like.

A visual diary is good because it puts pressure on the relative and on the disabled person to do something to record. The use of reminiscence *in relation to future events* can be seen in making a calendar for the next year which includes events of note, again, where possible, with a visual display. So John's birthday on 23 May is accompanied by a picture of John. This calendar should be in a prominent position and by showing two weeks at a time acts as a memory jogger – to get that card, remember the anniversary, get the suit pressed for Armistice Day etc.

The devaluation of a disabled person's life is again shown in units such as day hospitals or day centres who rarely give feedback as to what their clients did to the relatives. This is especially deleterious in the case of memory loss, because the person, when they get home, can either give no account or a very limited one. So again, the record is impoverished and you cannot communicate about what you do not know. Ask the day unit to send you a few lines on what your relative did that day.

Again, because of the low status of the disabled person in society, we tend to think that grandchildren will not want to know about their experiences (a personal intergenerational communication). But this is usually incorrect and this handing-on of experience of wisdom can be face-to-face, through audio tape or videotape, in book form etc.

Finally, where a person has difficulty linking names to faces, a 'facial address book' using pictures either from the albums, or taken when people visit, is both useful and good fun to make and talk about.

Statutory services may be of use to you in at least four ways:

1 They can provide you with information about your relative's condition – diagnosis/cause/prognosis, and give you access to the relevant literature and organizations.
2 They can network you into a support system.
3 They may be able to provide you with resources that you will want to use at home.
4 They may be able to widen your repertoire of skills. For example, an occupational therapist may be able to offer you a lot of advice.

In a residential context, you often have some scope to decorate a resident's room. This can prompt discussion of personal material to be brought in from home, how it should be arranged etc. This allows for a minor decrease in discontinuity, an increase in familiarity and 'ownership' of the space.

Kenneth Hepburn and colleagues (1997) describe a Families Story Workshop in which people whose relatives were in a nursing home were given six weekly 2-hour sessions in creating a family story with their relative. Once again, the need for time-limited interventions spoils this work – what happened after the workshop closed? But the model of giving relatives skills is a good one.

In 1998 there is an EU initiative teaching relatives how to use reminiscence activities in 12 countries. Errolyn Bruce, of Bradford University Dementia Group, is involved in this project and writes about such work in *Reminiscence in Dementia Care* (see list of reading at the end of the chapter).

Such attempts to improve relatives' skills are praiseworthy. What should *not* be allowed to happen is that your activities at home are used as an excuse not to provide services to your relative.

So far we have mainly considered reminiscence in terms of stimulation and communication. The life review aspect may become relevant as the person tries to sort out their life and get their affairs in order. The relative may find this awareness and concern with dying quite upsetting, and should seek support if they find this is the case. They certainly can help the person sift through and make sense of past events, and take part in deep sharing. Jane Crisp (1995) has written a moving article on making sense of the stories told her by her mother, who was in a nursing home because of her Alzheimer's.

The professional carer

Almost all we have said in addressing the relative as carer applies to a paid worker. Perhaps the only major difference is likely to be the lack of common experiences. Therefore, the most urgent task for the professional carer is to get to know the person they are caring for, their biography, and their past and present networks.

Conclusions

Reminiscence work, applied in the active way we have outlined in this chapter, tries to put boundaries on caring, so that caring is done in the context of two people both striving to maintain their identity and a quality of life. Sometimes, of course, their needs will conflict and we take it as read that these conflicts need to be acknowledged and resolved, not swept under the carpet. Life can on occasion be fun but it is always problematical.

For both professional and personal carer, we reiterate that reminiscence is but one form of input, but because it has a framework, and a philosophy, it has the advantage of creating purpose and meaning, rather than just being a time-filling activity. Obviously, though, the person engaged in many hours of caring should try to get familiar with the range of occupational therapy activity. But certainly being familiar with the uses of reminiscence should allow access to the vital goals of satisfaction, creation and communication – goals or needs that can seem terribly difficult to reach or fulfil when one is spending many hours each day in another person's company.

Useful reading and resources

Some of the ideas about identity-maintenance are discussed in Mike Bender, Val Levens and Charles Goodson's *Welcoming Your Clients* (Winslow, 1995).

Maslow developed his ideas about the Hierarchy of Needs in *Towards a Psychology of Being* (2nd edition, Van Nostrand, 1968).

The term 'the gift process' is taken from Richard Titmuss' study of blood donation, *The Gift Relationship*, first published in 1970 and now re-published, with new material, by L.S.E. Books (1997).

Backman's article on remembering is 'Memory training and memory improvement in Alzheimer's disease: rules and exceptions', *Acta Neurologica Scandanivica*, Supplement, 1992, 139, pp. 84–87. The reader who wants to look at memory re-training may find useful ideas in Barbara Wilson and Nick Moffat's *Clinical Management of Memory Problems* (2nd edition, Croom Helm, 1992).

Two useful books on reminiscence and creative activities are Caroline Osborn's *The Reminiscence Handbook: Ideas for Creative Activities with Older People* (Age Exchange, 1993) and Carole Archibald's *Activities I* and *Activities II*, which are focused on dementia, available from the Dementia

Services Development Centre, University of Stirling, Stirling FK9 4LA (tel. 01786 467740).

Winslow and Nottingham Rehab have large catalogues of occupational therapy material. Winslow Press, Telford Road, Bicester, Oxon OX6 0TS (tel. 01869 244733); Nottingham Rehab Ltd, Ludlow Hill, West Bridgford, Nottingham NG2 6HW (tel. 0115 945 2345).

The Families Stories Workshop is written up in 'Families Stories Workshop: stories for those who cannot remember', by K.W. Hepburn and colleagues, *The Gerontologist*, 1997, 37, pp. 827–832.

Errolyn Bruce contributed a chapter on 'Reminiscence and family carers' in *Reminiscence in Dementia Care*, edited by Pam Schweitzer (Age Exchange, 1998).

Jane Crisp's 'Making sense of the stories that people with Alzheimer's tell: a journey with my mother', is in *Nursing Inquiry*, 1995, 2, pp. 133–140.

Kahlil Gibran's *The Prophet* is published in paperback by William Heinemann (1980), distributed by Pan Books.

Purpose Eighteen

REMINISCENCE TO TRAIN STAFF IN GROUPWORK OR TO IMPROVE STAFF GROUPWORK SKILLS

Rationale

Groupwork aims to provide a framework in which individuals can improve their personal or communal situation. So groupwork is much more than 'just talking to people'. It can be a support tool, a healing agent. In the main, a grounding in groupwork has been a small part of social worker, psychiatric nurse and clinical psychologist training. Rarely is it seen to stand on its own merits and those who control finances are often reluctant to release staff on a course that is either seen as a distinct specialism or a somewhat obscure unnecessary 'extra'.

Staff should have a sound knowledge of the principles of groupwork prior to embarking on reminiscence work. However this is often not the case. Indeed, the usual situation is that they have had no groupwork training at all. Therefore staff with little or no experience do run groups. Many are successful in mastering the principles by their own innate ability. However, many groups fragment before they have had a chance to become cohesive and often this is through the group leaders' lack of knowledge of group processes. (Nevertheless we would say it is far better to take a chance with untrained staff, in the hope that the group may flourish, than to have no group at all.)

We would stress at this point that this chapter is not about explaining the theoretical principles of groupwork. The list of further reading offers resources for that. It is for staff who have knowledge of groupwork and wish to enhance their skills and for staff with little or no knowledge of groupwork, who have been instructed to run a group. Should professional training not be available, then read as much as you can on the subject. In her training manual *Using Reminiscence* (Part 3): *Individual and Groupwork* Faith Gibson outlines how 'The package has been prepared to meet the needs of a variety of professional and non-professional people who may wish to either undertake training led by a trainer or a tutor or to engage in independent distant learning.'

Training of any kind requires full management support, not only to regulate staff rotas in the absence of staff involved in training but to ensure that the rest of the staff group are aware that you are involved in an exercise with a specific purpose and goal. Therefore, prior to embarking upon groupwork, staff must ensure that they are fully supported by management in order that the process is a positive experience. In order that the skills learned can be applied effectively, continued management support is necessary throughout the running of their first group, and afterwards, as they apply and improve their new-found skills in later groups.

Supervision is another important component of learning groupwork skills. It should take place within an open and trusting relationship where the group process can be discussed, where direction and constructive criticism is given. It allows us to improve and maintain good practice and can be used as a sounding board or base to implement change to the group, allowing staff to develop their newly learned skills. Supervision is also a means of supporting the inexperienced or insecure and assists in the further development of those with groupwork knowledge.

Experience has taught us that reminiscence is a good place to start learning groupwork skills. The purpose of this chapter is to underline how, by running reminiscence groups, staff can develop groupwork skills that encourage growth in staff and in so doing promote the wellbeing of the members. The group leader's task is to organize and plan a series of sessions with specific aims and objectives, with carefully selected group members, where discussion takes place in a warm and friendly manner. In order that this purpose is achieved, the functioning of the group must be a purposeful experience, with planned space, time, subject and commitment.

The participation and behaviour of individuals within a group is never completely predictable. Group leaders must be prepared for the unexpected, the anger, sorrow or distress that reminiscing can release; the silent, argumentative or verbally overpowering member who holds the limelight; the wanderer, the toilet (or attention) seeker; and those clients who display anti-social behaviour.

We are not forgetting the use of reminiscence with the very confused, but one must bear in mind that we are, in this chapter, looking at developing staff skills. Consequently it is not felt that running a group for very confused older people would initially aid this process. Later, with successful groups behind you, then the more challenging reminiscence work can be undertaken.

By actually running a group and experiencing the behaviour of various members, staff will learn. They will learn from the positive experiences as from well as from their mistakes. It is the case that we learn more from our mistakes than from our successes. If the group went badly then we must ask why. Was it the dynamics within the group? Was it lack of preparation? Was it forces outside of the group, i.e. lack of support, bad location, bad timing? By running a group, staff will have a far greater knowledge of their client group and an understanding of why people act in a certain manner. For example, in one group we had a resident who preferred to be up all night and sleep during the day, which was disruptive to the other residents. In the reminiscence group, we discovered that he had worked nights all his working life. It won't change the person's behaviour by you knowing its cause, but it will give you insight and understanding of the person you are caring for.

Why reminiscence as the content for the training group?

- Because it is fairly easy to explain its purpose and its method.
- It allows the members to develop and practise a wide range of skills – planning, evaluating, making a budget, finding material, writing up sessions, presenting to colleagues and others.
- It quickly shows staff, willing to see, that the members are individuals with rich life experiences.

During the sessions, staff will find that preconceived views and stereotypical labels applied to their clients are often incorrect as they get to know them. What you see is *not* what you get; you will discover the hopes and dreams of your client, the pain and distress, joy and fulfilment and isolation that often comes with old age. You will get a holistic, a rounder, more complete view of this older person.

Most reminiscence groups, after a few sessions, give positive feedback to the leaders, because they can see the members are enjoying themselves. They can also see the increase in self-worth of the group members during the session as they take part in pleasurable conversation with their peers and the staff caring for them. Their memories will not only enrich the lives of those running the group but their interest in and reactions to the memories as they unfold will increase self-worth and enhance the uniqueness of the older person.

Goals implied in the purpose

1 To train/improve staff skills in groupwork through practical experience.
2 To promote and encourage growth and development of staff.
3 To increase staff understanding of their client.
4 To reinforce the staff/client relationship.
5 To provide a positive and rewarding experience for both client and staff.
6 To improve the culture/context of the unit.

The tasks: what staff need to learn

1 How to plan a group – purpose, selection, informing others etc.
2 To undertake life history taking and gaining a biographical profile competently. It is impossible to run a group unless you know the biography of each member in detail, so staff must learn the skill of interviewing. (They may be interviewing the client alone or with a relative, depending on the client's memory and verbal abilities.)
3 To provide a relaxed and comfortable setting allowing for open discussion.
4 To create security and trust within the group.
5 To allay anxieties within the group.
6 To demonstrate to members that group leaders are in control of the group process, thus achieving goals 3 to 5.
7 To show empathy and sensitivity to members' past experiences.
8 How to provide a positive experience for clients and staff.
9 How to allow the group to progress and develop – awareness of stages in a group's life.
10 To brief (plan for the next session) and to debrief (go over the session they've just been in: discussing how the group went and whether changes could be made to improve interaction, e.g. alter the seating arrangements). To understand the importance of briefing and debriefing in achieving a well-run group.
11 To record what is happening in the group and write up each session: subject, who attended, reactions, interaction and any planned changes. (The Individual Recording Sheet for Group Members, and the Record of Group Activity from our *Groupwork with the Elderly* may be useful here.) Recording should be part of the debriefing: what goes on within your group allows you to monitor the progress. If the group went well or not could be due to the subject under discussion and the reaction to it of your member(s). If there was distress, then the subject should be used with some caution (or not at all). Should the topic result in good humour and a more energized group, then it can be used freely again, or even to open up the next session. If there was limited interaction or arguments within the group then this may relate to who a member sits next to. Recording is also needed to observe and note change over time; and to communicate with interested others.
12 To evaluate the outcome.
13 To have access to supervision and to learn how to use it for personal and professional growth.

To discuss this last point somewhat further, it is unfortunate that supervision is rarely available for workers with older adults, because staff would find it extremely beneficial. Faith Gibson in her *Individual and Groupwork, Training Manual* describes how 'discussing with an outsider is helpful in developing skilled practice and also allows staff to get in touch with their own feelings about what is happening in the group and to themselves as a consequence of their close involvement with older people'. Therefore, if at all possible, identify someone who is conversant with the process of a working group, and who is willing to supervise you on a regular basis.

Supervision can take a number of forms. Most often it is in the form of a person talking about their cases or group to a more experienced worker, and this is probably the commonest form of supervision. But this form of supervision may be too 'hands-off' for the person leading only their first or second group. Here, working alongside a more experienced practitioner may be more useful. (If they both get supervision as well, that's even better.) When the person feels more confident, they can take a more active role in planning and leading the group, while the more experienced worker takes more of a back-seat role, advising and commenting. If a unit is lucky enough to have a number of experienced group workers but cannot get access to a supervisor, peer supervision may be useful. Here, the leaders of the various groups meet and discuss progress and give each other constructive feedback.

Note that it is not necessary for a groupwork supervisor to work with the same client group as yourself. It is not experience of a given type of client – though this can be a bonus – that makes a good groupwork supervisor. Rather it is an understanding of group dynamics and the ability to use that understanding to analyse what's going on in groups, and to communicate that understanding effectively.

Examples of work for this purpose

In the early 1980s, we began to recognize the worth of reminiscence and did our utmost to promote it, in order to bring something more stimulating than bingo into the lives of older people. We were initially met with distrust and inertia, but persevered. The principal manager for the residential homes we worked in, Mervyn Eastman, was innovative and gave us his full support to implement reminiscence programmes in residential homes for older people. However, all was not plain sailing as we were working with uninitiated care staff who had done little more than change beds and 'top and tail' clients, and who held themselves in low esteem. Although accepting the concept of reminiscence we, too, were new to groupwork with elderly people. Initially, we worked alongside staff in the groups.

The group was a learning process for all concerned. What do you do when an elderly lady shouts 'I hated my father'? Sadly, afraid to pick this up, we quickly passed on to another topic. Fortunately, problems which were encountered in the group were discussed during debriefing and supervision. From this shaky beginning, we developed our knowledge of older people and the many problems that can be encountered in groups. When to ignore, challenge, confront, agree, collude, sympathize, empathize, share, laugh, touch, take action and eventually say goodbye, together with the many physical, mental, emotional, sensory frailties elders are burdened with and how to manage them within the group: all this we learned from experience.

We were not just running the groups, but also helping the care staff learn about groupwork. Eventually, with the success of the first group, staff self-worth and confidence increased and our co-leaders, with regular supervision, went on to run other and more challenging groups. Later, with the success of many and varied groups behind us and the effect they had on both residents and staff, we ran ongoing training courses for staff and officers but we continued to have staff work alongside us in all our groups. So staff could start with us, and then move to running groups with a more experienced staff member, these groups being supervised by us. At some point, they would join a training course about groupwork; then, as they became more competent and experienced, so they in turn would welcome less experienced staff to run groups with them.

A clinical psychology trainee, Rob White, helped us to look at the anxieties these staff felt when they were undertaking groupwork training and running supervised groups. He undertook 15-minute interviews with five of the eight staff who were working in reminiscence groups at that time, four staff from each of two homes. Initially, staff were concerned about their ability to lead a group and were anxious, on the one hand, about the possibility of clients drying up and saying nothing; on the other hand, they were afraid of clients becoming upset. These anxieties reduced over the first few sessions. Staff also felt uneasy when a psychologist was present in a group, and perhaps we should have done more to develop trust before starting groupwork.

Each person interviewed was asked what advice they would wish to give to staff beginning work in reminiscence. The following points were offered:

1 that the anxieties preceding the group are worse than the realities;
2 that groups become easier to work with after a few sessions;
3 that silences should be accepted as a natural part of the group process;
4 that staff should not feel too responsible for the group's success or failure;
5 the importance of patience and a sense of humour.

One other point is that far more is learned if staff being trained come from different units.

It is certainly true that having all the staff from the same unit hinders learning. I ran a training course in the use of reminiscence groups at a day centre, the students all being staff at this day centre for the elderly. It seemed the rule at this centre was: Don't talk till the centre head has spoken first and then follow her lead. This made the development of any group discussion difficult. After two or three sessions of this, I had a briefing session with the centre head and asked her to delay her comments in future. The first question that I then addressed to the group was followed by a total silence, and the silence remained. I hadn't read the small print: If the centre head has no opinion on a topic, nor do we!

What I learnt from that experience was never to teach a group all of whom work in the same unit. You keep stumbling over the unverbalized, unrecognized assumptions by which the place functions. Secondly, if you then criticize those assumptions, you end up in a confrontation. Much better to get other members of the training course to ask why those assumptions are necessary when their own units seem to run perfectly well without them. Such an approach is far harder to resist and makes change much easier.

A very innovative approach to helping staff develop reminiscence skills and providing training is Reminiscence Approaches with Frail Elderly People (RAFE), run by Norfolk County Education Council. They created a number of 'itemed' memory boxes, which were circulated to homes and units for older adults via the Mobile Library Service. By February 1998, they had 15 such boxes. Each had 40 memorabilia objects in it relating to the period 1920–1950 and cost, all told, about £100 each. RAFE also run two training courses, one a Reminiscence Activities course and a more specialized one on Reminiscence and Day Care.

The importance of training to help staff develop, and the ability of reminiscence material to elicit memories, is nicely shown in a short article in a RAFE newsletter by Jane Craskem, a carer at a home. She attended a reminiscence training course and on the first day the trainer, Mike Wilson, asked the participants to attempt to use 'triggers' to elicit memories. She decided to try out this approach on one of her residents,

Mary, who has lived in the home for several years. In all this time, the only words she ever said, over and over again were 'If nobody comes for me, can I stay?'

The third trigger object, a bar of washing soap, elicited detailed descriptions of wash day. She concludes:

I hope Mary gained from it, I know I certainly did – to hear her say more in thirty minutes than I ever heard her say in the eighteen months I have been at the home is just unbelievable. This was my first attempt at reminiscence and I came out feeling elated. I know I couldn't ever have thought of doing this without Mike giving me such help and confidence.

A detailed account of this purpose in action

Working alongside care staff, I had introduced reminiscence groupwork into a good number of residential homes. Following cutbacks, many groups fell by the wayside, and staff who were successful in running groups were once again returned solely to the role of physical care. The team I had management responsibility for, the recreational assistants, fulfilled the role they were employed for – meeting the social and emotional needs of elderly people in residential care, through provision of handicrafts, bingo, quiz time, cookery, gardening, sing-a-long, music and movement, seasonal activities and outings. Recognizing the increasing limitations of those coming into care, many of these activities were now beyond their abilities.

I approached senior management with the idea of setting up a Reminiscence Centre, where I could use the team more effectively in the now unused dining room of a home that had been converted for group living. Approval was obtained and, with a very talented team, we set about adapting the room to resemble a pre-war kitchen and parlour. The team: Carol Brabender, Noreen Heaphy, Sylvia Griffiths and Joan Barker were all extremely able in DIY. With an electric drill, paint brushes, hammer, nails, a sewing machine and a very meagre budget the room was transformed. The kitchen and parlour provided the setting for the numerous objects – small items of furniture, mementoes and pictures – I had accumulated over 10 years of reminiscence work. Following the extremely successful opening of the centre, the planning and pro-gramming of visits from residents of the 13 other homes was set into operation. However there was one problem: Noreen was the only member of the team who had any real knowledge of reminiscence groupwork.

Having looked carefully at the team, there were two things they all had in common: (1) they were extremely good at the work they did and their interaction with frail elderly people was as good as I had ever seen; (2) they were all very willing to try new ventures. The differences were in their personalities. Having taken this into consideration, I paired Carol, the outgoing personality who was bouncy, ever-cheerful and confident, with Noreen. Noreen, on the other hand, was more reserved, quiet with a gentle calming approach. The two (as time proved) were an excellent mix and complemented each other perfectly. Carol could initiate and lift a group with her bouncy repartee and Noreen would listen attentively, using empathy as the painful episodes unfolded. Sylvia and Joan were different again: somewhat similar in personality, confident, outspoken with a keen sense of humour, they easily made friends of the clients they cared for.

I arranged to give each staff member training in reminiscence and groupwork by co-leading a group with them. I also used formal training on the principles that underpin good groupwork. I stressed the need for positive non-verbal communication, empathy, confidentiality and open-ended questions which encourage extended dialogue.

We set up sessions for people who had come from their residential centres to the Reminiscence Centre for the day. The sessions were initially opened by myself with one of the pairs. By co-leading they quickly picked up the core elements of groupwork and any areas of concern or uncertainty were fully discussed during the debriefing. I was soon able to leave them to function independently. Although initially reluctant to make written observation of the various groups' process, they did complete the groupwork session forms and from them learned to recognize how the groups were progressing. On other occasions, the leaders gained prior permission for me to sit in on a session, and this allowed me to observe the team function.

Through experience, their knowledge of groupwork increased and the group leaders did not just sit with the members asking open-ended questions. They worked the group. If response to a subject proved positive, they allowed it to gather momentum, drawing reluctant members into the conversation. But there were many times when direction had to be given. Positive criticism is a honing tool which the four team leaders accepted and used. The groups progressed and grew. Eventually, five reminiscence groups were running each week with 35 elderly people being transported to the Reminiscence Centre over five days.

I was learning too. Previously I had, when running a group, seated the members on chairs in a circle, where reminiscence prompts and cues would be passed to them. At the Reminiscence Centre, however, the staff seated the members around the dining table in the 'parlour'. This proved far better for frail elderly people who were not always able to hold the objects passed to them, such as the hobbing foot or flat iron. Even the pictures could be reflected upon at greater length when laid in front of them. I learned from the experienced team they had become that with this arrangement objects or pictures could be pondered over and discussed by the elderly members in pairs or passed freely across the table, thereby increasing interaction.

With numerous successful reminiscence groups behind them, the team were asked if they would take over the running of a new type of group, the Residents' Committees, which were being introduced into each residential home. These meetings would include visitors such as family members and friends. Notes of those present and minutes of the meetings would have to be taken, written up and sent for typing and subsequently distributed to each person present, to the officer-in-charge, and their line manager. Having given the proposal much thought, they agreed and the meetings proved to be a very positive addition to the empowerment of the elderly people in residential care. As time went on, I progressed within my career. However, the team continues to function and the Reminiscence Centre remains a popular venue, under the management of two of the original team.

Conclusions

Reminiscence groups can be a useful vehicle to facilitate the development of groupwork skills through practical experience. A well-run group promotes progress and growth not only in the clients but also in the staff who care for them.

Having taken on the ideas and suggestions put forward in this chapter, staff can develop and grow from their experiences, and become more adept and confident in the skills of groupwork. They can embark on the more varied and challenging groups; specializing in work with the hard-of-hearing, the poorly sighted, the confused, a group for residents from a different culture: widening and honing their command of groupwork techniques. All these experiences should result in staff who are more knowledgeable and professional in the care of their clients. With their confidence and ability heightened, they will often request to go on a course that can further assist them in caring for older people with a specific frailty.

Being adept at groupwork not only allows you to facilitate recreational pursuits but heightens your knowledge of how people act collectively, a knowledge which is useful in many situations. For example, you may be asked to run a staff committee or staff meeting. Understanding the principles of groups, you should now be able not just to control a group but to manage it effectively and efficiently. The ages of the group members will differ but a wide range of temperaments will become evident: quarrelsome, positive, shy, uncooperative, uninterested, the know-all and the persistent questioner. These are not just the characteristics of older people. You will meet them all again in all age ranges. Having previously run reminiscence groups, the skills acquired will go a long way to preparing you for such work.

Useful reading and resources

Mike Bender, Andrew Norris and Paulette Bauckham (1987) *Groupwork with the Elderly*, Winslow Press. A practical manual on running successful groups, and a good manual for training in groups. Its focus is reminiscence work.

Mike Bender, Paulette Bauckham and Gill Lancaster (1996) 'Fifteen ways to lose your group', *Reminiscence*, August, No. 13, pp. 4–6. A quick checklist on the things that can – and do – go wrong in reminiscence groups.

Faith Gibson (1989) *Using Reminiscence* (Part 3) *Individual and Groupwork, Training Manual*, Help the Aged.

Faith Gibson (1994) *Reminiscence and Recall: A Guide to Good Practice*, Age Concern.

Faith Gibson has trained generations of residential workers in Northern Ireland and both these manuals are very useful.

Peter Hawkins and Robin Shohet (1989) *Supervision in the Helping Professions*, Open University Press. A leading work on supervision.

Reminiscence Approaches with Frail Elderly People (RAFE) can be contacted by telephoning Margaret Plummer on 01603 666330.

PART FOUR

REMINISCENCE AS THE PHILOSOPHY OF THE UNIT

Purposes Nineteen and Twenty

REMINISCENCE TO IMPROVE STAFF UNDERSTANDING OF THE INDIVIDUAL *AND* REMINISCENCE AS THE WORKING PHILOSOPHY OF THE UNIT

This chapter discusses two purposes. Considering the first – aiding staff understanding of the individual – it is undoubtedly one of the strengths of the reminiscence approach that it focuses on the individuality of each client, and it does this simply by pointing out that a person's lived experiences are important in making them what they are; and since each person's life history is unique, it highlights this. However, focusing on the individual client has been a theme throughout this book and to give it its own chapter as a purpose would be to repeat ourselves. This is especially the case since we have talked a lot in earlier chapters about reminiscence groupwork helping staff 'see' the individual client. This should particularly be the case where they have undertaken a biographical profile of some of the members of the group. Again, in this chapter we will be emphasizing the need for staff to see each client as an individual person with their own history and their own wishes and needs.

In this chapter, we are addressing the senior staff of a unit. In many respects what we will be discussing applies to any management change.

What is perhaps somewhat innovative is to describe the steps needed to achieve effective change within a philosophy of reminiscence and to achieve the establishment of a culture based on its values.

Let us therefore turn to using reminiscence as the philosophy for your unit. Before we start, perhaps we should say that this chapter has nothing to do with converting your ward to 1930s decor. It is about creating a value system.

The chapter is in three sections:

1 What we see the core beliefs of a philosophy based on reminiscence to be.
2 How you might create such a working philosophy in your unit.
3 How you can maintain such a philosophy.

When we try to outline the core values of reminiscence, they sound goody-two-shoes, and harmless, because every rational or well-meaning person is bound to agree with them. They might indeed agree with them on paper, in the abstract; but to get them to act on them, to make them happen, that's quite a different proposition. It's then that you start to see the underhand/underground resistance.

Looked at in one way, such resistance is inevitable. A staff group in any unit will reach a consensus of what their work is about, what it means – in other words, the philosophy by which they will try to operate the unit. Obvious 'places' where we can see this philosophy in action will be:

- who gets admitted;
- on what conditions;
- under what circumstances they get discharged;
- what 'doing well' means;
- what 'not trying' means.

In sum, the ways in which the unit rewards and punishes clients; and what they reward or punish them for.

Some staff will espouse this philosophy enthusiastically, others merely go along with it. Those who dislike it will find the unit uncongenial and will leave, with or without a bit of encouragement from the other staff.

The unit's philosophy, then, is a living thing, not a dry piece of paper; and it does directly affect staff's lives. So, in imposing a new philosophy – one based on reminiscence ideas – you are challenging the validity of the previous philosophy *and* the rationality and motives of those who upheld it.

In some units that have been going for a long time, you may not only be challenging the wisdom of the current upholders of the unit's philosophy, but also the wisdom of their parents and even grandparents.

It follows that a few staff undertaking effective reminiscence work are most unlikely to change a unit's culture. Rather, the unit's culture allows such work to succeed or dooms it to failure. Hence the need to gain control of the culture and its content. Faith Gibson puts it well:

> Reminiscence work is often subversive and unsettling because it challenges conventional relationships between staff and older people, between carers and cared for and it challenges staff to revise and reorder priorities. People and listening to people may become more important than maintaining present policies and prevailing regimes where the first priority is physical care. (from Buchanan and Middleton in Bornat, 1994)

We hope you can see now that what you are doing is not tinkering, is not neutral. *It is challenging and will be vigorously opposed.* You may be taken by surprise by the thinness of the line between love and hate. The opposition may be up front or underground, but it will be there. So bear in mind that however reasonable you think you're being, and however necessary the changes, you are actually starting a revolution.

The core values of reminiscence

Goals

A unit wishing to introduce and develop the core values of reminiscence as a working philosophy will work out strategies that:

1 Maximize the breadth and depth of staff understanding of the individuals that come to their unit
   - in terms of their personal history
   - in terms of their social, cultural and religious experiences
   - in terms of their present wishes and needs.
2 Offer clear and continuing messages of respect to each and every client.
3 See their clients' past as a source of valuable and still relevant experience.
4 Allow clients to share their experiences and gain individual strength (empowering) and group strength (cohesion).
5 Provide the opportunity to explore their lives in a one-to-one situation, where the client wishes this.
6 Maximize the informed choices open to the client.
7 Empower clients to decide for themselves and to act on those decisions.

Point 5, the opportunity for one-to-one work, concerns the presence of trauma in people's lives. There is good agreement that such trauma should be explored on a one-to-one basis. It may also require the hiring of skilled mental health workers on a sessional basis.

Implementing these values

We can only take you some of the way down the route to implementing these values. Only you/the management team can decide the best strategy for achieving the implementation and also the time scale in which you wish to achieve it. Too fast and you can have open revolt and good staff can get injured/lost in the cross-fire. Too slow and it will never actually take hold – it will never become part of the day-to-day decision making. But only you can know what's happening where you are. One thing is for certain – these changes will need to be carefully planned if they are to be successfully implemented.

How you might achieve these goals

1   It is very unlikely that these changes can be achieved by one person; rather it needs a small team to work out what these goals imply; which goals will be implemented first; how they will be implemented; and in what time scale.

2   At an early stage, you will need to gain informed management support. By 'informed' we mean that they understand in some detail what you are intending to achieve and what the difficulties may be; and how you intend to tackle them. If you do not gain this support, at the first crisis you may 'be stabbed in the back' by management failure to back you. And if you do not gain this initial management support, you need to ask yourself very carefully whether it is worth proceeding in terms of the likelihood of achieving a successful outcome.

3   In deciding who should be in the project team, it is important that there are representatives of staff and clients, and, if relevant, carers. These representatives don't have to agree with everything proposed, but you do need to be aware of how the proposals look 'from the receiving end'.

4   More generally, you will need to implement the Principle of Parallelism. By this we mean that the core concepts – of individuality and respect – with which you intend to treat clients must also be applied to the staff, if the project is to succeed. If you don't, staff will be bitter that clients are treated better than them, and will see you as cynical and presumably imposing this philosophy for your own ends. In short, it's very hard to believe that you could actually succeed in achieving an environment in which clients felt empowered in a context where staff did not feel their views were being listened to and taken seriously. So, you are creating a climate of trust and respect and empowerment within

the unit *generally*, a philosophy for all who have access to and use the place, in whatever role.

5   There will almost certainly need to be staff training/induction into what the philosophy is and what it implies. Try to present the philosophy in sufficient detail that it is understandable, but in sufficiently general terms that you can ask the staff to come up with concrete suggestions as to how it could be made 'real' and made to work. Staff can work in small groups on different parts of the implementation. For example, one of the core principles is respect, but what can we do to communicate that respect? Similarly, what does treating each client as an individual actually mean in practice?

It is very important that sufficient time is allowed for this phase. It may mean changing rotas; having bank or agency staff while your staff are in their training sessions, or closing the unit for these sessions. Bringing in an outside facilitator may be very useful in achieving this stage successfully.

It is a good idea to have such sessions away from the unit. Even if you bring in agency staff, your staff will be half-listening to the sounds coming from the unit, as they do every usual day, which means less attention to the work that needs to be done. Taking them away is likely to increase innovative thinking; and taking them to a business-like conference unit indicates your respect for and valuing of them.

6   If we consider the concept of informed consent, this can only happen if clients can clearly see what is being offered; and what isn't being offered. (This applies to the staff, too!) A good welcoming procedure is an important aspect.

7   To get to know a person in any depth requires the completion of a biographical profile (see Purpose Four), which itself requires the creation of a trusting relationship, and time allocated for the profile to be completed.

Marie Mills has run training courses for residential staff where they are asked to prepare a 'two page case-study on one of your key clients with dementia'. She has found such work greatly increases the staff member's understanding of and involvement with their client. A biographical profile tells you how the client sees their history. Also of interest is, of course, the world they live in and have to cope with. A home visit to explain the purpose of the unit allows a much fuller understanding of their present reality than a referral form.

All this information needs to be shaped into a care plan – a set of goals and how to reach them – to be discussed in the client's presence and agreed with them. How well these goals have been reached must be reviewed and new goals substituted at regular reviews.

8   For a person's life to be understood by another, that other will need a grounding in the culture and history the person comes from and lives in. This is especially important for staff in multi-cultural units. Only in this way can staff understand the background against which

and within which the individual made their choices. Trips to places important in clients' lives can be very informative and helpful for staff. This awareness must inform the day-to-day running of the unit, in terms of respect for religious and cultural high days and holidays, understanding what they are celebrating, knowing cultural and religious values and taboos.

9   To help clients overcome devaluation, groups aimed at giving value to their culture have a useful role. This of course overlaps with the use of reminiscence to achieve cultural legacy (Purpose Twelve) and also encourages cohesion and support between clients (Purpose Seven). Interestingly, an implication of reminiscence is that each individual's life is of equal value. It therefore promotes cooperation, rather than competition, communal problem solving rather than authoritarian decision making.

10   In terms of agency and empowerment, you would be looking at structures such as informed consent being sought before a person is expected to attend a given activity or event. A clients' committee with a clear mandate is another aspect.

11   So far we have talked as if who the 'staff' are is obvious. We would suggest that staff training should include *all* paid staff who work full- or part-time in the unit. Of particular importance are receptionists, the gatekeepers of the unit, who give would-be clients and outside agencies their first taste of your philosophy. Secondly, porters, cleaners and cooks are often key figures. Clients come into contact with them and seek their advice. They are also seen – rightly or wrongly – as either a bit outside the power hierarchy and/or at the bottom of it. Either way, their opinion is often treated as more independent and more sympathetic and understanding of the clients' position. So it is very important that these staff understand what you're trying to achieve. Finally, visiting staff – the GP, physiotherapist, psychologist etc. – are often quite prestigious. If they opt out or only pay lip-service to the philosophy this is very damaging to the credibility of your purpose.

If each person is of value, and is of equal value, then if two people disagree and one is better educated or trained, it is up to that person to explain to the other's satisfaction the rightness of their view, and not just impose it. So staff must learn how to persuade, not coerce, colleagues and clients. This is rather contrary to the usual attitude of 'the professional knows best' and this change in approach will need to be taken on board by the professionals who work in your unit.

It is important to understand that the kinds of structures we are advocating do not make a unit's functioning 'wishy-washy'; indeed, it can have quite the opposite effect. Some units' written-down philosophies – their 'mission statements' – are so vague as to mean all things to all people. But in developing the unit as described above, both staff and clients can see, in black and white, what the purposes and processes of the unit are, perhaps for the first time. It follows that what is expected of them is also much clearer. For example, communicating respect, which is actually an exhausting business for staff, is now expected of them all the time they are with clients. For clients, some agreement with staff as to what the purpose of their attendance at the unit is has to be reached, and this makes it difficult for clients who wish to attend for quite different reasons to continue to do so. And the respect for individuality effectively 'outlaws' anti-social or aggressive behaviour.

There is always a possible tension between client need and client wishes. This can be particularly acute where the client 'lacks insight'. For example, in a unit serving people with dementia, their natural wish to move around freely or leave the unit could conflict with the need to keep them safe. These issues can be tackled within a philosophy of individual care, detailed assessment and detailed care plans (see, for example, Nicky David, 1997).

In no way therefore do we see running a unit in terms of a reminiscence philosophy as a soft option. Certainly there has to be much discussion and debate as to how best to implement the purpose, but the structures within which they take place should be very solid and detailed.

Maintaining the culture

A culture that is not actively maintained will degenerate. It may degenerate into a few empty symbols and/or degenerate so that the words and deeds – what actually happens – are quite at odds, as appears to happen, for example, in special hospitals. If setting up a culture based on the philosophy of reminiscence is hard work, maintaining it can be even harder, if only because it is more of a grind and less exciting or innovative. But it is absolutely essential if the philosophy is to continue to be a living, growing, developing thing. In the next few pages, we look at ways in which maintaining and strengthening it can be achieved.

1   One needs to keep in mind the four levels at which a unit works: with its clients; with its staff; with its management; and with the political system of local and central government. Links need to be kept with all these levels, as changes in them will inevitably affect the unit.

2   We stress again that maintenance, just as implementation, requires the continued involvement of *all* staff who interact with the clients, so that includes full- and part-timers and all visiting staff. Your unit may well be multidisciplinary but all must agree on its purpose.

3   The use of reminiscence groups to allow clients to feel they have lived valued lives can and should set up a positive cycle (see Figure 8).

4   For the staff, the need for ongoing supervision and support is of great importance. Getting feedback that your work *is* of use and does make a difference is particularly important where clients are very disabled (and as a consequence, very devalued). In our experience, *regularity* of supervision is even more important than (high) frequency.

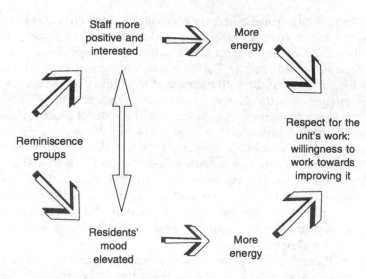

Figure 8   *Cycle of positive institutional change through reminiscence*

So a cast-iron once a month supervision session is more useful than an erratic fortnightly session.

As we have stressed before, supervision should, if possible, be off-line, rather than by a line manager.

5   Of course, such an arrangement means that the managers must find other opportunities for discussing progress and encouraging staff. One way of doing this is to build an evaluation of all activities into the unit. Simple measures such as attendance and consumer enjoyment, combined with write-ups of each session and the workers' views at the end of the group, allow evaluation to take place and prevent staleness.

6   At regular intervals, a more detailed and comprehensive evaluation of the work of the unit should take place. This might be either six-monthly or yearly, and should involve all levels of staff, the clients/consumers/users and, if appropriate, carers.

If carers are included, then heed must be taken that the client's voice is not diminished through staff–carer collusion. So, at least initially, it may be better to work up a unit evaluation system that does not include the carers.

A thorough-going review may happen more easily if it is chaired and led by a respected outsider. The presence of such a person will lend importance to the review and to its conclusions. It is, of course, vital that staff see the evaluation review as belonging to the unit and for the unit, not as a management budget-cutting tool; and that the outside facilitator also works within that framework.

7   Maintenance of morale and purpose is furthered by outside interest. The preparation of presentations and papers helps this in two ways. First, unit staff and clients can be involved in the preparation of

the presentation, which gives them prestige. Secondly, it makes the keeping of records less introspective and routine, if it is possible/likely that they will be disseminated outside the unit. Such presentations can lead to requests to visit; and visitors can be told, ahead of their visit, that the unit would welcome detailed feedback.

8   Similarly, if bona fide research workers want to evaluate the unit then, as long as that is acceptable to the clients, and does not interfere with the running of the unit, this should be encouraged, as it brings new perspectives into the unit.

9   It is often hard to recall change as one's framework changes over time, and as this happens, some details come to the fore and others recede. A good database of who has been in the unit and how they changed allows a more accurate statistical account to be kept of how the unit has changed. In addition, we can try to hold on to the experience by compiling an illustrated and annotated diary. This function can be delegated to a group of clients, if they are interested.

10   The goal of empowering clients is undermined in some units by staff and relatives agreeing 'what is best'. This can be most frequently seen in units for people with learning difficulties, and where there are speech or conceptual difficulties such as in units for people with severe strokes or dementia. It is for this reason we stress the need to make the strategy and means by which you are seeking to empower your clients the first priority. Clearly, you will wish to have a good working relationship with relatives. It may well be beneficial for them to receive education as to the goals of the unit and how the unit intends to achieve those goals. Also, as Peter Coleman and Marie Mills (1997) point out, and as we discussed in Purpose Seventeen, relatives may well need help learning how to encourage and benefit from reminiscence, so it makes sense to give them the opportunity to learn that skill.

11   In previous chapters, we have stressed the need for two group leaders for any group; and if the group contains confused members, then the staff ratio should be 1 (leader) to 2 (clients). This requirement can stretch staffing resources. Volunteer helpers may be of use, and again, suitably encouraged, can provide outside views on how the unit is going. However, volunteers must receive a well-thought out induction and ongoing support and supervision. Initially, they do not save time. Indeed, they may actually be a negative time cost for the first few months. But once trained for the work, they can be a most useful resource.

Finally, we would like to emphasize that maintaining the culture is, first of all, about the innumerable small, on-the-spot decisions that staff have to make, far more than written policies or big, policy decisions. Secondly, it is these small decisions that determine the ethos of the unit, and so require continual observation and monitoring.

Lister Bainbridge, the warden of a psychiatric hostel, put it well. He is talking about his residents, but what he says is equally applicable to staff:

If you like, each person is presented with twenty choices a day, and he can either make a life-enhancing choice or an anti-therapeutic choice, and we try to load the choices.

Examples of work for this purpose

We have discussed nuts-and-bolts in some depth above, as we are aware how stretched staff resources are in many, if not most, units caring for disabled people, especially if they are older. So, it seemed important to spell out the implications of trying to run a unit on reminiscence lines.

To give examples of such work, we return here to a project we described briefly in Purpose Six. On one continuing care ward we were involved in, we found relatives spending many hours by the bedside of stroke patients with severe difficulties in speaking. This was clearly a frustrating and exhausting situation for both parties. We encouraged the ward staff to invite these relatives to form a 'carer volunteer task force'.

The amount of energy that was released was most impressive. They undertook a number of activities for the patients, such as going to the library for cassettes, getting the patients out into the grounds, but the activity with a reminiscence content was 'old fashioned' tea and cakes. This was served once a month in the lecture hall with white linen, 'silver' cutlery, home made cakes and old-time music. Very quickly word got round what a pleasant experience it was, and patients, relatives and staff all made sure they got across to the hall.

This activity undoubtedly enriched the life of the unit and would never have happened in the normal course of events. The need to respect and empower, as values to be maintained, was neatly demonstrated when the nurse liaising with the volunteers left, and a more directive one took her place. There was a clash of styles and within a few months the volunteers lost interest in organizing events of which they no longer felt in control, and disbanded. The need for managers to monitor what is happening is ever-present.

To give a clinical example of this approach, one of us was asked to help with a woman who had to be force-fed. This force-feeding occurred at the ward's regular mealtimes – 7 am, 1 pm and 6 pm. By talking to a visiting relative, we established that she was for many years the wife of a Fenland farmer and the mealtime pattern was a breakfast after milking at 10 am and high tea in the evening. By getting staff to readjust when they tried to feed her, it was possible gradually to get her to eat without force-feeding at the times when she had always been used to eating.

Another example of this work is Charles Murphy's (1994) description of the use of life story books by community psychiatric nurses, domicilary services and day centres.

Faith Gibson (1993) applied the philosophy of reminiscence work to 'the most troublesome resident' in residential units for older adults with dementia. The two key ingredients were (1) compiling a detailed life history and (2) special observation 'to identify rhythms, patterns of recurring behaviours, or particular times of the day when the person might be especially troubled or disorientated' (p. 47). In this way, 'the fine-grained detail of the person's life was gathered' and a plan of intervention was worked out and also an ethos of evaluating success built in. Small but important gains, especially in sociability, were shown by the five people helped in this way. You will need to read the original paper for the details. Given these were particularly 'troublesome' residents and were suffering from dementia, the gains were impressive, but there is no doubt that there was considerable staff input.

It is not just that you get out what you put in: the input has to be structured, has to be purposeful. We hope in this chapter to have outlined what the objectives of a unit focusing on the values of reminiscence would be, and how such a unit could be set up and maintained.

Useful reading and resources

Some of the ideas about maintaining a philosophy in a unit are spelt out in more detail in Mike Bender, Val Levens and Charles Goodson's *Welcoming Your Clients* (Winslow, 1995).

The quote from Faith Gibson is from Kevin Buchanan and David Middleton's chapter 'Reminscence reviewed: a discourse analytic perspective', in *Reminiscence Reviewed*, edited by Joanna Bornat (Open University Press, 1994, pp. 61–74). The differential effect of the environment on the impact of a reminiscence group is neatly shown in 'The impact of reminiscence groups in two different settings', by Donna Head, Sara Portnoy and Bob Woods in the *International Journal of Geriatric Psychiatry*, 1990, 5, pp. 295–302.

Nicky David described how 'nursing practice successfully challenged the need for "baffle locks" on a ward for older people with dementia' in the *Journal of Dementia Care*, November/December 1997, pp. 18–19.

Peter Coleman and Marie Mills wrote about reminiscence work when discussing 'Life review and the painful past in day and residential care settings', in Linda Hunt, Mary Marshall and Cherry Rowlings' edited collection *Past Trauma in Later Life* (Jessica Kingsley, 1997).

Charles Murphy writes about life story work and people with dementia in a booklet called *It Started with a Sea-shell* published in 1994 by the Dementia Services Development Centre, University of Stirling, Stirling FK9 41A.

Esme Moniz-Cook and Alec Gill published a couple of fascinating articles linking traditional superstitions (in this case, on the East Coast) with 'problem behaviours' in people with dementia in the *Journal of*

Dementia Care, March/April 1996, pp. 12–13 and June 1996, pp. 16–18.

Faith Gibson describes the intensive work to understand the past and present factors making up the world of 'troublesome' mentally frail residents in 'The use of the past', a chapter in *Dementia: New Skills for Social Workers*, edited by Alan Chapman and Mary Marshall (Jessica Kingsley, 1993).

The quote from Lister Bainbridge comes from an interview with him in Mike Bender's *Community Psychology* (Methuen, 1976).

We recognize that these references have a heavy skew towards work with dementia. We reiterate yet again that reminiscence work – and a philosophy based on it – is applicable to all age ranges and all conditions; in short to everyone. We all feel better and function better when we are being respected and valued.

FINISHING TIME – 'PEOPLE AND LISTENING TO PEOPLE . . .'

We have concluded our tour of the reminiscence country and city scapes. We hope you have found the guide's comments useful.

Looking back over the pages, we can crystallize what reminiscence has to offer into four strands:

- as a set of techniques to elicit clear goals;
- as a set of purposes which can be properly and profitably researched because the desired goals are specified, and there is some clarity as to the method;
- as various ways of helping people, inasmuch as achieving these goals will benefit them and increase their wellbeing;
- as a philosophy of how people can relate to each other.

It is perhaps this last attribute of reminiscence that will be its most important and lasting; for what is interesting and puzzling, nearly 20 years after reminiscence work in the UK got started, is why it is still so controversial, not in the sense of not being used, but in the sense of being marginalized and trivialized and commercially degraded into merchandizing memorabilia. It is as if the importance that reminiscence places on treating people as individuals, and of having to slow things down to get to know them, is a dangerous notion.

'We brought nothing into this world, and it is certain that we can carry nothing out', and that must mean that what is not developed, what is not expressed, what is not shared, is wasted.

Is it that once we dared to stop to *see* each other, the present systems of care could not just steam-roller on? As Faith Gibson, puts it, reminiscence work is often subversive and unsettling, because it shows too clearly that we are devaluing each other and wasting each other's potential.

There is little evidence of the health and welfare system moving in this direction of greater cooperation and compassion. Rather, the rhetoric and the reality slide ever farther apart. Therefore, how you can develop this kind of work and, in the process, develop yourself, becomes a series of decisions that you make alone, in order to try to create a situation for yourself and others in which such developments can occur. You will need to trust and believe in yourself, to hold on to what you've got. Seek out and work with like-minded people, and together make your own discoveries. Don't be afraid of making your own mistakes too. Good luck.

INDEX